61 1990s war locale
62 Agile, for a senior
63 Los ___ Reyes Magos
64 Days of old
65 Flock sounds
66 Mathematician Pascal
68 Rags-to-riches author Horatio
69 iPod heading
71 Divine
72 Sarge's superior
74 Direction at sea
75 Narrow margin
76 Like many conglomerates: Abbr.
78 One of the housewives on "Desperate Housewives"
80 Thumb's middle?
83 2001 biopic
84 Be sparing
86 John Grisham best seller
87 Smoke
88 Disinclined
89 Gourmet mushrooms
90 Made up (for)
91 It's measured in pound-feet
93 Feed
97 Line at a picnic?
98 Neb. neighbor
99 Accelerated bit
100 Prefix with mom
101 Current: Prefix
102 Quagmire
104 "The West Wing" chief of staff ___ McGarry
105 McKinley and Washington: Abbr.
106 And other things: Abbr.
107 "So that's it!"

☽ FIRST QUARTER

tuesday

7

wednesday

8

thursday

9

friday

10

saturday

11

sunday

12

January

s	m	t	w	t	f	s
			1	2	3	4
5	6	7	8	9	10	11
12	13	14	15	16	17	18
19	20	21	22	23	24	25
26	27	28	29	30	31	

3. COME TO ORDER

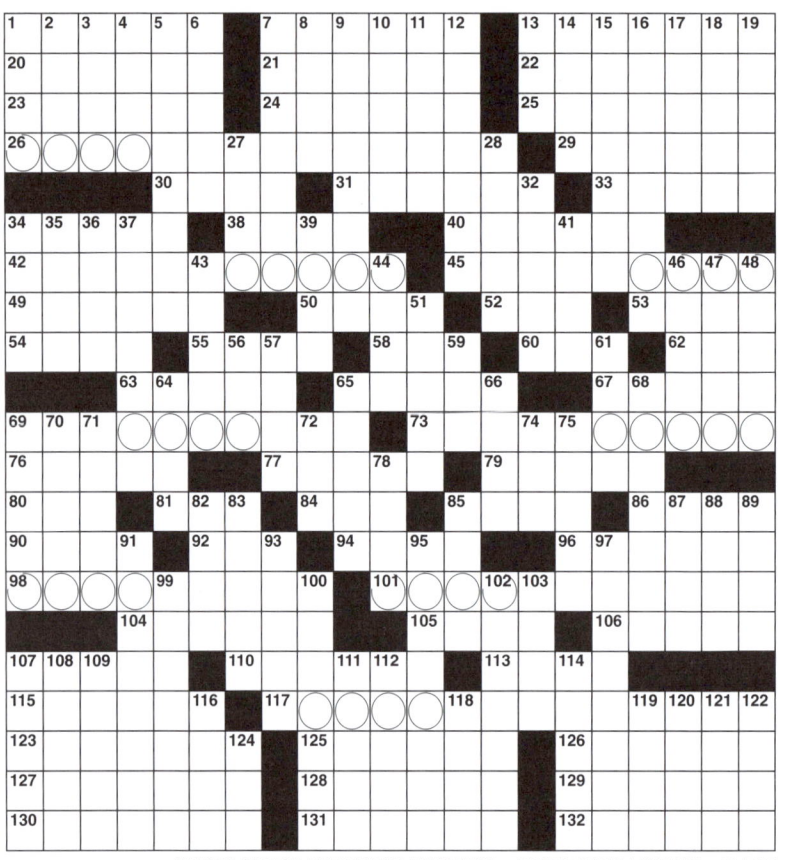

The New York Times

BY TONY ORBACH AND PATRICK BLINDAUER • EDITED BY WILL SHORTZ • 03/7/10

ACROSS

1. Quarter deck?
7. Cross sites, often
13. "And?"
20. 1957 Wimbledon winner Gibson
21. Say "Oh, all right"
22. Folded like a fan
23. Smack
24. More homely
25. Escaped
26. Slogan encouraging binge drinking?
29. Business partner of Marcus
30. Wind up on the stage?
31. Steamship name
33. Conquers
34. Set straight
38. "… ___ saw Elba?"
40. French city on the Moselle River
42. What spectators high up in Ashe Stadium see?
45. Tutorial on becoming a resident manager?
49. Congressman who went on to be mayor of New York
50. Make a muffler, maybe
52. By means of
53. Got home in a cloud of dust
54. Like "el" or "le": Abbr.
55. Is light
58. Online "Ha!"
60. Harry's chum at Hogwarts
62. Number of states whose last two letters are its own postal abbreviation
63. Show fear
65. Butterfingers
67. Pickup line locale?
69. Alex Trebek?
73. Eco-friendly computers from Taiwan?
76. 1998 De Niro film
77. Character in the Torah
79. Nuts
80. Abbr. on a pay stub
81. Brethren
84. You might bow your head when receiving one
85. Will who played Grandpa Walton
86. Appetizer abroad
90. Casual tops
92. Dictionnaire entry
94. Starchy stuff
96. Explosive mixture
98. Nashville neurosis?
101. Teakettle's sound?
104. Chinese craft
105. Mount ___ (highest point on Baffin Island)
106. Jaded sort
107. Outpouring
110. Head cases?
113. ___ support
115. They point the way
117. Clueless emcee?
123. Giant advantage, scorewise
125. Daniel's mother on "Lost"
126. Even
127. French king called "the Fat"
128. Apple product since 2001
129. Series of notes
130. Put up
131. Comes together
132. Midway enticements

DOWN

1. Jumble
2. Citizen of Sesame Street
3. Surmounting
4. P's, but not Q's
5. Like some plates
6. Colonial word for "master," in India
7. Swiss district known for its cheese
8. ___ Park (Queens neighborhood)
9. Casual reference
10. Conrad of "Casablanca"
11. Month that includes Capricornio
12. Certain crew training
13. Big inits. in news
14. "The Good Earth" heroine
15. Place to sample bouquets of rosés?
16. Portrayer of Cuthbert J. Twillie and Egbert Sousé
17. Damages
18. Really rankled
19. New voters, often
27. Leopold's partner in crime
28. Add zing to
32. More mature
34. "Lemme ___!"
35. 13th moon of Jupiter
36. Contents of some cartridges
37. Food whose name means "lumps"
39. Game with racks
41. Franco of "Camelot"
43. On display
44. See 85-Down
46. Skip the service, say
47. Not serious
48. "Waiting for Lefty" playwright
51. "Too bad, so sad!"
56. Like some noodles
57. Franklin who sang "Piece of My Heart"
59. Common Amer. paper size
61. Intl. Peace Garden state
64. Sow sound
65. Some midpoints
66. Bratkowski in the Packers Hall of Fame

January

68 Rhapsody
69 "___ Remember"
70 Egyptian for "be at peace"
71 Rear-___
72 Wisk alternative
74 Inits. in the classifieds
75 Grammy winner Jones
78 Cotillard's "La Vie en Rose" role
82 Mosqued man?
83 Sexist or ethnically stereotyping
85 With 44-Down, kindness
87 Abbr. at the top of a memo
88 ___ sci
89 Twin vampire in "The Twilight Saga"
91 Having a rhythmically recurrent contraction
93 Diamond holder
95 Bad winner's response
97 Pulitzer winner for "Tales of the South Pacific"
99 Portrayer of Flower Belle Lee and Peaches O'Day
100 Angels are at home there
102 Court reporter?
103 PBS flagship station
107 Shade of black
108 Earlier conviction
109 State one's case
111 Golden Globe-winning actor who was People's 1992 Sexiest Man Alive
112 "God ___ refuge …": Psalms
114 Zoo attraction
116 Computer command
118 "Ah"
119 Subject of a museum in Figueres, Spain
120 The works … or how each set of circled letters in this puzzle is arranged
121 Tease
122 Pocket jinglers
124 Carried out

monday
13

tuesday
14

wednesday
15

○ FULL MOON

thursday
16

friday
17

saturday
18

sunday
19

January

s	m	t	w	t	f	s
			1	2	3	4
5	6	7	8	9	10	11
12	13	14	15	16	17	18
19	20	21	22	23	24	25
26	27	28	29	30	31	

4. BOOK BINDING

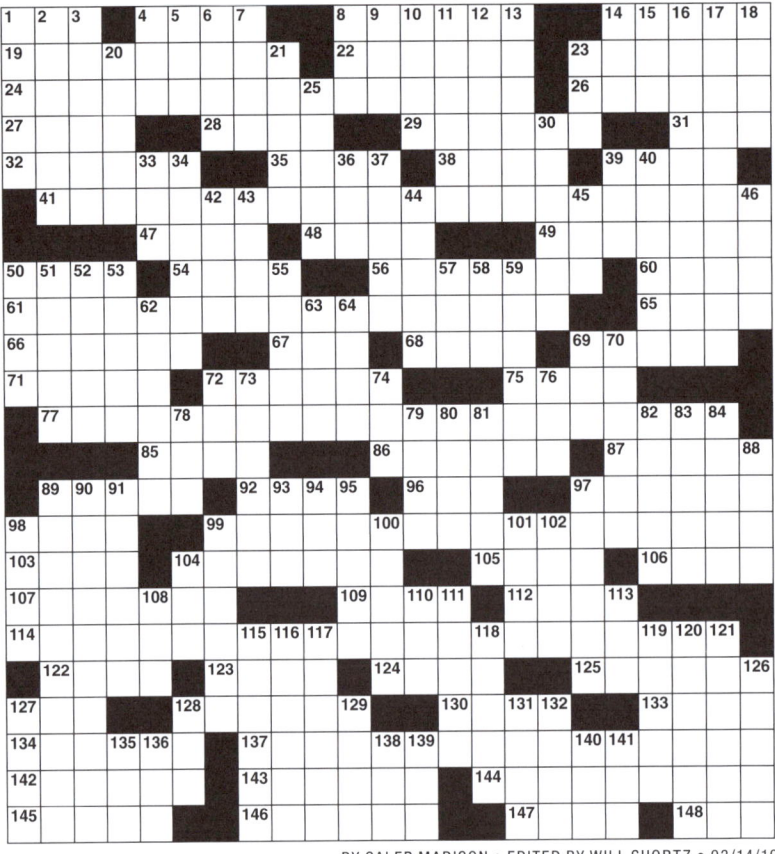

The New York Times

BY CALEB MADISON • EDITED BY WILL SHORTZ • 03/14/10

ACROSS

1. Window boxes, for short?
4. Prefix with business
8. F.B.I. scandal of the 1970s-'80s
14. Actress Fox of "CSI"
19. "Let's Talk About Sex" hip-hop group
22. Tony who directed "Michael Clayton"
23. Not just a little bow
24. Plot of a Willa Cather novel?
26. Cool-looking
27. Río contents
28. "Look what ___!"
29. Not so dry
31. Lb. parts
32. Desert bloomers
35. Ship to the New World
38. Beachgoer's item
39. Tennis star nicknamed "Ice Man"
41. Unabridged version of a Philip Roth novella?
47. Maneuver
48. Prepare for planting
49. "Don't believe that!"
50. Warts and all
54. Bobby and others
56. Drifting
60. "Authority is never without ___": Euripides
61. Pocket edition of a D. H. Lawrence novel?
65. Singer Lambert
66. Trapped
67. Things that go through tubes
68. Analogy part
69. Ed who provided the lead voice in "Up"
71. Eyes
72. Most likely
75. "The Closer" star Sedgwick
77. "Frost/Nixon" director's copy of a Graham Greene novel?
85. No longer fresh
86. Takeoff
87. Bachelor's end?
89. Weary
92. It's molded
96. Ear part
97. Not casual
98. Convertible, maybe
99. Final copy of a Cervantes novel?
103. O.T. book read at Purim
104. It's read to the rowdy
105. Suffix at a natural history museum
106. Literary collections
107. 1948 Literature Nobelist
109. Red ___
112. Form of many Tin Pan Alley tunes
114. Creased copy of a Jack Finney novel?
122. Tennis star Tommy
123. One-named supermodel
124. Sky: Fr.
125. C. S. Lewis land
127. Louvre article?
128. Mass producer, for short
130. Himalayan legend
133. Community hangout, informally
134. "Same here"
137. Illustrations in a Leo Tolstoy novel?
142. Sour
143. Brought up
144. 1957 film dog
145. How a call may be picked up at the office
146. They get added to pounds
147. "A Serious Man" co-director, 2009
148. Head of state?

DOWN

1. Mineralogist's job
2. String once used for cellos
3. Not sit up
4. Whatever
5. Mailing HQ
6. Altered mortgage, briefly
7. Touch, for one
8. Past
9. Storage unit
10. Plethora
11. Unsettling
12. Blood lines
13. Seer
14. Start of the yr.
15. Suffix with Cray-
16. Fuzz buster?
17. Duke Ellington band instrument
18. Carter and Adams
20. Slightest residue
21. Mimicry
23. Lith., e.g., once
25. Boob
30. Kay Thompson title character
33. Savoy peak
34. Was helpless?
36. "There is ___ in 'team'"
37. Stevenson of Illinois
39. Kind of line
40. Marlon Brando, by birth
42. Neighbor of Swed.
43. Spinner
44. Russian pancakes
45. Some blockers: Abbr.
46. Feel like
50. Too
51. Indian P.M. Manmohan ___
52. Author Calvino
53. Throw around
55. Hit hard
57. Goal-oriented grp.?
58. Shooting site
59. Brought to mind
62. "Gil Blas" author
63. Still
64. Former Wall St. inits.
69. Toy sound?
70. Firefox alternative
72. Byrd's rank: Abbr.
73. Film with the line "Oh, we have 12 vacancies. 12 cabins, 12 vacancies"
74. Beat

January

76 Celebratory cry
78 "Lovely!," in dated slang
79 It's undeniable
80 Stepped
81 Vagrants
82 Vega of "Spy Kids"
83 Fight announcement
84 Bob Marley, e.g.
88 Deli supplies
89 "Buffy the Vampire Slayer" creator
90 Roughly
91 Flower once cultivated for food
93 Rent
94 ___ mode
95 Marina sight
97 South African city of 2.5+ million
98 Biological bristle
99 Mr. and Mrs.
100 Giving nothing away, in a way
101 Bread with chicken tikka masala
102 College locale
104 Seoul soldier
108 Election winners
110 "I don't need to hear that!," informally
111 "Ciao!"
113 Ottoman honorific
115 Locks up
116 Ottoman hospice
117 Sweet drink
118 Old Olds
119 Soviet co-op
120 Not just puff
121 "Uncle!" criers, perhaps
126 Australia's ___ Rock
127 Stretch ___
128 One of the Jonas brothers
129 Dance typically done to "Hava Nagila"
131 Rash preventer
132 Intro to Chinese?
135 Drag
136 Bolivian bear
138 Noted Palin impressionist
139 O.E.D. entries: Abbr.
140 Coloring
141 Where you might find a long sentence?

monday 20
MARTIN LUTHER KING JR.'S BIRTHDAY (OBSERVED) (USA)

tuesday 21

wednesday 22

thursday 23

friday 24
☾ LAST QUARTER

saturday 25

sunday 26
AUSTRALIA DAY

January

s	m	t	w	t	f	s
			1	2	3	4
5	6	7	8	9	10	11
12	13	14	15	16	17	18
19	20	21	22	23	24	25
26	27	28	29	30	31	

5. THEM'S THE BREAKS

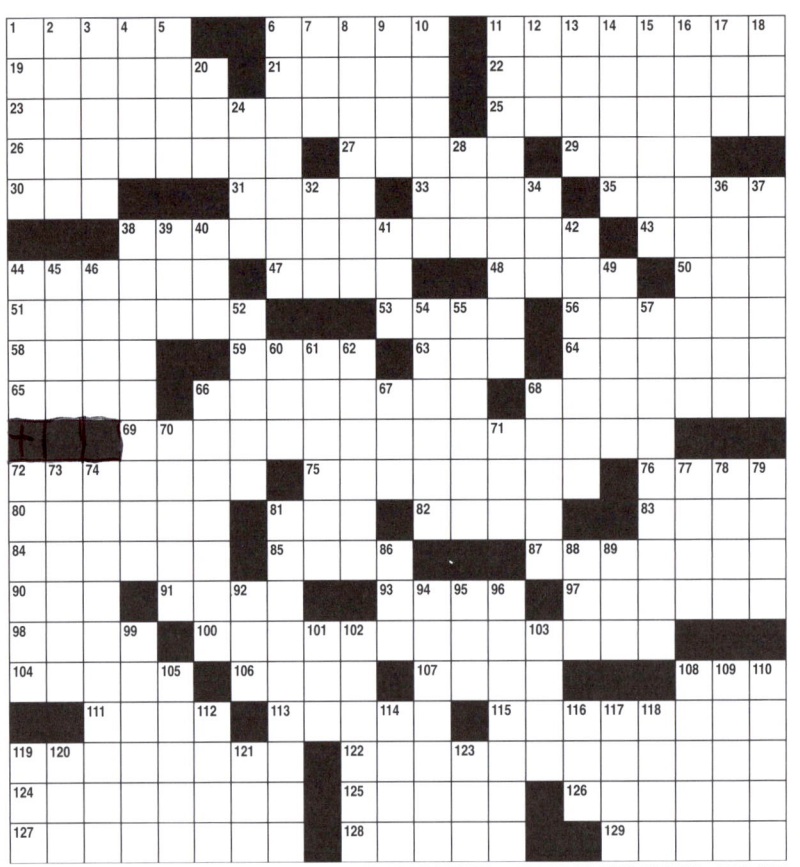

The New York Times

BY ADAM FROMM • EDITED BY WILL SHORTZ • 03/21/10

ACROSS

1. Colorful bird
6. Beguiled, maybe
11. Seven-card melds
19. Shortly
21. "All systems ___"
22. Zoo home for gibbons
23. Goes from walk to trot and trot to gallop?
25. Lever in a trunk
26. "You're on!"
27. Flinch, say
29. Tend to a hole
30. Visit
31. S-s-s-subject of a 1918 hit song
33. The "her" in the lyric "I met her in a club down in old Soho"
35. Change south of the border
38. Teaches a ceramics class?
43. Outline clearly
44. Greeting of respect
47. Pour on the love
48. Where Haiku is
50. "Was ___ blame?"
51. Word-processing acronym
53. Dutch construction
56. Not easily stirred
58. Carrier whose name means "skyward"
59. Frist's successor as Senate majority leader
63. Vote in Versailles
64. Bulwark
65. Chow
66. One of two by Liszt
68. James who was C.I.A. director under Clinton
69. Monitors food orders to go?
72. Piscivorous flier
75. Election problem
76. Founder of New York's Public Theater
80. "Onward!" in Italy
81. Narrator in Kerouac's "On the Road"
82. The blond Monkee
83. Potentially going into screen saver mode
84. Less mellow
85. Albatross
87. International food company based in Paris
90. Ky. neighbor
91. Unable to decide
93. Doesn't quite go straight
97. "The Five Orange Pips" sleuth
98. ___ buco
100. Illuminates a Halloween display?
104. San Diego's region, for short
106. Melville work
107. Book after Chronicles
108. Group defeated in '65
111. Eighty-sixes
113. Bridge declaration
115. Wardrobes
119. Ingredient in furniture polishes
122. Puts hats on display?
124. Music Appreciation 101, perhaps
125. Calms
126. Pre-euro coin
127. Big snafu
128. Any member of 4-Down
129. Insurance holder's burden

DOWN

1. Not-quite-ankle-length skirts
2. Make ___ of
3. Free Tibet, e.g.
4. "Chiquitita" group
5. Natural
6. Santa's traditional home, to some
7. Procter & Gamble laundry brand
8. Crack, in a way
9. S-curve
10. Dietary restriction
11. Ones promoting brand awareness?
12. Bee: Prefix
13. Brainiac's put-down
14. Oodles
15. Big do
16. Prepares to play Scrabble?
17. Japanese volcano
18. D.C. V.I.P.
20. Casual top
24. "The Open Window" writer
28. "M*A*S*H" prop
32. General on a menu
34. Coach Parseghian
36. 45° wedge
37. Substandard
38. Closely follows secret banking information?
39. Like some emotions
40. Funnywoman Sedaris
41. U.K. reference
42. Solve, in British slang
44. ___' Pea
45. "The Clan of the Cave Bear" heroine
46. It includes a sect. of logic games
49. "Some Like ___"
52. Common place for a pull
54. Whole
55. Gold-certified debut album of Debbie Harry
57. Makes drugs easier to swallow?
60. S.A.S.E., e.g.
61. Nickname for Björn Borg
62. Big production company in 1950s-'60s TV
66. Hair care brand since 1931
67. N.F.L. linemen: Abbr.

January-February

- 68 Knowledgeable on arcane details of a subject
- 70 Maids a-milking in a Christmas song, e.g.
- 71 It borders the Atl.
- 72 House add-ons
- 73 Be that as it may
- 74 Manages to grab some bullfight attire?
- 77 First of all?
- 78 Bend for Baryshnikov
- 79 Strokes
- 81 Recording engineer, sometimes
- 86 ___ admin
- 88 Cry from one who just got the joke
- 89 "Eldorado" poet
- 92 Kia model
- 94 "Like, totally cool!"
- 95 Michael Jackson film, with "The"
- 96 German street
- 99 Mexican state south of Veracruz
- 101 Jump #1 in a triple jump
- 102 Parts of many celebrations
- 103 Haul
- 105 Fast times?
- 108 Skeevy sort
- 109 Sealy competitor
- 110 Evaluate
- 112 Houlihan player on TV
- 114 Only man to win both a Nobel Prize and an Oscar
- 116 Swab
- 117 Its HQ are in Austria, which isn't a member
- 118 ___ facto
- 119 One of the Beverly Hillbillies
- 120 Lighter of the Olympic flame in Atlanta
- 121 Constitution in D.C., e.g.
- 123 Hitch up with

January

s	m	t	w	t	f	s
			1	2	3	4
5	6	7	8	9	10	11
12	13	14	15	16	17	18
19	20	21	22	23	24	25
26	27	28	29	30	31	

February

s	m	t	w	t	f	s
						1
2	3	4	5	6	7	8
9	10	11	12	13	14	15
16	17	18	19	20	21	22
23	24	25	26	27	28	

monday 27 — AUSTRALIA DAY (OBSERVED)

tuesday 28

wednesday 29

thursday 30 — ● NEW MOON

friday 31

saturday 1

sunday 2

6. WHAT MAKES IT ITCH?

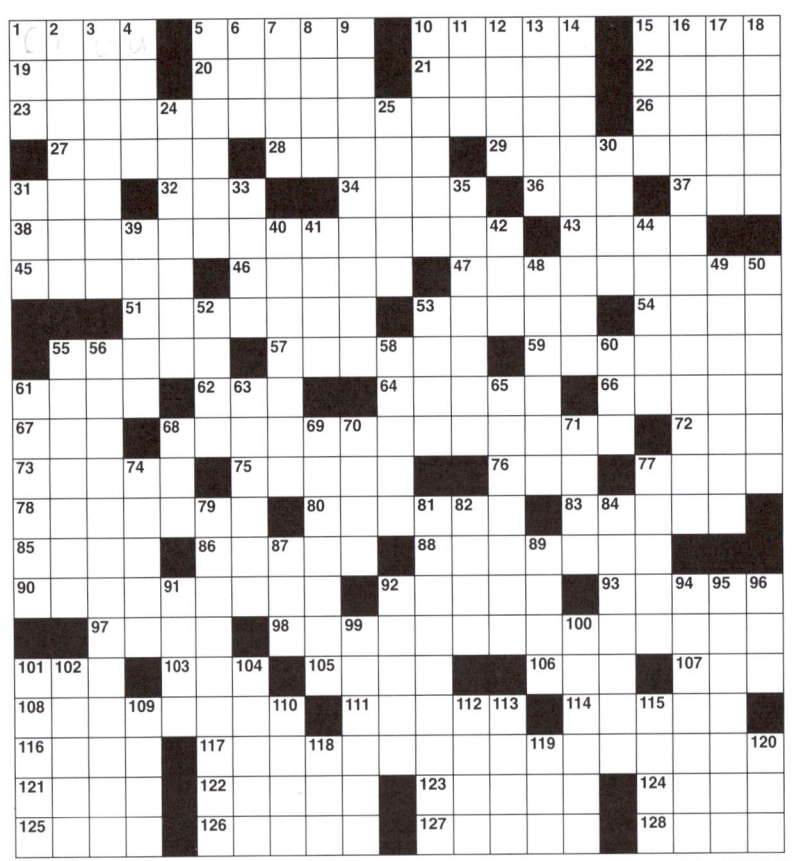

The New York Times

BY ED SESSA • EDITED BY WILL SHORTZ • 03/28/10

ACROSS

1. "Coffee ___ my cup of tea": Samuel Goldwyn
5. World capital at 12,000 feet
10. Rugby gathering
15. Schoolyard comeback
19. Phone abbr.
20. & 21. Native Oklahoma group
22. Eponymous engineer
23. Problem for a crane operator?
26. Green-light
27. Pillow fill
28. In a lather
29. Get ready to go
31. Noodge
32. ___ culpa
34. Average fellows
36. Haberdashery offering
37. "___ Lincoln in Illinois" (1940 biopic)
38. Exceptional soldier on his only tour?
43. Kvetch
45. Showed over
46. Lead and tin alloy
47. Cuban's home?
51. Food giant based in Downers Grove, Ill.
53. Feigned
54. Chief Norse deity
55. Hot dog topping
57. G.M. tracking system
59. Like many a 36-Across
61. Plug along
62. Motorist's no-no, for short
64. Helps in a heist
66. Get used (to)
67. Rubbish
68. What kind, decent people wear?
72. Colt's fans, for short?
73. Grouchy Muppet
75. Head turner
76. 45 ___
77. Leave a mark on
78. Cuddly cat
80. "___ Mucho," #1 hit for Jimmy Dorsey
83. ___ ark
85. Switch add-on
86. Machu Picchu people
88. Wall Street landmark?
90. Arrive unexpectedly en masse
92. Play center, often
93. Dentist's directive
97. iTunes selection
98. Hidden help for one who's trying to quit smoking?
101. Handicapper's hangout, for short
103. Spanish wave
105. Big Apple neighborhood
106. Twice tre
107. Eggy quaff
108. Court figures
111. Scrutinized, with "over"
114. Colorado resort
116. Years, in Rome
117. Instruction #1 for roofers?
121. Beat
122. Centers of early development
123. Wish granter
124. News tidbit
125. Yearn
126. Vocally bother
127. Cry from beyond a closed door
128. Leader of the Untouchables

DOWN

1. Electrical particle
2. Expo '74 city
3. Shirley MacLaine, notably
4. Take a header
5. Keepsake on a chain
6. Volcanic fallout
7. Court transfer?
8. Currency exchange premium
9. Academy Award winner for "Chicago," 2002
10. Hung around
11. Computer screen, for short
12. Jacob who wrote "How the Other Half Lives"
13. Maritime threat of the early 1940s
14. Beggar
15. Off-base in a bad way
16. Hit below the belt?
17. Six-time baseball All-Star Rusty
18. Like universal blood donors
24. Hardly worth mentioning
25. Ahead, but barely
30. Charlie Chan creator Earl ___ Biggers
31. Postman's creed conjunction
33. Courthouse records
35. Gets hold of
39. Member of a strict Jewish sect
40. Hint offerer
41. Follower of Christopher or Carolina
42. Slowing down, in mus.
44. Flip ___ (decide by chance)
48. Tittle-tattle
49. Rugged range
50. Win over
52. Razz
53. Sunscreen additive
55. Conclusion
56. Really angry group?
58. Ohio political dynasty
60. Old Japanese coin
61. Investigated
63. Straighten out

February

- 65 Included for free
- 68 Field ration, for short
- 69 Some quick-change places
- 70 Peach and orange
- 71 It means everything
- 74 Bygone brand with a torch in its logo
- 77 Bygone title of respect
- 79 Bachelor
- 81 Home of Elmendorf Air Force Base
- 82 "Fly ___ the Moon"
- 84 Beastly
- 87 Filch
- 89 Google stat
- 91 Genesis son
- 92 Sound while jerking the head
- 94 Tony and Emmy winner Fabray
- 95 Candleholders on a wall
- 96 Ticker tape letters?
- 99 Like atriums
- 100 Punk's piece
- 101 City in Florida's horse country
- 102 Gin's partner
- 104 Prince Valiant's love
- 109 "Swoosh" brand
- 110 One ___ at a time
- 112 Heavenly place
- 113 Succinct warning
- 115 Pest
- 118 Parseghian of Notre Dame
- 119 "For shame!"
- 120 Britannia letters

monday
3 34

tuesday
4 35

wednesday
5 36

WAITANGI DAY (NZ)
☽ FIRST QUARTER

thursday
6 37

friday
7 38

saturday
8 39

sunday
9 40

February

s	m	t	w	t	f	s
						1
2	3	4	5	6	7	8
9	10	11	12	13	14	15
16	17	18	19	20	21	22
23	24	25	26	27	28	

7. AFTER WORD

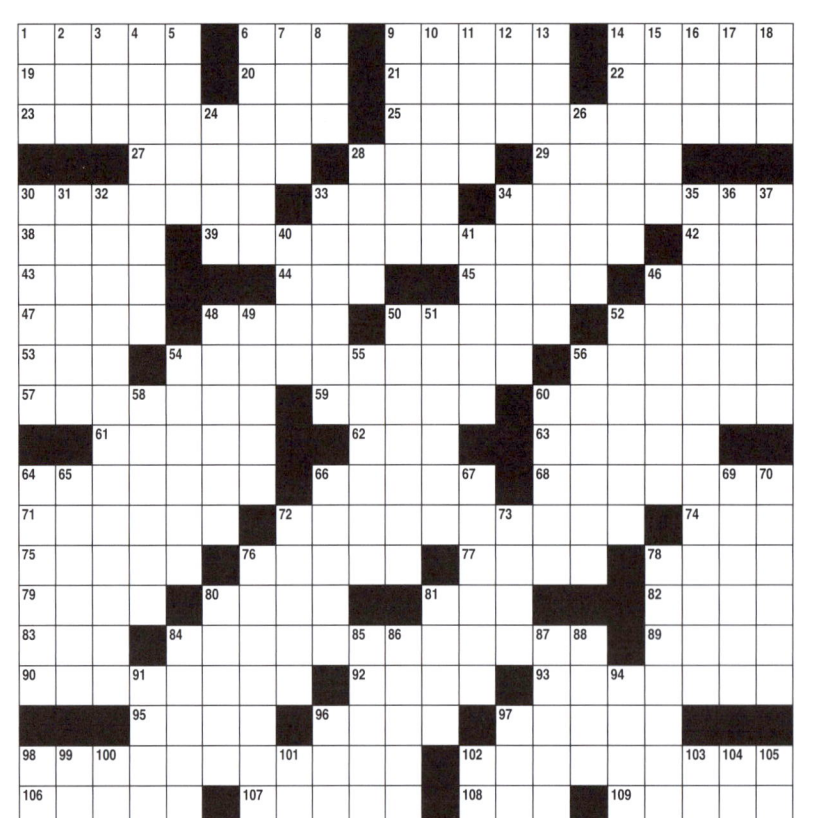

The New York Times

BY BOB KLAHN • EDITED BY WILL SHORTZ • 04/04/10

BONUS QUESTION: WHAT WORD CAN FOLLOW EACH HALF OF THE ANSWER TO EACH STARRED CLUE?

ACROSS
1. Economy
6. "Spare" part
9. Direction for violinists
14. Rubbish
19. Relieve
20. "Cold Mountain" heroine
21. Hot stuff
22. High trump card
23. *"Either that ___ goes, or I do" (Oscar Wilde's reputed last words)
25. *Legislative V.I.P.
27. "As You Like It" role
28. Curved nail, perhaps
29. Dentiform : tooth :: pyriform : ___
30. Certain
33. Chin
34. *Object of superstition
38. Wiped out
39. *Annual N.F.L. event
42. Project Blue Book subj.
43. Get a flat
44. "___ Love" (1978 hit for Natalie Cole)
45. German unity
46. Kind of crazy?
47. Org. that gives approval
48. Dirt
50. Obloquy, e.g.
52. ___ dish
53. Print maker
54. *Zigzag trail up a mountain
56. Better writing, e.g.
57. Wry
59. Big band
60. Navigator William with a sea named after him
61. Jazzy Chick
62. Decline in value
63. Sitting around for years waiting to get drunk?
64. Tedious trips
66. Something that might be hard to drink?
68. Open up
71. Jostles
72. *Green Bay Packers fan
74. Chartres shout
75. Femme fatale
76. They may offer rides
77. Site of numerous firings
78. A guard may protect it
79. Imitated
80. Real first name of Alfalfa of the Little Rascals
81. Trouble
82. Bring around
83. Display in the Auckland Museum
84. *Tally
89. Choice
90. *Lamp holder
92. "The Flying Dutchman" tenor
93. Armpits
95. Exotic berry in some fruit juices
96. Missed signals from Little Boy Blue, maybe
97. Director Kurosawa
98. *Lure
102. *Cover-up
106. 1986 rock autobiography
107. New addition
108. Lunkhead
109. Babushkas
110. Actress Streep
111. Cultivates
112. Interjection added to the O.E.D. in 2001
113. Land called Mizraim in the Bible

DOWN
1. Harsh call
2. Suffix with boff
3. Purely
4. Birthplace of William Thackeray and Satyajit Ray
5. Wired
6. Spanish fleet?
7. Brain matter?
8. Block
9. June "honoree," briefly
10. Sense of taste
11. Big wind
12. Spanish bear
13. F-14, e.g.
14. 1977 Liza Minnelli musical
15. Family name in Frank Miller's "Sin City" series
16. Gary's home: Abbr.
17. "The Purloined Letter" writer
18. Foozle
24. A Baldwin
26. Pages (through)
28. Gregg Allman's wife who filed for divorce after nine days
30. Sudden
31. Oscillate
32. *Wonder product
33. Critical situation
34. Sharp and stimulating
35. *Risking detention
36. Something unprecedented
37. Major party
40. Yahoo
41. Dickens
46. Some naturals
48. Wins everything

February

- 49 Cursed alchemist
- 50 Sands, e.g.
- 51 Stars in many westerns
- 52 Stop sign?
- 54 Cast about
- 55 One stocking stockings
- 56 Coat named for a British lord
- 58 Made an individual effort
- 60 Scene of confusion
- 64 "Open ___"
- 65 Like some earrings
- 66 Serving from a pot
- 67 Football do-over
- 69 Epithet for Elizabeth I
- 70 Sassy lassies
- 72 Meat, as in 66-Down
- 73 Liliuokalani Gardens site
- 76 Half-circle window over a door
- 78 Rogue
- 80 Resident of Daiquirí
- 81 Frequent disclaimer
- 84 Like some census categories
- 85 Closed in on
- 86 Marks
- 87 Dashing
- 88 Out
- 91 Light brown
- 94 Galsworthy's Mrs. Forsyte
- 96 One raised on a farm
- 97 "Got it!"
- 98 Empty-headed
- 99 Rural address abbr.
- 100 It's in circulation
- 101 French firm: Abbr.
- 102 Bankroll?
- 103 A little or a lot
- 104 Dupe
- 105 Pres. with the Marshall Plan

monday
10

tuesday
11

wednesday
12

thursday
13

ST. VALENTINE'S DAY
○ FULL MOON

friday
14

saturday
15

sunday
16

February

s	m	t	w	t	f	s
						1
2	3	4	5	6	7	8
9	10	11	12	13	14	15
16	17	18	19	20	21	22
23	24	25	26	27	28	

8. TEE TIME

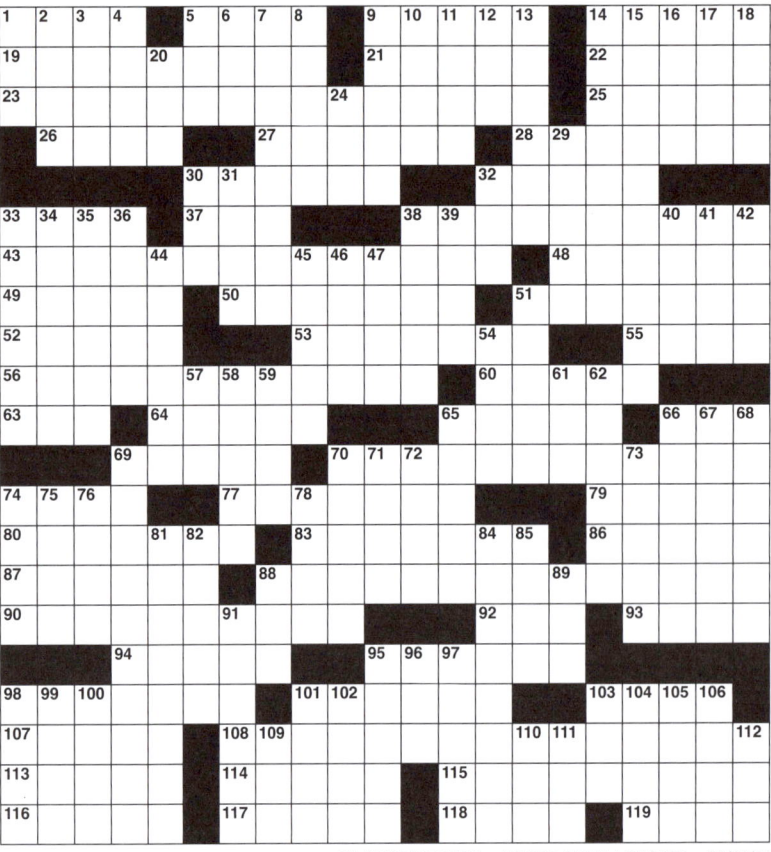

The New York Times

ACROSS
1. Pitch evaluators
5. Children's illustrator Harrison ___
9. "The great aphrodisiac," per Henry Kissinger
14. Easily broken
19. Bathing beauty at a swimming facility?
21. Nicholas Gage memoir
22. Something thrown for a loop?
23. Armistice signed on December 25?
25. Leave-taking
26. Important match
27. Easily attached
28. Allergy medication brand
30. Poultry delicacies
32. Bear Lake State Park locale
33. Excellent summers, for short?
37. Grp. that entertains troops
38. Scottish body of water with beverage concentrate added?
43. Awful illustration from cartoonist William?
48. Mideast capital
49. "Return of the Jedi" moon
50. Something not to be missed?
51. Lone player
52. ___ Field (former name of Minute Maid Park)
53. Discover
55. Reasons to cry
56. Opting not to sunbathe?
60. Readies, as a firearm
63. Reagan-era program, in brief
64. Some of this may be picked up at a beach
65. Better at scheming
66. Union opposer: Abbr.
69. ___ Tribunal (international court)
70. Exactness in giving orders to toymaking elves?
74. Remote button
77. Japanese ruler
79. First lady after Bess
80. Crankcases' bases
83. Civil code entry
86. Minneapolis neighbor
87. Brazilian beach resort
88. What a bunny buyer at a pet shop might want?
90. Choice of songs at a piano bar?
92. It's lode-bearing
93. Pinkish
94. R&B singer Marie
95. 12th-century Crusader state
98. Sets free
101. Actor Haley Joel ___ of "The Sixth Sense"
103. Use a cell phone outside one's local calling area
107. ___ rima (verse form for Dante)
108. Hybrid sheepdog that moves ver-r-ry slowly?
113. Oscar : United States :: ___ : Mexico
114. Rack up
115. Drinking and dancing instead of sleeping?
116. Punks
117. "You good to go?"
118. "Nascar Now" broadcaster
119. Conventional explanation for a tragic event

DOWN
1. Scanned lines, for short
2. Hardness scale inventor
3. Tiny perforation
4. Unpromising, as a chance
5. Director's cry
6. Device at a drive-thru
7. Large-scale flight
8. Phrased for a quick answer
9. Lawbreakers
10. Tub filler
11. Remove gradually from, with "off"
12. Med. specialty
13. City that's home to King Fahd Road
14. Like some boots
15. Rush jobs?
16. Like
17. Neutral reaction to a revelation
18. Easily picked up, say
20. TV program set in Vegas
24. Light earth tone
29. Division of an Edmund Spenser work
30. Tiny tiger
31. With all haste
32. Bitterly cold
33. Where some hooks connect
34. Had nothing good to say about
35. Peace Nobelist Sakharov
36. One who's in your business?
38. Swinging dance
39. Sharkey of TV's "C.P.O. Sharkey"
40. Chamber group, often
41. Lessen, as pain
42. Unpaid workers?
44. Yellow-flowered perennial
45. Overwhelmingly
46. "House of Meetings" novelist, 2006
47. Ripped

BY PATRICK BERRY • EDITED BY WILL SHORTZ • 04/11/10

February

- 51 Follower of the philosopher Epictetus
- 54 Pac-10 competitor
- 57 Drink from a bowl
- 58 Puts together, in a way
- 59 It may be measured by a meter
- 61 Animator's sheet
- 62 John ___, villain in the "Saw" films
- 65 Look-at-me walk
- 66 "Heaven's Gate" director
- 67 Is parsimonious
- 68 Roger on a ship
- 69 Open to suggestions, say
- 70 Kept for future use
- 71 Burnoose wearer
- 72 Response to the Little Red Hen
- 73 Speedster's undoing
- 74 "That's just silly!"
- 75 Actress Taylor
- 76 Settled on a branch
- 78 H.S. exam
- 81 Epinephrine-producing glands
- 82 Identified
- 84 Some Scott Joplin compositions
- 85 Prominent parts of a George W. Bush caricature
- 88 Cape Town's home: Abbr.
- 89 Stephen of "Stuck"
- 91 Doing time
- 95 The Eagles of the N.C.A.A.
- 96 "Ad majorem ___ gloriam" (Jesuit motto)
- 97 Follow
- 98 ___ Beach (D-Day site)
- 99 Historical subject of a Boito opera
- 100 Vigor
- 101 Boat in "Jaws"
- 102 Small earring
- 103 Sales force member
- 104 Minnesota's St. ___ College
- 105 Razor brand
- 106 Necessity when playing hardball
- 109 Together
- 110 Maker of fuel additives
- 111 Turtledove
- 112 Smiley dot

February

s	m	t	w	t	f	s
						1
2	3	4	5	6	7	8
9	10	11	12	13	14	15
16	17	18	19	20	21	22
23	24	25	26	27	28	

PRESIDENTS' DAY (USA)

monday
17 48

tuesday
18 49

wednesday
19 50

thursday
20 51

friday
21 52

☾ LAST QUARTER

saturday
22 53

sunday
23 54

9. WHATS-ITS

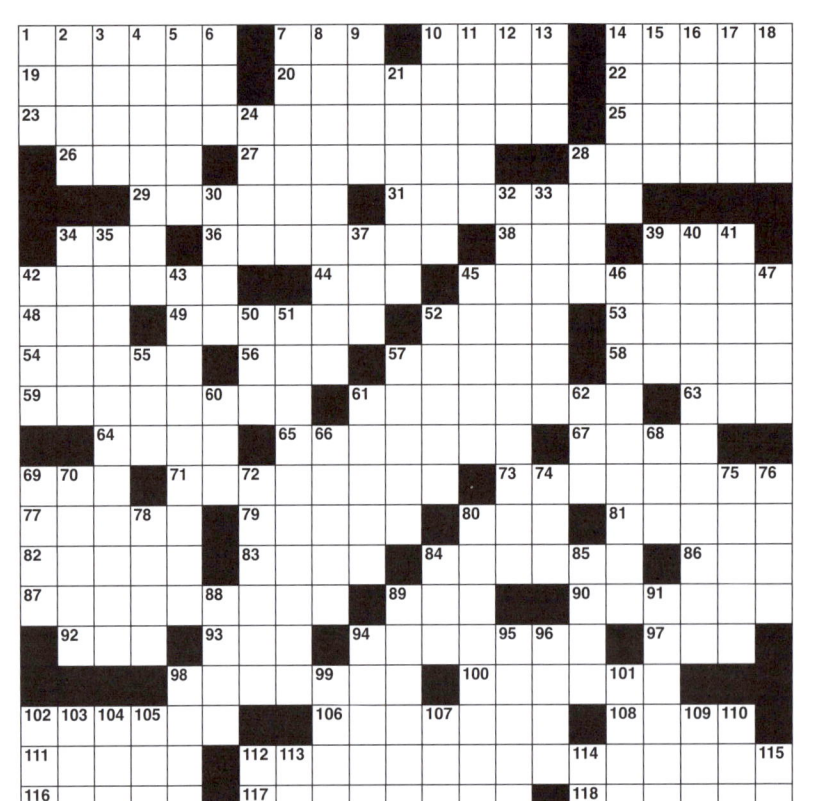

The New York Times

BY RANDOLPH ROSS • EDITED BY WILL SHORTZ • 04/18/10

ACROSS

1. Your tongue
7. Trip preparation
10. Early 10th-century year
14. Uncle
19. "Lemme!"
20. Sloping
22. Gland: Prefix
23. An idea
25. The picture
26. Identify
27. 1986 parody of a Sylvester Stallone film series
28. First name among the Axis powers
29. Not going anywhere?
31. Direct to the exit
34. It often follows you
36. Summer coolers
38. Dragon roll ingredient
39. Spots
42. Greek high spot
44. Gambler's hangout, for short
45. Retro upholstery material
48. Dressing choice
49. Contract winner, often
52. Leave in a hurry
53. Opera ___ (complete works: Lat.)
54. TV "Miss"
56. Story accompanier
57. "A Beautiful Mind" star
58. You, in Yucatán
59. Tool for making eyelets
61. Old-fashioned clothes presser
63. Org. with an oath
64. California's ___ Valley
65. Created
67. Old buffalo hunter
69. Closed-captioning problem
71. Expanse
73. Surgeon's tool
77. Kind of ring
79. Rube of bygone funnies
80. Common cricket score
81. Cause of a pain in the neck
82. Yawn producer
83. Pouches
84. Curly pasta
86. Writer Anaïs
87. Like cornstalks after about six weeks
89. Weapon carried in a speakeasy
90. Accommodations with low overhead?
92. Abbr. in many a Québec address
93. Fighter with a shuffle
94. Math operations that yield remainders
97. Shaker ___, Oh.
98. Field tools
100. Moses at the Red Sea, e.g.
102. "In the Bedroom" actress, 2001
106. Rare announcement after balloting
108. Slams
111. Crow
112. A message
116. Prince Valiant's wife
117. Didn't get a good deal
118. Name associated with fire
119. The light
120. Putter (around)
121. Sot's woe
122. Face

DOWN

1. Inexpensive pen
2. Joyful cry
3. Author Janowitz
4. Exes, sometimes
5. One ___ (long odds)
6. Eastern path
7. Home of Shalimar Gardens
8. The point
9. Like dungeons, typically
10. Some garlic
11. Scorsese subject
12. ___ Kamoze of reggae
13. Big corp. in defense contracts
14. Bob ___, narrator on TV's "How I Met Your Mother"
15. Present-day site of the ancient port city Eudaemon
16. Hirsute Himalayan
17. J. Edgar Hoover used one: Abbr.
18. Fictional terrier
21. 1973 NASA launch
24. Gillette's ___ II
28. Major portion
30. Former Chinese Communist military leader Lin ___
32. A deck of cards
33. Olympic discus great Al
34. Not straight
35. The aisles
37. Announcement at a terminal, in brief
39. Poor support
40. Sure loser
41. Sloppy spots
42. ___ Southwest Grill (restaurant chain)
43. A pillow
45. Ticket site
46. An abacus
47. "Humpty Dumpty ___ great fall"
50. Angkor ___ (Cambodian temple)
51. Lunch
52. Actress Sonia
55. Wharf workers' org.
57. Crossword creator, at times
60. Water source

February-March

- 61 Course calls
- 62 Part of a tuba sound
- 66 Dressing choice
- 68 Spanish bear
- 69 Theater mogul Marcus
- 70 Kournikova and others
- 72 Without breaking a sweat
- 74 2010 Denzel Washington title role
- 75 Athletic shoe brand
- 76 Second place?
- 78 River of York
- 80 *Snuff*
- 84 Far out
- 85 G.O.P. elephant originator
- 88 Commit a computer crime
- 89 Dirt
- 91 Does very well
- 94 They may be fed downtown
- 95 Scots with lots
- 96 City SSW of Moscow
- 98 Tuned to
- 99 Ups
- 101 Classical sister
- 102 Seven ___
- 103 Washed out
- 104 Suit to ___
- 105 Field opening?
- 107 Not much
- 109 Soccer immortal
- 110 California's ___ Valley
- 112 Nursery rhyme boy who "stole a pig, and away he run"
- 113 N.Y.C.'s A, B, C or D
- 114 Night sch. class
- 115 Rug rat

monday 24 55

tuesday 25 56

wednesday 26 57

thursday 27 58

friday 28 59

ST. DAVID'S DAY (UK)
● NEW MOON

saturday 1 60

sunday 2 61

February

s	m	t	w	t	f	s
						1
2	3	4	5	6	7	8
9	10	11	12	13	14	15
16	17	18	19	20	21	22
23	24	25	26	27	28	

March

s	m	t	w	t	f	s
						1
2	3	4	5	6	7	8
9	10	11	12	13	14	15
16	17	18	19	20	21	22
23	24	25	26	27	28	29
30	31					

10. MONUMENTAL ACHIEVEMENT

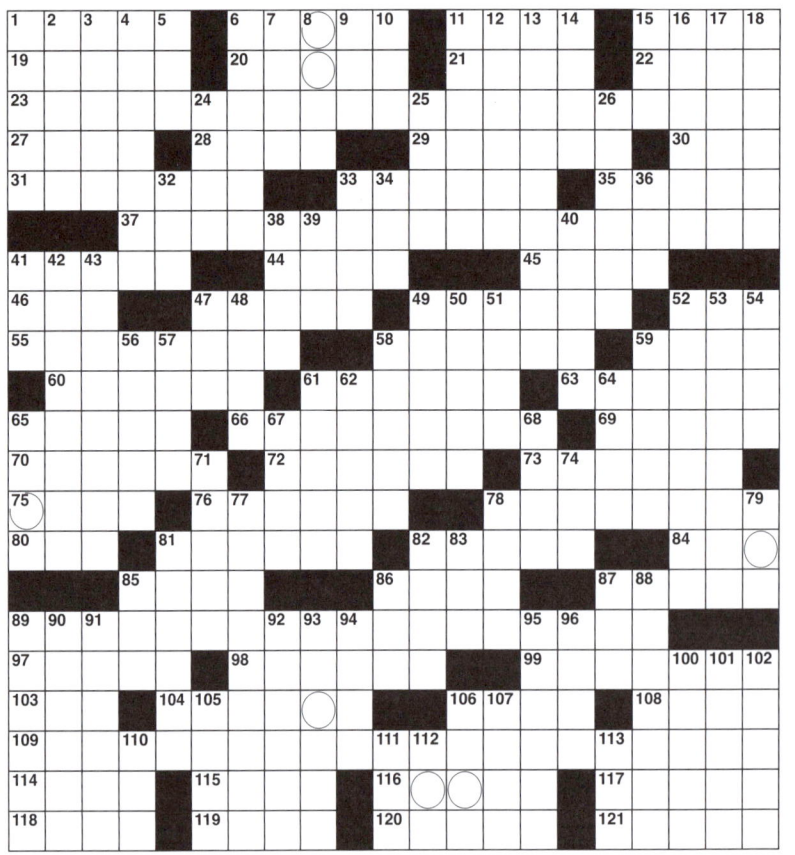

The New York Times

BY ELIZABETH C. GORSKI • EDITED BY WILL SHORTZ • 04/25/10

WHEN THIS PUZZLE IS DONE, THE SEVEN CIRCLED LETTERS CAN BE ARRANGED TO SPELL A COMMON WORD, WHICH IS MISSING FROM SEVEN OF THE CLUES, AS INDICATED BY [ ]. CONNECT THE SEVEN LETTERS IN ORDER WITH A LINE AND YOU WILL GET AN OUTLINE OF THE OBJECT THAT THE WORD NAMES.

ACROSS

1. Tubs
6. Dead
11. Large amount
15. Imported cheese
19. Tribe of Israel
20. Resident of a country that's 97% mountains and desert
21. Sailor's direction
22. "Here I ___ Worship" (contemporary hymn)
23. [ ]
27. Fling
28. English connections
29. "Le Déjeuner des Canotiers," e.g.
30. You may get a charge out of it
31. Gwen who sang "Don't Speak," 1996
33. Top of a mountain?
35. Saintly glows
37. [ ]
41. Leaving for
44. "Go on!"
45. "A pity"
46. Charles, for one
47. Very friendly (with)
49. Start of a famous J.F.K. quote
52. Price part: Abbr.
55. [ ]
58. Pizza orders
59. Glossy black birds
60. New York City transport from the Bronx to Coney Island
61. Throat soother
63. Like clogs
65. After, in Avignon
66. Paris attraction that features a [ ]
69. Passes over
70. Football shoes
72. Nervousness
73. Low clouds
75. Fannie ___ (some investments)
76. Prenatal procedures, informally
78. [ ]
80. Coast Guard rank: Abbr.
81. Snow fall
82. Run ___ of
84. Willy who wrote "The Conquest of Space"
85. Whites or colors, e.g.
86. NASA's ___ Research Center
87. Trumpet
89. [ ] that was the creation of an architect born 4/26/1917
97. Humdingers
98. Atomic centers
99. Mozart's birthplace
103. Network that airs "WWE Raw"
104. Breakdown of social norms
106. Naval officer: Abbr.
108. Bop
109. [ ]
114. O'Neill's "Desire Under the ___"
115. "___ Death" (Grieg movement)
116. Flat storage place
117. Headless Horseman, e.g.
118. Way: Abbr.
119. Larry who played Tony in "West Side Story"
120. Compost units
121. Professional grps.

DOWN

1. Almanac tidbits
2. "Give it ___"
3. "___ Foolish Things" (1936 hit)
4. Deems worthy
5. Canadian-born hockey great
6. Walter of "Star Trek"
7. "Diary of ___ Housewife"
8. Crash sites?
9. Prefix with sex
10. Cookie holder
11. Seattle's ___ Field
12. Like some cell growth
13. Part of a Virgin Atlantic fleet
14. Prefix with monde
15. "Let's ___!"
16. Composer Shostakovich
17. Like Berg's "Wozzeck"
18. Williams of TV
24. Smallville girl
25. Sudoku feature
26. Genesis landing site
32. "I love," in Latin
33. Tizzy
34. "Krazy" one
36. Financial inst. that bought PaineWebber in 2000
38. Upper hand
39. "I'm impressed!"
40. At ___ for words
41. Suffix with contradict
42. Nutritional regimen
43. Parts of some Mediterranean orchards
47. French pronoun
48. Exists no more

March

49 High: Lat.
50 It doesn't hold water
51 1980s Chrysler debut
52 April first?
53 Double-crosser
54 Payroll stub IDs
56 Fields
57 History
58 Covered walkways
59 Joltin' Joe
61 "Thin Ice" star Sonja
62 Bars from the refrigerator
64 "___, is it I?"
65 Tip-top
67 Pinup boy
68 "___ Wood sawed wood" (start of a tongue twister)
71 Light lunch
74 Bygone daily MTV series, informally
77 Clapped and shouted, e.g.
78 "___ fan tutte"
79 Ophthalmologist's study
81 Anatomical cavities
82 Both: Prefix
83 Tina of "30 Rock"
85 Baton Rouge sch.
86 "Wheel of Fortune" purchase
87 Wanna-___ (imitators)
88 They're nuts
89 Sitting areas, slangily?
90 How rain forests grow
91 Bells and whistles, maybe
92 Kind of romance
93 Least friendly
94 Valley
95 House keepers
96 Knitting loop
100 Some have forks
101 How some people solve crosswords
102 Singer/actress Karen of Broadway's "Nine"
105 Neighbor of Sask.
106 Mrs. Dithers of "Blondie"
107 Run before Q
110 Ballpark fig.
111 Brown, e.g.: Abbr.
112 Chemical suffix
113 Spanish Mrs.

monday
LABOUR DAY (AUSTRALIA—WA)

3 62

tuesday

4 63

wednesday
ASH WEDNESDAY

5 64

thursday

6 65

friday

7 66

saturday
INTERNATIONAL WOMEN'S DAY
☽ FIRST QUARTER

8 67

sunday

9 68

March

s	m	t	w	t	f	s
						1
2	3	4	5	6	7	8
9	10	11	12	13	14	15
16	17	18	19	20	21	22
23	24	25	26	27	28	29
30	31					

11. FIX-A-TION

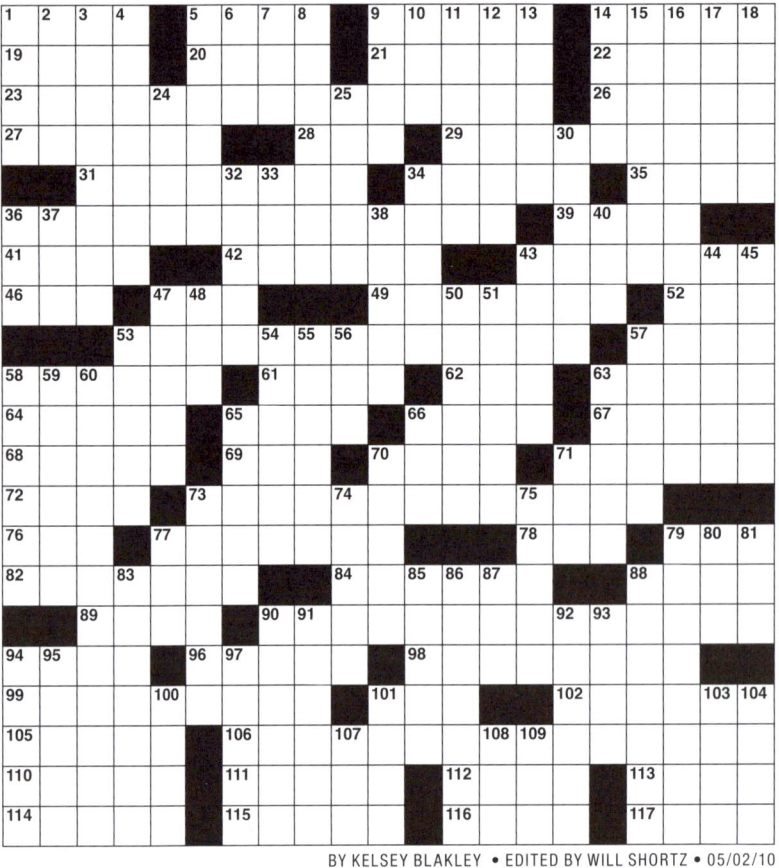

The New York Times

106 Enthronement of a metalworker?
110 They're sometimes found on belts
111 Sleep disruption
112 ___ Reader (bimonthly magazine)
113 Ad in, e.g.
114 Titleholder
115 E-6 officers in the U.S.A.F.
116 Burn
117 Duff

DOWN

1 So-called "style moderne"
2 Press
3 O.K. to put in one's mouth
4 Retire
5 Harum-___ (reckless)
6 Dallas player, for short
7 Grp. with the old slogan "A deadline every minute"
8 Early Christian
9 The Golden Bears, briefly
10 Cuckoo bird
11 "It's digestible" sloganeer, once
12 Event won five straight times by Roger Federer
13 Pervading tone
14 Society: Abbr.
15 Red Cross, e.g.
16 Being forced into a smaller house, say?
17 Having an irregularly gnawed edge
18 Recap numbers
24 Australian P.M. Kevin
25 ___ the heart of
30 Comic Conan
32 Take for another year, say
33 Commercial suffix with Gator
34 Inflate
36 Batty
37 Hail, e.g.
38 Cheerios
40 "___ showtime!"
43 Is too much
44 Amsterdam in New York
45 Credentials
47 Latches
48 Little one
50 A drunk might be in one
51 ___ Nevada
53 Some sleepers
54 Party of nine
55 Family secret, perhaps
56 Windy City transportation inits.
57 Brougham, e.g.

BY KELSEY BLAKLEY • EDITED BY WILL SHORTZ • 05/02/10

ACROSS

1 [That is correct!]
5 Overconfident
9 Not edited for TV
14 Bengay targets
19 Old switch attachment?
20 Whom mateys address
21 Jinx
22 Underfunded
23 Following the rules?
26 2009 "Survivor" locale
27 Traveling, say
28 R.S.V.P. component
29 Ladle cradle
31 Unbending
34 Astringent
35 St. ___ (malt liquor brand named after an Irish nun)
36 Variety of arbitrating techniques?
39 Observance
41 Vinegar, for one
42 Hummingbird food
43 Car rental freebie
46 Universal Human Rights Mo.
47 Sault ___ Marie
49 Scraps
52 Fertilization targets
53 Title under a photo of rain?
57 Whole tone, e.g.
58 Propose a date to
61 Fishing aids
62 A person might hang one on a road
63 Subject of paintings by Corot and Manet
64 Montgomery of "The Young Lions"
65 Peru's ___ Trail
66 Colo. ___, Colo.
67 British smell
68 Skipjack and albacore
69 Montemezzi's "L'Amore ___ Tre Re"
70 Restaurateur Toots
71 Some fighters
72 Societies: Abbr.
73 Detergent factory, e.g.?
76 Rock Island and Reading: Abbr.
77 Depression at the mouth of a volcano
78 "Galaxy Quest" characters, in brief
79 Arrangement provider
82 Keyboard features
84 Wedding proposal?
88 Gin flavorer
89 Units in physics
90 "$100 per dozen plus shipping," e.g.?
94 ___ Lang of Smallville
96 Hoopster Gilmore
98 Second best
99 Place for hangings
101 Fr. firm
102 Annoys
105 Mobile homes?

March

58 Cast
59 Wet cement mixture
60 Passing reference in the "I Have a Dream" speech?
63 Goes off on one's own
65 The Beatles, once
66 Who sells seashells by the seashore
70 Rash
71 Classic Parker Brothers card game
73 Dances with spins
74 Tough tests
75 "Grand" backdrop for "Shane"
77 Gear tooth
79 Opposite number
80 Moreover
81 Outlaw's refuge
83 Thorny bush
85 "Hamlet" courtier
86 Watery
87 Work on a tan
88 Say "Th-th-th-that's all, folks," e.g.
90 Leaves without an answer
91 Intending
92 19th-century Swedish writer Esaias ___
93 Vicinity
94 Milk: Prefix
95 It might be presented with a bow
97 Met again, as a legislature
100 It disappeared on Dec. 26, 1991
101 Alternative to Chuck
103 Word repeated in an "Animal House" chant
104 Corker
107 Lunar New Year
108 Travel plan: Abbr.
109 Off ___ tangent

monday
EIGHT HOURS DAY (AUSTRALIA—TAS)
CANBERRA DAY (AUSTRALIA—ACT)
LABOUR DAY (AUSTRALIA—VIC)
COMMONWEALTH DAY (AUSTRALIA, CANADA, NZ, UK)

10 69

tuesday
11 70

wednesday
12 71

thursday
13 72

friday
14 73

saturday
15 74

sunday
PURIM*
○ FULL MOON

16 75

March

s	m	t	w	t	f	s
						1
2	3	4	5	6	7	8
9	10	11	12	13	14	15
16	17	18	19	20	21	22
23	24	25	26	27	28	29
30	31					

*Begins at sundown the previous day

12. MS. CONCEPTIONS

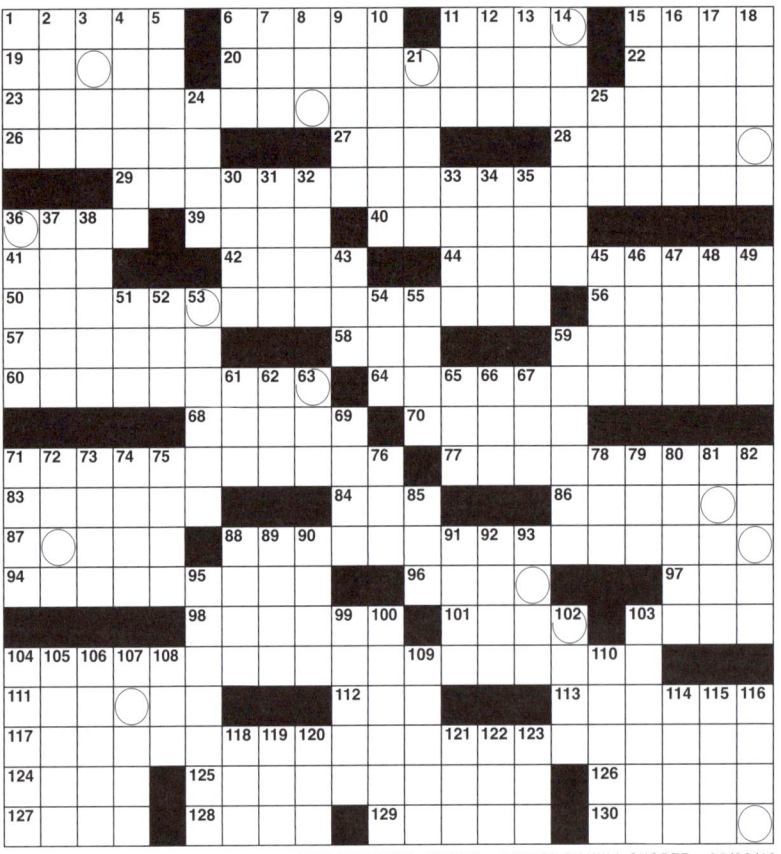

124 Lunar effect
125 Entry-level carpentry jobs?
126 Proctor ___ (small appliance brand)
127 Shangri-la
128 Twists the truth
129 Act badly?
130 Journal jotting

DOWN

1 Common type
2 Old Testament prophet
3 Bell ___
4 Whitlings, e.g.
5 Zippo
6 Before now
7 Pilfer, old-style
8 Microwave
9 Accustom
10 Frolickers by a stream
11 Yevtushenko's "Babi ___"
12 Copy ctr. blowup
13 Lead role in "The Piano"
14 Telephone part
15 "Pardon me, Arturo ..."
16 Banquo, e.g.
17 "La Grande Parade" artist Fernand
18 Yellow-and-white flower
21 Tubular pasta
24 Julie of "The Early Show"
25 Joe and Jane
30 "Golda's Balcony" subject
31 Roundish
32 Agatha Christie title
33 Sombrero part
34 Eastern princess
35 Where Polynesian Airlines is based
36 ___ Speaker
37 F.D.A. guideline
38 Primitive percussion instrument
43 "Don Giovanni" aria "Dalla ___ pace"
45 Start of a spell
46 Home in the woods
47 Bride and groom exchange
48 Jorge's house
49 Crock pot dinner
51 Donate, to Burns
52 LAX watchdog
53 Popping pills
54 Letters on a bucket
55 Celtic land
59 On the same side
61 Little rascal
62 Court grp.
63 Beer source
65 Dorm V.I.P.'s

BY ELIZABETH C. GORSKI • EDITED BY WILL SHORTZ • 05/09/10

WHEN THIS PUZZLE IS DONE, A BONUS MESSAGE WILL APPEAR IN THE CIRCLED BOXES READING FROM TOP TO BOTTOM.

ACROSS

1 New ___, N.Y.
6 W.W. II beachhead south of Rome
11 "Amen!"
15 Battle of Normandy site
19 Japanese porcelain
20 Washington zoo attraction
22 Squares for breakfast
23 Programming tool created by Grace Hopper (1906-92)
26 In that capacity
27 Stimpy's pal
28 ___ World
29 Item of apparel created by Mary Phelps Jacob (1891-1970)
36 Kissers
39 River of St. Petersburg
40 Mexican wrap
41 Active Japanese volcano
42 Pet food brand
44 Like this
50 Medical discovery of Gertrude Elion (1918-99)
56 Having no talent for
57 Rocky's love
58 It's south of Eur.
59 Songlike
60 Really prospered
64 Woodworking tool created by Tabitha Babbitt (1784-1853)
68 Block
70 2008 Wimbledon champ
71 Office item created by Bette Nesmith Graham (1924-80)
77 Practice game
83 Chaperons, typically
84 ___ king
86 Singer Kitt
87 Actress Téa
88 Driving convenience created by Mary Anderson (1866-1953)
94 Slightly faster than moderately slow
96 Ramblers and Hornets
97 Cape ___
98 Like some companies' day care facilities
101 Pike, e.g.
103 Music and dance, e.g.
104 Rock group whose name is an appropriate alternative title for this puzzle
111 Fly
112 Money machine co.
113 First family starting in 2009
117 Food formula created by Ruth Wakefield (1903-77)

March

66 Public health agcy.
67 Former Mideast inits.
69 Interpret
71 Refrain syllables
72 Esquire in "Henry VI, Part 2"
73 "Eris ___ sum" ("You will be what I am")
74 Forearm part
75 "Put ___ writing!"
76 Literary inits.
78 Gaping mouth
79 Brief look inside?
80 Stock phrase
81 War of 1812 treaty site
82 Takes in
85 "Brilliant!"
88 First part of a record
89 Preceder of many words?
90 "There Is ___ …" (song by the Cure)
91 Hungarian patriot Nagy
92 Coll. major
93 Future atty.'s challenge
95 Removed with force
99 Add a hint of color to
100 Make secret
102 Midnight Poison maker
103 Relief pitcher?
104 Having a dull surface
105 Egglike
106 What appears above a piñata?
107 Rock's Van ___
108 Land in East 58-Across: Abbr.
109 Drag race sound
110 Like many a sumo wrestler
114 Jazz vibraphonist Jackson
115 Impressionist
116 Like a hottie
118 Swiss canton
119 Have a good cry
120 Nav. rank
121 "Koochie-___!"
122 Subway line to Columbia U.
123 Needle point?

March

s	m	t	w	t	f	s
						1
2	3	4	5	6	7	8
9	10	11	12	13	14	15
16	17	18	19	20	21	22
23	24	25	26	27	28	29
30	31					

ST. PATRICK'S DAY

monday
17 76

tuesday
18 77

wednesday
19 78

thursday
20 79

friday
21 80

saturday
22 81

sunday
23 82

13. DOUBLE CROSSERS

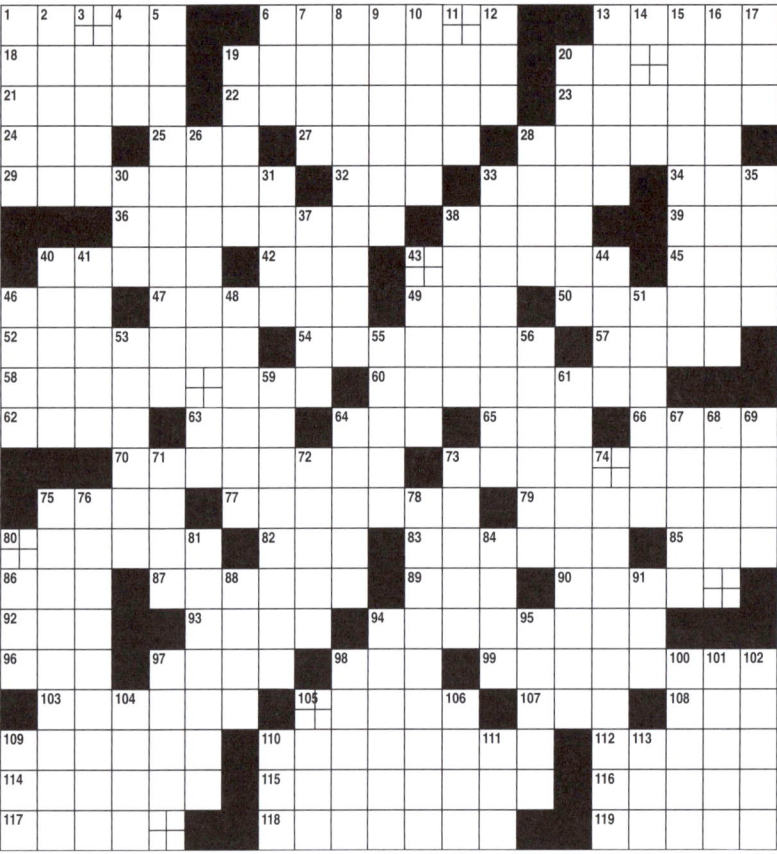

The New York Times

BY MATT GINSBERG • EDITED BY WILL SHORTZ • 05/16/10

ACROSS
1. *Winning dad in a race
6. *Like Enron
13. Joe of "NCIS"
18. "All systems ___!"
19. Only person to be named Driver of the Year in three different decades
20. *Whispers heard during an in-class test
21. Dashboard choice
22. ___ Sea, north of Alaska
23. Ajax's opponent
24. Grandmother of Spain's Juan Carlos
25. When Paris is burning?
27. "South Park" boy
28. Comparatively dull female
29. Wine drinks
32. "___ Miz"
33. Snorkeling spot
34. Camera inits.
36. Kvetch
38. Minus
39. Aunt, in Andalucía
40. "What if this present were the world's last night?" poet
42. LeBron James, beginning in '03
43. *Serving tray left next to the frying pan
45. ___ Snorkel
46. 108-Across, e.g.
47. ___ Johnson, a k a the Rock
49. Aladdin's kleptomaniac sidekick
50. Foam turbulently
52. Edison, notably
54. Junkers
57. Brisk pace
58. *Revival meeting
60. Tennis's Capriati
62. Latin being
63. Aboriginal food source
64. "My dear man"
65. ___ Friday's
66. Medieval chest
70. Extent
73. *"You're not that sorry!"
75. Old Pontiacs
77. Zebra's home
79. "This'll cost you"
80. *One who apprentices woodworkers
82. Get (to it)
83. Excepting
85. Squeeze (out)
86. Einstein's birthplace
87. Discourages
89. Month after avril
90. *Bozo, for one
92. The Indians, on a scoreboard
93. Say grace, say
94. Speed
96. 3,281 ft.
97. Pointed implement
98. The nth degree?
99. Solvents often found in antiknock additives
103. Like the down and out
105. *Singer Britney succeeds at the high jump
107. PC key
108. Altar words
109. DC ___
110. Caused to be depressed?
112. Kind of column
114. Xylophone sounds
115. Becomes more inclined
116. TV pitchman David
117. *Just one or two pups, say
118. Flies across sub-Saharan Africa?
119. Hornets' homes

DOWN
1. Drops back, as in a horse race
2. Circus site
3. *Edberg enjoying a sports match
4. ___ booster
5. 1989 Michael Moore documentary
6. Like Schoenberg's Chamber Symphony No. 1
7. The Missouri R. runs through it
8. Carpenter's standard
9. Hugh M. ___ First Amendment Award
10. Stiff collars
11. *Knock again
12. Morse code sound
13. Paper bundle
14. *Nectarine grove
15. Confirms
16. Strip sight
17. Only defenseman to have won the N.H.L. scoring title
19. Crosswise, at sea
20. Dairy section
26. *Stupid show from a cable TV giant
28. Pain, so to speak
30. OB/___ (medical specialist)
31. Telephone answerer: Abbr.
33. Start of some sequel titles
35. Have special privileges
37. Talked incessantly
38. Brother of Rebekah
40. Einsteins they aren't
41. "Laugh-In" announcer Gary
43. *Orthodontist, at times
44. Neural network
46. Greed, for one
48. Inner personalities, in psychology

March

- 51 Slips
- 53 Photographer Richard
- 55 Muslim spirit
- 56 Register
- 59 Leading in a race
- 61 Strikingly, as in dress
- 64 Some afternoon fare
- 67 Teed off
- 68 *Oven, at times
- 69 What you may need to do to get a hand
- 71 Broken in, say
- 72 Shade of white
- 73 Lock site
- 74 *Small-claims court
- 75 1981 Mel Gibson film
- 76 Exam constraint
- 78 Tries to impress, as in conversation
- 80 *Lorry in a ditch
- 81 Make unconscious
- 84 Legislature
- 88 Put one's foot down
- 91 Change the locks?
- 94 Alpine domicile
- 95 Things between shoulders
- 97 *Vlasic employee
- 98 Volcano that devastated Martinique in 1902
- 100 Diamond complements
- 101 Decree
- 102 Punches
- 104 Salon job
- 105 *Where Robert Burns and kin are buried
- 106 Popeye's ___ ' Pea
- 109 One answering to a 45-Across: Abbr.
- 110 Presidential inits.
- 111 Coast Guard rank: Abbr.
- 113 Pitchblende, for one

☾ LAST QUARTER

monday
24

tuesday
25

wednesday
26

thursday
27

friday
28

saturday
29

MOTHERING SUNDAY (IRELAND, UK)
● NEW MOON

sunday
30

March

s	m	t	w	t	f	s
						1
2	3	4	5	6	7	8
9	10	11	12	13	14	15
16	17	18	19	20	21	22
23	24	25	26	27	28	29
30	31					

14. FLIP-FLOPS

The New York Times

BY YAAKOV BENDAVID • EDITED BY WILL SHORTZ • 05/23/10

ACROSS
1. Frozen dessert in France
6. Vise parts
10. Personnel IDs
14. Michelle Robinson, now
19. Nearby school, maybe
20. Jai ___
21. "While you're ___ ..."
22. First sign
23. Where ETs do knitting and art?
26. Country singer Chesney
27. Old fogy
28. Bell site
29. David, for one
30. Give ___ (say O.K.)
32. Current regulator
34. Thug living next to humorist Will?
42. Org. for Venus and Serena Williams
43. Comical Johnson
44. Keats's nightfall
45. Place for grain
46. "Get that first down … and don't fumble"?
53. Book contents: Abbr.
55. Home of the N.C.A.A. Spartans
56. Wine city north of Lisbon
57. Pacific atoll in 1943 fighting
59. Frozen dessert
61. Shortish piano piece
64. Home of the N.C.A.A. Minutemen
66. Bright lights
67. Watching over Warsaw's national emblem?
71. Relevant, in law
74. Former Yankee pitcher Hideki
75. Biennial golf competition
79. "Parade de Cirque" artist
81. Future seeds
84. Verdi tragedy
85. Ill-mannered one
86. "Platoon" setting, for short
88. Waiting in line for hooch?
91. Alan of Hollywood
93. Pen name
95. Skin ___
96. Dorm V.I.P.'s
97. Competition among shrinks?
105. Paid attention to, with "of"
106. Santa ___
107. Long bones
110. Halloween purchase
114. Fireplace cavity
118. Gave heartburn, say
119. Visitors' fair warning?
121. Capital city more than 9,000 feet above sea level
122. Prefix with logical
123. Maintain
124. Start of the French Lord's Prayer
125. Temptress
126. Relish
127. Round of golf, informally
128. County of Newark, N.J.

DOWN
1. Five-time U.S. Open champ
2. Disney title character from Hawaii
3. Hertz rival
4. Husband of Pompeia
5. Cause of some storms
6. Big bump
7. Word said with a tear, maybe
8. Ride the breeze
9. Web presence
10. Plato's "tenth Muse"
11. Lost zip
12. "Good comeback!"
13. Chateau ___ Michelle winery
14. Art supply store stock
15. Inspirations
16. "___ No Woman," 1973 hit for the Four Tops
17. Computer offering
18. "___ sow …"
24. Jam
25. Blood fluid: Prefix
29. Undercover jobs
31. Not to be persuaded
33. Ooze
34. Philippines' highest peak: Abbr.
35. Blathered
36. Growling sound
37. [Ignore edit]
38. Blood: Prefix
39. Airhead
40. Colleague of Lane and Kent
41. No contests
42. "___ next?"
47. Clothier, in Cambridge
48. Hassock
49. Thwart
50. Salad green
51. Super Bowl XXXIV champs
52. Famous movie river
54. Milton works
58. Observatory subj.
60. Kick oneself over
62. "In the," in Italy
63. Place to stick a comb
65. "Charlotte's Web" setting
68. Pumice source
69. Be flush with
70. Pedestal topper
71. Royalties org.
72. Passes out
73. Like some complexions
76. "Bewitched" aunt
77. ___ nerve
78. Sci-fi escape vehicles
80. They're just not done

March-April

- 82 Spanish demonstrative
- 83 Small-runway aircraft, briefly
- 87 Standard part of a food pyramid
- 89 Like Saint-Saëns's "Urbs Roma" Symphony
- 90 Norman of TV fame
- 92 Impel
- 94 Say "I lost," say
- 98 Dr. Seuss title animal
- 99 Spurs
- 100 "Boy, am I shvitzing!"
- 101 Job legislation estab. in 1973
- 102 Stray
- 103 Dead Sea Scrolls writer
- 104 Exuberant cries
- 107 Recommended reading for newbies
- 108 Thread holder
- 109 Kiev-born Israeli P.M.
- 111 ___ Bator, Mongolia
- 112 10 years before the Battle of Hastings
- 113 Nobel Prize category: Abbr.
- 115 A lot of mil. personnel
- 116 "Able was ___ …"
- 117 Creature in a "King Kong" fight
- 119 Guru
- 120 Fall behind

March

s	m	t	w	t	f	s
						1
2	3	4	5	6	7	8
9	10	11	12	13	14	15
16	17	18	19	20	21	22
23	24	25	26	27	28	29
30	31					

April

s	m	t	w	t	f	s
		1	2	3	4	5
6	7	8	9	10	11	12
13	14	15	16	17	18	19
20	21	22	23	24	25	26
27	28	29	30			

monday
31

tuesday
1

wednesday
2

thursday
3

friday
4

saturday
5

sunday
6

15. FULL CIRCLE

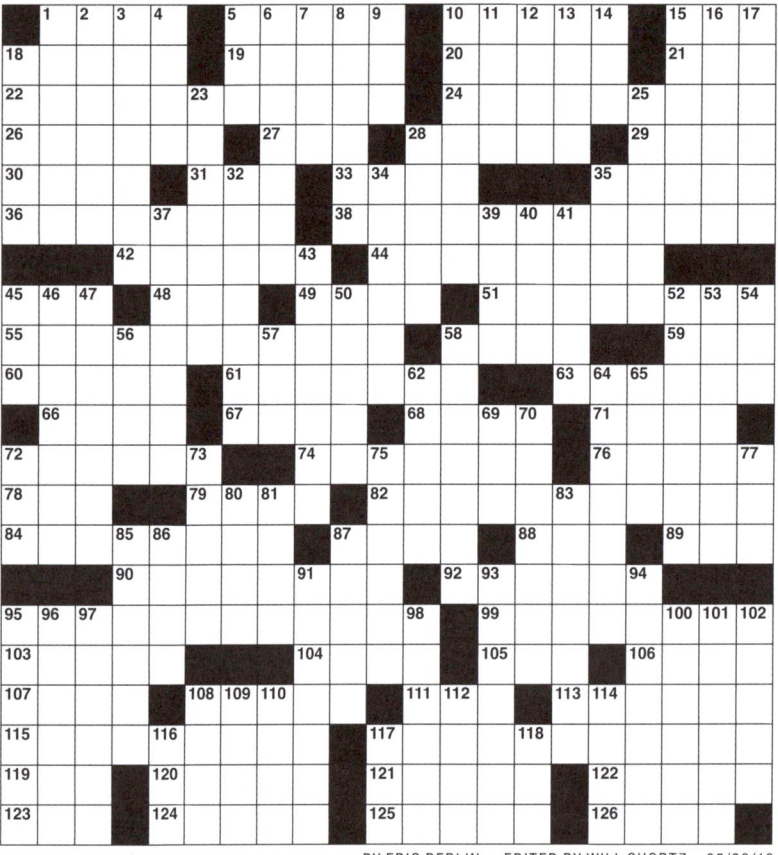

The New York Times

ACROSS

1. City SE of New Delhi
5. "To your health!"
10. Cumberland Gap explorer
15. iPod control: Abbr.
18. Supermax resident
19. Chekhov's "Uncle ___"
20. Instructional tool
21. W.W. II command
22. With 24-Across, two things that are stuffed
24. With 36-Across, two things on a farm
26. Getting up there in years
27. Tests for college credit, briefly
28. Domain
29. Laugh ___
30. Word game component, sometimes
31. Tijuana "that"
33. Seeing red
35. Guy
36. With 38-Across, two things associated with needles
38. With 55-Across, two things that spin
42. Like some roofs and roads
44. Balloonists' baskets
45. Que. neighbor
48. Fund-raising grp.
49. Scientist Pavlov
51. Some poetic feet
55. With 82-Across, two things at an amusement park
58. Believers
59. "Hair" song with the lyric "Hello, carbon monoxide"
60. Many a Miley Cyrus fan
61. Speaker's spot
63. Sicilian tourist attraction
66. Out of concern that
67. Little argument
68. Accusatory words
71. ___ Kalugin, former K.G.B. general with the 1994 book "Spymaster"
72. Vivacious person
74. Annual foursome
76. Opponent of Pericles
78. Santa ___
79. ___ de malaise
82. With 95-Across, two things that are sticky
84. Admonishment
87. Egg cream component
88. Argentine aunt
89. Edinburgh-to-London dir.
90. Second track on "Beatles '65"
92. "No Escape" star, 1994
95. With 99-Across, two things with brushes
99. With 115-Across, two things with ladders
103. Bargaining group
104. Church recess
105. Noted period
106. 1922 Physics Nobelist
107. Physics units
108. Certain Apples
111. HDTV brand
113. Adjective for a bikini, in a 1960 song
115. With 117-Across, two things that are red
117. With 22-Across, two things associated with Thanksgiving
119. Wire service inits.
120. Drug company behind Valium
121. "Pearls Before Swine," e.g.
122. What some titles are written in, briefly
123. Standing need
124. Signed
125. "Zorba the Greek" setting
126. Smooth

DOWN

1. Region in ancient Asia Minor
2. With a smile
3. Most promising
4. Certain soldiers
5. "Law & Order" spinoff, for short
6. Draw of some bars
7. Being punished, military-style
8. "O.K., captain!"
9. Not ecclesiastical
10. Inspired by
11. Deep-sea predator
12. Spoken
13. Usual
14. Woolly one
15. In truth, in Shakespeare
16. Peter with four Golden Globes
17. Claim in a cigarette ad
18. Latte topper
23. Juilliard's focus
25. Hockey goalie's area
28. Scout's job, briefly
32. Hasty signatures
34. Entertain
35. To-do
37. Use as a resource
39. Nutritional stds.
40. Word of warning
41. Ending with proto-
43. Like some metal toys
45. Many times, in verse
46. Studio that produced the Austin Powers movies
47. Source of some resins

BY ERIC BERLIN • EDITED BY WILL SHORTZ • 05/30/10

April

50 American sports car, for short
52 Shiny fabrics
53 Small-time tyrants
54 Mexican Mrs.
56 Others
57 In the know, in old slang
58 Counting everything
62 Put new turf on
64 Improvisatory piece of classical music
65 "Enchanted" girl of children's lit
69 "Southland" airer
70 Shows near the front?
72 Target for certain athletes
73 Actor Burton
75 They're nuts
77 Scientist with multiple Emmys
80 Rash soother
81 Rash soother
83 Fertilizer ingredient
85 Biochemical sugar
86 Sign
87 Gets through slowly
91 Kissed noisily
93 "Honest!"
94 Neighbor of Montana
95 Very sorry
96 Green, say
97 18-wheeler
98 Real brat
100 Sea between Italy and Greece
101 Protect
102 Long lock
108 Monopoly token
109 Gooey dirt
110 Workout aftereffect
112 Arrived
114 She threw the apple of discord
116 Not quite quadri-
117 XXX x X
118 Letters in an old date

☽ FIRST QUARTER

monday

7 97

tuesday

8 98

wednesday

9 99

thursday

10 100

friday

11 101

saturday

12 102

PALM SUNDAY

sunday

13 103

April

s	m	t	w	t	f	s
		1	2	3	4	5
6	7	8	9	10	11	12
13	14	15	16	17	18	19
20	21	22	23	24	25	26
27	28	29	30			

16. TYPECASTING

The New York Times

ACROSS

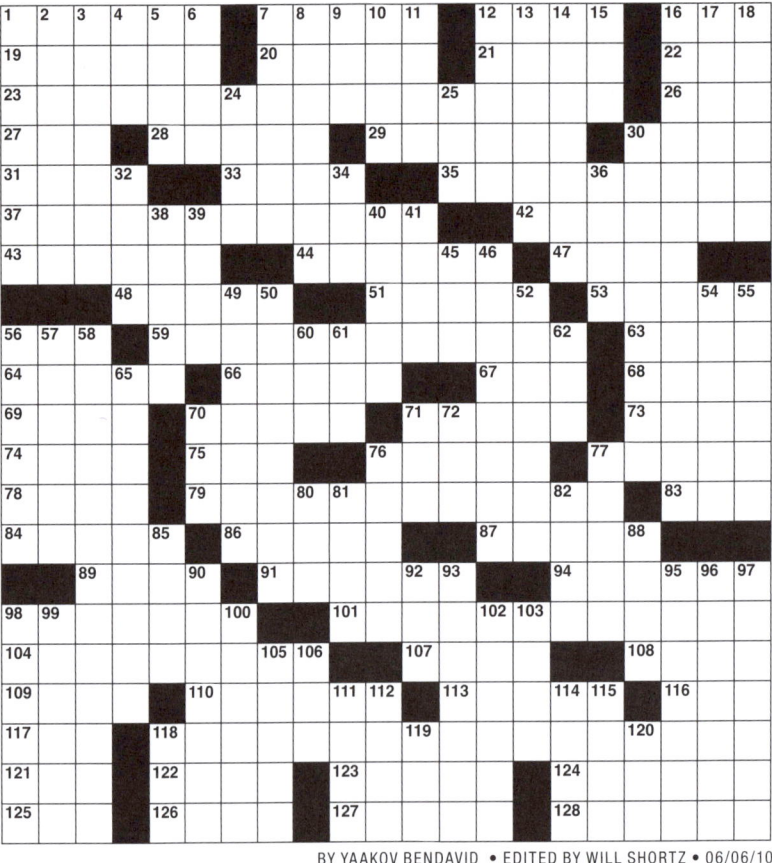

1. See above
7. Slicker, in a way
12. "… so long ___ both shall live?"
16. Youth grp.
19. Bit of excitement
20. Japanese comics style
21. Have ___ to grind
22. Cries of a toe-stubber
23. JAIL OR FINE
26. Edge
27. Grown-___
28. Staff connections
29. "Carrie" star
30. Year Attila the Hun was born
31. Figure on an electric bill
33. Chris ___, player of Mr. Big on "Sex and the City"
35. Excuse maker, maybe
37. *Perspectives*
42. Sound city
43. Kitt who sang "Santa Baby"
44. Tarzan's simian sidekick
47. ___ spell
48. Actress Christina
51. Lee who got a kick out of acting?
53. "You are mistaken!"
56. Trail
59. Putting in a carton
63. Bygone name in hair removal
64. Salivation cause
66. Turkish money
67. ___ spell
68. Exam for a Wharton applicant: Abbr.
69. Himalayan legend
70. Come out with
71. PC insert
73. French suffix
74. Critical comments
75. ___ culpa
76. 2005 "Survivor" setting
77. Not superficial
78. "___ would seem"
79. *Wordsmith*
83. Results of some rushes, for short
84. Ltr. accompaniers
86. Bro
87. Audacious
89. Pool surface
91. Some riding mowers
94. Noxious atmosphere
98. Mercury and Saturn
101. **Birthday cake toppers**
104. Endorse
107. Jedi foes, in "Star Wars"
108. Is indisposed
109. Goya's field
110. Mr. ___ of advertising
113. Desiderata
116. Printemps month
117. 2006 Nintendo debut
118. Couple-swapping
121. 1976 album "Olé ___"
122. Zig or zag
123. It may be snowy
124. Board as a group
125. Rembrandt van ___
126. Language from which "loot" comes
127. Smooths, in a way
128. Stashes

DOWN

1. Bedamn
2. Mexico's largest lake
3. Snoop, e.g.
4. "… ___ quit!"
5. Pepper and Friday: Abbr.
6. One clapping at a circus?
7. Comedy specialty
8. Biting
9. Comfort ___
10. Sponsorship: Var.
11. Not smooth-talk?
12. Company with a "beep-beep" in its ads
13. Responses of contempt
14. Team whose logo features a bat in a hat
15. No. after a no.
16. Assertion
17. Turn 90°, say
18. Have a goal
24. Bergman's role in "Casablanca"
25. Is sick with
30. Separating machine
32. ___ 'acte
34. Snicker part
36. Reclined
38. "Is ___ joke?"
39. For one
40. "Our Town" family
41. Prefix in hematology
45. What a penguin doesn't really wear
46. Deleterious precipitation
49. Prestigious West Coast school, for short
50. Race that takes a northern trail in even years and a southern trail in odd years
52. Neither here nor there?
54. Prepared, as some tuna
55. Warren : rabbits :: couch : ___
56. A parking garage may have special pricing for it
57. Home of the U.S.'s last active nickel mine
58. *Untruths*
60. Garnierite, for nickel

BY YAAKOV BENDAVID • EDITED BY WILL SHORTZ • 06/06/10

April

61 It's good for "absolutely nothing" according to a 1970 hit
62 Sweaters' place
65 Christmas hanging
70 Sounds of hesitation
71 Field call
72 Abbr. on some license plates
76 Wing: Prefix
77 Pro Football Hall-of-Famer Michael
80 The Beatles' "___ Mine"
81 It's on top of piles
82 Columnist Bombeck
85 Dude ranch nickname
88 When tripled, a "Seinfeld" catchphrase
90 Satan, with "the"
92 Ambulance letters
93 Like Joan of Arc
95 More like a slug
96 U.S. tennis player Oudin
97 Gives, as homework
98 Chest part
99 How haunted houses creak
100 Blow one's stack
102 Bikini blasts
103 Copenhagen, e.g.
105 Country that's just 8 square miles in area
106 Leadership org. opposed to the G.O.P.
111 Island instruments, for short
112 Classical attire
114 Party bowlfuls
115 State of ill humor
118 "Law & Order: ___"
119 Ash holder
120 Shine, in ads

monday
14 104

tuesday
PASSOVER*
○ FULL MOON

15 105

wednesday
16 106

thursday
17 107

friday
GOOD FRIDAY (WESTERN)
HOLY FRIDAY (ORTHODOX)

18 108

saturday
EASTER SATURDAY (AUSTRALIA—EXCEPT TAS, WA)

19 109

sunday
EASTER (WESTERN, ORTHODOX)

20 110

April

s	m	t	w	t	f	s
		1	2	3	4	5
6	7	8	9	10	11	12
13	14	15	16	17	18	19
20	21	22	23	24	25	26
27	28	29	30			

*Begins at sundown the previous day

The New York Times

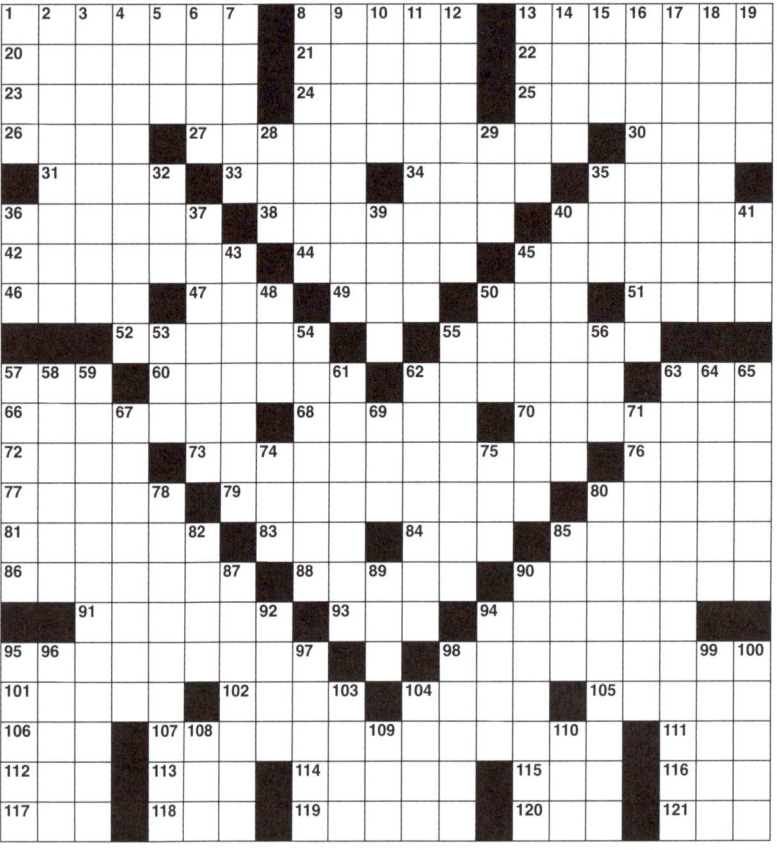

ACROSS

1 Desert Storm transports
8 Is sociable
13 Annoyed with persistent petty attacks
20 Qualify
21 Contest site
22 1994 Red Hot Chili Peppers album
23 Rabbi or mullah
24 Like most Western music
25 Went over completely
26 March ___
27 John McCain and John Kerry
30 Dog command
31 Gig for a deejay
33 Sped
34 For-EV-er
35 Steeplechase, e.g.
36 Idle
38 Emulated a hungry wolf
40 Common rolls
42 River crossed by the Longfellow Bridge
44 Clogs at the bottom?
45 Arrive at by air
46 Repair shop figs.
47 British P.M. after Lloyd George
49 Ward, to the Beaver
50 Payday, often: Abbr.
51 Crash-investigating org.
52 Striped stones
55 What "Arf! Arf!" or "Meow!" may mean
57 "The Real World" airer
60 2009 hit film with subtitled scenes
62 Earn
63 Word on either side of "à"
66 Contributes
68 Transfer, as at a nursery
70 "The Charge of the Light Brigade" figure
72 Block component
73 "Wedding Crashers" co-star, 2005
76 Evolutionary chart
77 Key of Chopin's "Polonaise-Fantaisie"
79 Tina Fey and Amy Poehler, once, on "S.N.L."
80 "Spider-Man" director
81 "Get lost!"
83 Ft. Collins setting
84 Abbr. on a currency exchange board
85 Toy company behind yo-yos
86 Entered carefully
88 Canyonlands National Park features
90 Bands on the run?
91 Aircraft control surface
93 Good name for a surveyor?
94 Some Muslims
95 Those near and dear
98 Quality of new-fallen snow
101 "___ Pieces" (Peter and Gordon hit)
102 Congolese river
104 Nondemocratic rule
105 Short answers?
106 Kind of scan, for short
107 Keepers of the flame?
111 E.R. readout
112 Old nuclear watchdog: Abbr.
113 Dutch city ESE of Utrecht
114 Toil
115 The Beavers of the N.C.A.A.
116 QB's miscue
117 Newcastle-to-London dir.
118 Play that introduced the word "robot"
119 Anathematic
120 Break, of a sort
121 Some Windows systems

DOWN

1 Eighth Hebrew letter
2 Discovers
3 Post-flood locale
4 The other way around
5 Old verb ending
6 About 16,900 ft., for 3-Down
7 Letter's end?
8 The situation
9 Tree with very hard timber
10 TV title character who said "I'm not an Amazon"
11 Covered, as cookware
12 Some gunfire
13 Overhead ___
14 Cadence syllables
15 "Let's make ___ true Daily Double"
16 Plant with purple flowers
17 Name of 13 popes
18 Gold and silver, but not bronze
19 ___ City, Fla.
28 Antiquity, poetically
29 Demise
32 Course for new U.S. arrivals
34 King on un trono
36 A-one service?
37 Setting for part of 2005's "Munich"
39 Royal name in Norway
40 Use for skating
41 Break down
43 Infernal
45 Big name in mustard
48 Sloppy, as a kiss
50 Sword: Fr.
53 ___-X
54 "Oh, joy!," e.g., typically

BY PETER A. COLLINS • EDITED BY WILL SHORTZ • 06/13/10

April

- 55 Inane
- 56 ___ Miller (Julie Christie title role with 57-Down)
- 57 Warren Beatty title role with 56-Down
- 58 Group with a board of governors
- 59 Weekly since 1955, with "The"
- 61 Type in again, as a password
- 62 "After you"
- 63 Vessel seen just below the surface?
- 64 Hired gun, in gang slang
- 65 Coils
- 67 Clotting agent
- 69 Plastic used in piping
- 71 Subs
- 74 Marcel Marceau, e.g.
- 75 [This makes me mad!]
- 78 Satisfied, for a while at least
- 80 #2's
- 82 Home recorder
- 85 Repair shop job
- 87 Teetotaler
- 89 U.S.S.R. part: Abbr.
- 90 What may help one live and learn?
- 92 Classic hair removal brand
- 94 Catch some flies
- 95 Some beans
- 96 Meanies
- 97 Hack
- 98 Overly caffeinated
- 99 Pooped
- 100 Some NCOs
- 103 "___ Enchanted" (2004 film)
- 104 V
- 108 U.R.L. ender
- 109 Brewhouse fixture
- 110 Code-breaking grp.

EASTER MONDAY (AUSTRALIA, CANADA, IRELAND, NZ, UK—EXCEPT SCOTLAND)

monday
21

PASSOVER ENDS
EARTH DAY
☾ LAST QUARTER

tuesday
22

ST. GEORGE'S DAY (UK)

wednesday
23

thursday
24

ANZAC DAY (NZ, AUSTRALIA)

friday
25

saturday
26

sunday
27

April

s	m	t	w	t	f	s
		1	2	3	4	5
6	7	8	9	10	11	12
13	14	15	16	17	18	19
20	21	22	23	24	25	26
27	28	29	30			

18. PUBLISHING TRADE

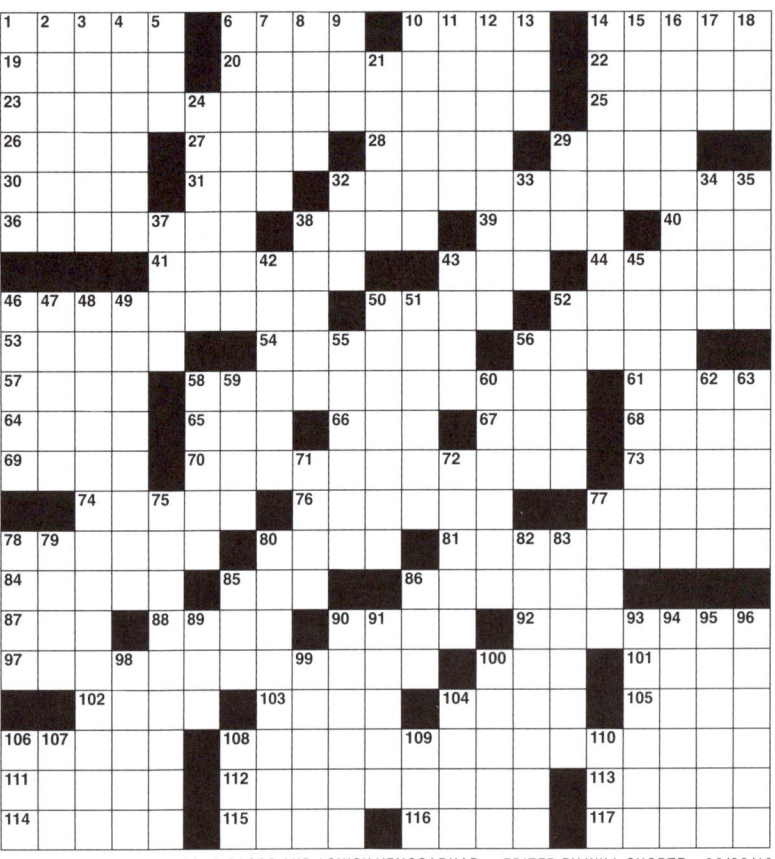

The New York Times

BY TODD GROSS AND ASHISH VENGSARKAR • EDITED BY WILL SHORTZ • 06/20/10

ACROSS

1. Out of fashion
6. Trailer org.?
10. C.I.A. director Panetta
14. Immerse
19. Leave ___ (be permanently damaging)
20. "Ale" for the underaged
22. Apple messaging software
23. "Carson's Successful Safari"? [Dalton Trumbo]
25. New Hampshire's ___ State College
26. Spanish liqueur
27. Knoxville team, to fans
28. Ralph Vaughan Williams's "___ Symphony"
29. Care
30. ___ en place (putting in place: Fr.)
31. Lacto-___
32. "Big Pile of Dirt"? [Charles Frazier]
36. Writer who wrote "A bear, however hard he tries, / Grows tubby without exercise"
38. Rad
39. Vet
40. Brandy letters
41. Beyond belief
43. Whichever
44. Govt. instrument
46. British coin discontinued in 1984
50. Have no input?
52. Pupil cover
53. 2006 million-selling Andrea Bocelli album
54. Presidential middle name
56. Talk about it
57. French rail station
58. "Battle Backstabber"? [Sun Tzu]
61. German quaff
64. Some receivers
65. Scandinavian rug
66. Deli order
67. Get to
68. Port in the eastern Mediterranean
69. Caustic soda, to a chemist
70. "Secretive Student Monitor"? [John le Carré]
73. Swelter
74. Big lie
76. Like racehorses, periodically
77. Soul singer Adams
78. Verdi opera
80. Corp. V.I.P.
81. Came down
84. "Toward Freedom" autobiographer
85. Not 85-Down
86. Hot ___
87. Kicker's aid
88. Zip
90. Main rat in "Ratatouille"
92. Letter of indictment?
97. "Endless Streams"? [David Foster Wallace]
100. Deg. in biology or physics
101. Letters
102. Superstar
103. Election goal
104. End of a boast
105. Central Sicily city
106. Sits
108. "Football Team Leaves L.A."? [Ernest Hemingway]
111. Brother of Malcolm on "Malcolm in the Middle"
112. White House nickname
113. Script
114. Three-piece parts
115. Hot
116. Former Swedish P.M. Palme
117. ___-Dale (1902 Kentucky Derby winner)

DOWN

1. ___ party
2. Tone deafness
3. Division
4. Grandchild of Japanese immigrants
5. Coastal flier
6. Candidate with the slogan "Come home, America"
7. Film director Pier ___ Pasolini
8. Some soldiers
9. Backrub response
10. Snares
11. Just beat
12. Christmas ball, e.g.
13. Sch. where Ross teaches on "Friends"
14. Two-piece part
15. Not worth ___
16. "Renaissance College Girl"? [Dan Brown]
17. Yangtze tributary
18. Somme summer
21. Cockpit features
24. Batgirl player Craig
29. Puss
32. Spreadsheet feature: Abbr.
33. ___-10 (acne medication)
34. Key
35. The Big Easy, briefly
37. Rapper Fiasco
38. Company whose logo contains its name crossing itself
42. Charm
43. Since
45. Venal
46. Tom ___, Vito's adopted son and consigliere in "The Godfather"
47. Appliance appellation

April-May

- 48 "Head Secretary"? [William Golding]
- 49 You might step out to get some
- 50 Lean, as meat
- 51 How much you might kick it up?
- 52 Like spoiled wine, say
- 55 Chemistry class charge
- 56 Camping supply
- 58 Carefree syllables
- 59 Oversell
- 60 Sagacity
- 62 Verdi aria
- 63 Pass again, in a race
- 71 Muffs
- 72 "Who's ___?"
- 75 Holier-than-thou types
- 77 ESPN's Hershiser
- 78 Start to freeze?
- 79 12-20 filler?
- 80 Laments the loss of
- 82 Low pitch indicator
- 83 Bring out
- 85 Not 85-Across
- 86 Corp. logos, e.g.
- 89 Start of many a rap moniker
- 90 Brought up
- 91 Ending with Rock
- 93 "Bam!" blurter
- 94 "Hey Jude" sounds
- 95 Dealers in metal goods
- 96 Minor-league category
- 98 To wit
- 99 Astrologer Dixon
- 100 Fictional hero in search of stolen treasure
- 104 Osso buco, basically
- 106 Record exec Gotti
- 107 Nearly failing
- 108 ___ tuna
- 109 GATT successor
- 110 Ending with Rock

April

s	m	t	w	t	f	s
		1	2	3	4	5
6	7	8	9	10	11	12
13	14	15	16	17	18	19
20	21	22	23	24	25	26
27	28	29	30			

May

s	m	t	w	t	f	s
				1	2	3
4	5	6	7	8	9	10
11	12	13	14	15	16	17
18	19	20	21	22	23	24
25	26	27	28	29	30	31

monday
28 118

● NEW MOON

tuesday
29 119

wednesday
30 120

thursday
1 121

friday
2 122

saturday
3 123

sunday
4 124

19. TO THINE OWN SELF BE TRUE

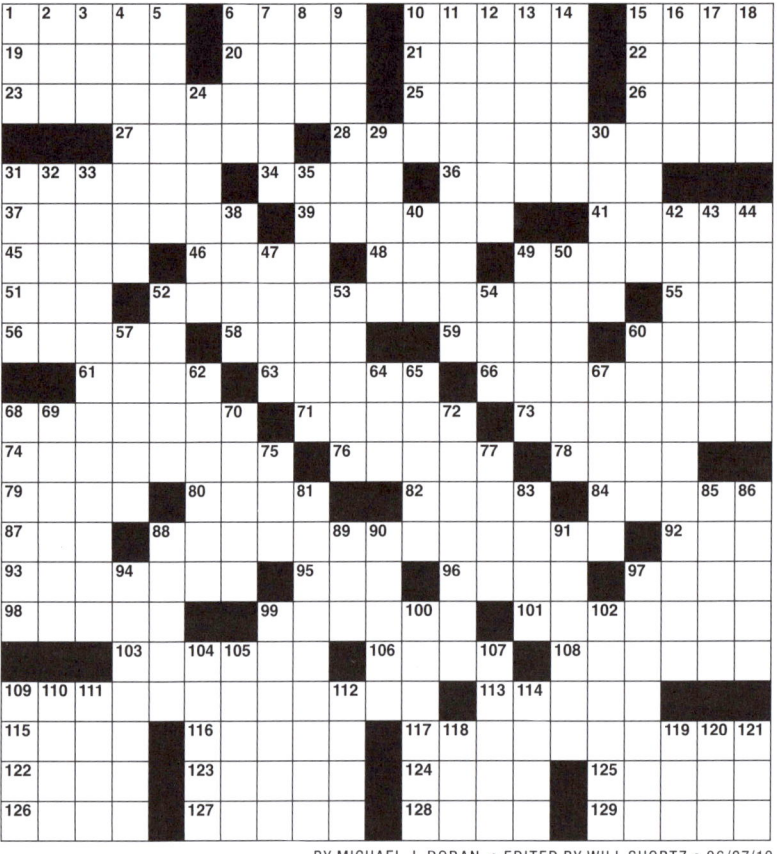

The New York Times

ACROSS

1. Low-lying land
6. "Dirty rat," e.g.
10. Moves quickly
15. Take the edge off?
19. Tower city resident
20. Ensure that a G is actually a G, say
21. ___ Lane, home of London's Theatre Royal
22. Pulitzer-winning James
23. Irate
25. Universal soul, in Hinduism
26. Troubadour's subject
27. Coffin frames
28. Isled
31. Bank
34. Benz of Mercedes-Benz fame
36. Ready
37. Lovingly, in music
39. Macedonian capital
41. Texas' state tree
45. Talk until you're blue in the face
46. Part of Q.E.D.
48. Shanghai-born N.B.A. star
49. Way in the past
51. Tina's role on "30 Rock"
52. Islander
55. Father's speech: Abbr.
56. Defendant's testimony, maybe
58. Elton John and Paul McCartney
59. Miró Museum architect José Luis ___
60. Word of greed
61. In ___ (unmoved)
63. What most Mormons do
66. Breaks up
68. Rout
71. Naproxen, commercially
73. Double-breasted winter wear
74. Greatly desires
76. Moran and Gray
78. Think, in olden times
79. Financial aid factor
80. One taking a bow?
82. When the tempest occurs in "The Tempest"
84. Grandson of Adam
87. Bit of video gear, for short
88. Iran
92. When written three times, fraternity in "Revenge of the Nerds"
93. Lets off
95. Hinduism, e.g.: Abbr.
96. Dentist's request
97. Swedish toast
98. Actress Hatcher and others
99. Large planes have two
101. Attorney general under Reagan
103. Like some investments
106. "___ the picture!"
108. Rose and rose and rose
109. iPhone
113. Word with kilowatt or business
115. Mix
116. "___ no?"
117. Ibid.
122. Certain Scot
123. Cat-tails connector
124. Trident feature
125. Bush with the memoir "Spoken From the Heart"
126. Title girl on the first Beatles album
127. Baja babies
128. Suffix with hip
129. Madrid misses: Abbr.

DOWN

1. Lotion letters
2. What to play Super Mario Galaxy on
3. Communication for the deaf: Abbr.
4. St. Louis airport
5. City near Sherman Oaks
6. Mix
7. Ukrainian city in W.W. I fighting
8. College, across the pond
9. Close again, as a wine bottle
10. Event depicted in "Saving Private Ryan"
11. Drawers in some college dorm rooms?
12. Make wrinkly
13. Crumbs, in "Hansel and Gretel"
14. Makes match up
15. Private greetings?
16. Awestruck
17. Actress Campbell
18. A couple of bucks?
24. Part of Eritrea's border
29. Christopher of "Back to the Future"
30. Recipient of Jesus' healing
31. Alfalfa's sweetie
32. Google or Yahoo! service
33. Icon
35. Area in Queens
38. Earth and moon
40. What a dog might "shake" with
42. Ideal
43. Outline of a sort
44. What the weary get, in a saying
47. Got off
49. Off the bottom, as an anchor

BY MICHAEL J. DORAN • EDITED BY WILL SHORTZ • 06/27/10

May

- 50 Words before "go"
- 52 South American monkeys
- 53 Basketry fiber
- 54 Roadside bomb: Abbr.
- 57 Competed in a velodrome
- 60 "Heart of Georgia"
- 62 Like a mild earthquake, maybe
- 64 Every other hurricane
- 65 Fiji competitor
- 67 Less furnished
- 68 Surgeon's tool
- 69 Sherpa's tool
- 70 Al et al.
- 72 Pen
- 75 ___-A-Fella Records
- 77 Pull over
- 81 Call from home?
- 83 Therapist's reply
- 85 Part of many an action movie
- 86 In hiding, with "up"
- 88 English racing town
- 89 Suffix with pant
- 90 Half of an old comedy duo
- 91 Becomes
- 94 Long Island town where the Wright Brothers experimented
- 97 Ocean dweller with five points
- 99 Is a polite host to
- 100 Marsh sights
- 102 Fable teachings
- 104 Silky material
- 105 "Me, Myself & ___," 2000 Jim Carrey movie
- 107 "The ___ of Fife had a wife": Shak.
- 109 "Spartacus" attire
- 110 Panache
- 111 Certain claim
- 112 Square root of nueve
- 114 Open hearing, in law
- 118 Drill part
- 119 Cause of a bump in the road
- 120 "… boy ___ girl?"
- 121 "If I Ruled the World" rapper

monday
5 125

LABOUR DAY (AUSTRALIA—QLD)
MAY DAY (AUSTRALIA—NT)
EARLY MAY BANK HOLIDAY (IRELAND, UK)

tuesday
6 126

wednesday
7 127

☽ FIRST QUARTER

thursday
8 128

friday
9 129

saturday
10 130

sunday
11 131

MOTHER'S DAY (USA, AUSTRALIA, CANADA, NZ)

May

s	m	t	w	t	f	s
				1	2	3
4	5	6	7	8	9	10
11	12	13	14	15	16	17
18	19	20	21	22	23	24
25	26	27	28	29	30	31

20. MAKING ENDS MEET

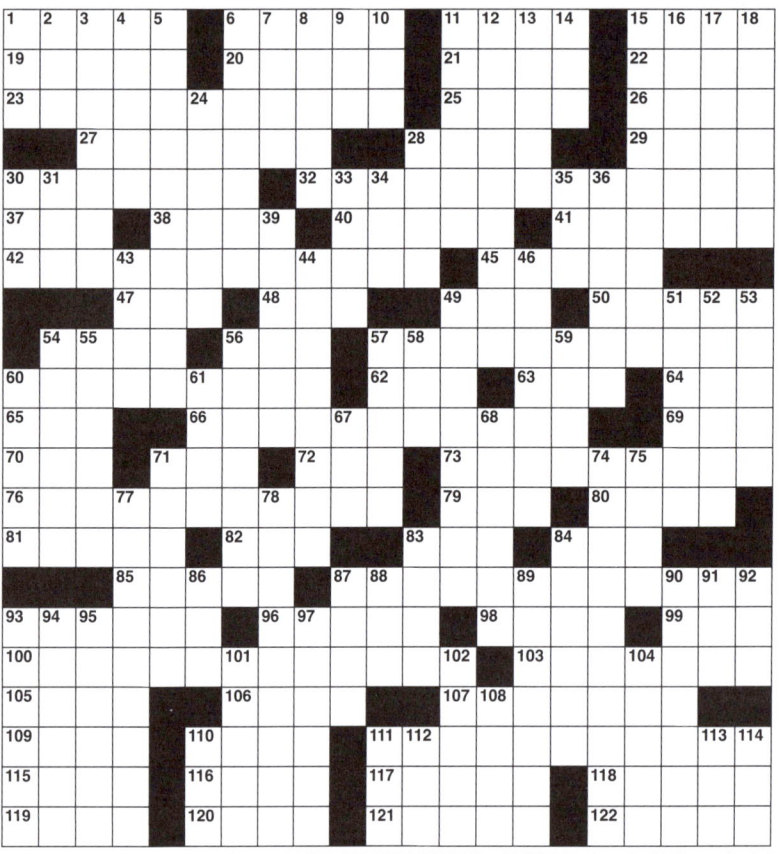

The New York Times

BY PATRICK BLINDAUER AND TONY ORBACH • EDITED BY WILL SHORTZ • 07/04/10

ACROSS

1. Routine responses?
6. 1961 Charlton Heston/Sophia Loren film
11. "Who ___?"
15. Goes back
19. Words of certainty
20. Unit of energy
21. Sculpture garden setting in N.Y.C.
22. Response to freshness?
23. Technical trouble
25. Uncle of Levi
26. Author John Dickson ___
27. Puts together
28. Items at one's disposal?
29. Prefix with thesis
30. Actor/comic Brad
32. Helper in herding
37. Bird with meat high in protein
38. Not e'en once
40. Not straight up
41. Sideshow features
42. Collectible book
45. Block legally
47. Carrier in the Star Alliance
48. Cassette knob abbr.
49. Yokel's laugh
50. Big name in trading cards
54. Indonesian vacation spot
56. Bao ___ (former Vietnamese emperor)
57. Line in London
60. Symbol of a boring routine
62. Special ___
63. Cassette button abbr.
64. Key: Fr.
65. Split
66. Like many an online password
69. World Cup cry
70. Service
71. Rose who rose to fame in the 1980s
72. 50-50, e.g.
73. Small carriage
76. It might have a theater and planetarium
79. Campers, for short
80. "Love surfeits not, ___ like a glutton dies": Shak.
81. Show expanded to four hours in 2007
82. Chess opening?
83. Itinerary word
84. Marxist, e.g.
85. Bars
87. Singer who played Cyrano in "Cyrano de Bergerac"
93. Caesar, e.g.
96. When daylight saving begins: Abbr.
98. Commercial time of day
99. "___ House," 1970 Crosby, Stills, Nash & Young hit
100. Introvert or extrovert
103. Grenache, for one
105. ___ fruit
106. They may be flipped
107. Off
109. Start
110. "Come here often?", e.g.
111. Protector
115. Kin of -ess or -trix
116. Future platypi
117. Offer one's thoughts
118. "Somewhere in Time" actor
119. Suffix with prank
120. Part of 58-Down: Abbr.
121. In a stack
122. Approvals

DOWN

1. Boozehound's sound
2. "Just ___!" ("Hold on!")
3. Prosaic
4. On the say-so of
5. Gift from the well-endowed
6. Bounced
7. Old tales
8. What a mummy might have
9. Agcy. of the U.N.
10. "___ Kommissar" (1983 hit)
11. "Bam!" man in the kitchen
12. Petered out
13. Very successful
14. Seine filler
15. Way out in space
16. Football Hall-of-Famer George
17. Composer of "The Miraculous Mandarin"
18. Parsley parts
24. Some pupils
28. Swedish-born "Chocolat" actress
30. Cowlick tamer
31. Confidant, peut-être
33. Get exactly right
34. 'Vette alternative
35. Little newt
36. Hot
39. Play featuring Mrs. Malaprop, with "The"
43. Española, e.g.
44. Demoiselle's dressing
46. Sudden turns
49. Not just noteworthy
51. Embroidery loops
52. What a forklift may lift
53. Disapproving look
54. Depp title role
55. Famous 12-book story
56. Brooklynese, e.g.
57. Wannabe
58. Alma mater of some engrs.
59. "Cheers" actor Roger
60. Word in many bank names

May

- 61 Year that Emperor Frederick I died
- 67 Not even once, in Nürnberg
- 68 For nothing
- 71 "Moving on then …"
- 74 Simple
- 75 German import
- 77 Resident of New York's Murray Hill, e.g.
- 78 Batch that's hatched
- 83 Seductress
- 84 Relative of fusilli
- 86 Vessel in an alcove
- 87 Kitchenware
- 88 Not in the profession
- 89 Made fractions … or factions
- 90 Pests
- 91 T. S. Eliot's "Theatre Cat"
- 92 What's mined to keep?
- 93 Sonatas and such
- 94 University V.I.P.
- 95 Dahl of "A Southern Yankee," 1948
- 97 Most outspread
- 101 True
- 102 Brick-and-mortar alternative
- 104 Dancer Jeanmaire
- 108 "Rule, Britannia" composer
- 110 Bit of neckwear
- 111 Herd of elephants?
- 112 Initials in news
- 113 1950 Anne Baxter title role
- 114 Évian-___-Bains, France

monday 12

tuesday 13

○ FULL MOON

wednesday 14

thursday 15

friday 16

ARMED FORCES DAY (USA)

saturday 17

sunday 18

May

s	m	t	w	t	f	s
				1	2	3
4	5	6	7	8	9	10
11	12	13	14	15	16	17
18	19	20	21	22	23	24
25	26	27	28	29	30	31

21. AS ELMER FUDD WOULD SAY …

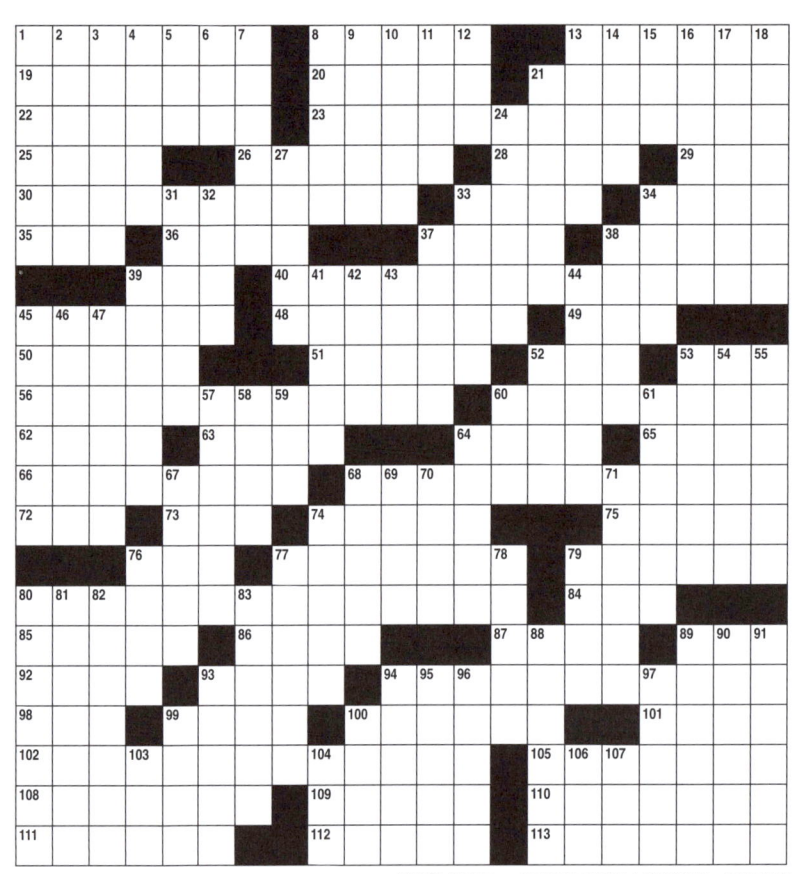

The New York Times

101 '33 Chicago World's Fair style
102 Advice to someone going to the Egg-Beaters' Convention?
105 Blanket
108 Thinks
109 Reduce to mush
110 Traditional
111 Spotlight sharer
112 Assists
113 Some dollhouse miniatures

DOWN

1 Recover from a blackout
2 Photographer Richard
3 Gets more InStyle, say
4 Lying
5 Make a choice
6 Singer
7 Singer Yearwood
8 Singer's accompaniment
9 "Put ___ in it!"
10 Nine daughters of Zeus
11 Curmudgeonly cries
12 ___ king
13 Actress Meadows
14 ___ of Solomon
15 Maker of the Z4 roadster
16 Snoopy's hip alter ego
17 So-so
18 Turn off
21 Totally wasted
24 Things letters have
27 Added-on Medicare provisions
31 Courtesy car
32 Saddam reportedly hid them, briefly
33 Tips, in a way
34 ___-flam
37 Beer brand originating in Brooklyn
38 Marshy tract
39 Collected
41 Gossipy Hopper
42 Nobel laureate Wiesel
43 Stereotypical debate outburst
44 Calf bone
45 Be philanthropic
46 Clay, e.g.
47 Golden Globe winner Pia
52 Rite for a newborn Jewish boy
53 1958 #1 hit by Domenico Modugno
54 King Arthur's burial place
55 Solidify
57 "Prove it!"
58 Knocks dead

BY ED SESSA • EDITED BY WILL SHORTZ • 07/11/10

ACROSS

1 House extension
8 Deadly African biter
13 Container holding slips of paper with tasks written on them
19 Like a bogey or double bogey
20 Commonplace
21 "Shouldn't have done that!"
22 "Amahl and the Night Visitors" composer
23 Part of a biblical warning against growing onions?
25 Garden with an apple tree
26 Livens (up)
28 Ages upon ages
29 French wine classification
30 Some locker room tomfoolery?
33 See
34 What a mare bears
35 Turn-___

36 Jerusalem's Mosque of ___
37 Letters
38 Arduous travels
39 Down
40 Bio for a Looney Tunes coyote?
45 Bakery trayfuls, say
48 Philosophy
49 Cartesian conclusion
50 "___ Ben Jonson!"
51 Radio features
52 OPEC unit: Abbr.
53 Closet item, in brief
56 Politico Ralph's fishing gear?
60 Light of one's life
62 Lots
63 Georgetown hoopster
64 The ___ One (sobriquet for Satan)
65 Buck
66 Razed
68 Pretty fat, actually?

72 Victorian ___
73 Sounds at a vaccination center, maybe
74 Garb for Gandhi
75 First Baseball Hall-of-Famer, alphabetically
76 Intent
77 Tabriz native
79 Marco Polo's destination
80 React to a bitter mouthwash?
84 Big hirer of techies
85 Mae West's "___ Day's a Holiday"
86 2003 disease scare
87 Battle of Normandy town
89 Egg container, of sorts
92 PBS staple since 1974
93 Barney of Mayberry
94 Sloven in the coven?
98 Author Umberto
99 Timbales player Puente
100 Loose smock

May

- 59 "The Fountainhead" writer Rand
- 60 New Deal inits.
- 61 "To life!"
- 64 So-called "Giant Brain" of 1946
- 67 Bit of crochet work
- 68 Détentes
- 69 "___ soit qui mal y pense" (old motto)
- 70 "Put ___ writing!"
- 71 English archer's weapon
- 74 Rapper with the 6x platinum album "2001"
- 76 Taj Mahal city
- 77 Spaced out
- 78 Fits one inside another
- 79 Unctuous
- 80 Kind of code
- 81 Shade of green
- 82 Cancels
- 83 The way things stand
- 88 Everything
- 89 Nicks on a record?
- 90 Sign of stress
- 91 Farmer's to-do list
- 93 Moral ___
- 94 Renaissance ___ (historical reenactment)
- 95 "No more for me, thanks"
- 96 Takes a shine to
- 97 Many people in People
- 99 "Cheerio!"
- 100 Carp family fish
- 103 "Mangia!"
- 104 New Deal inits.
- 106 Any of the Marquises, par exemple
- 107 Child-care writer LeShan

monday
VICTORIA DAY (CANADA)
19 139

tuesday
20 140

☾ LAST QUARTER
wednesday
21 141

thursday
22 142

friday
23 143

saturday
24 144

sunday
25 145

May

s	m	t	w	t	f	s
				1	2	3
4	5	6	7	8	9	10
11	12	13	14	15	16	17
18	19	20	21	22	23	24
25	26	27	28	29	30	31

22. CRITICAL PERIODS

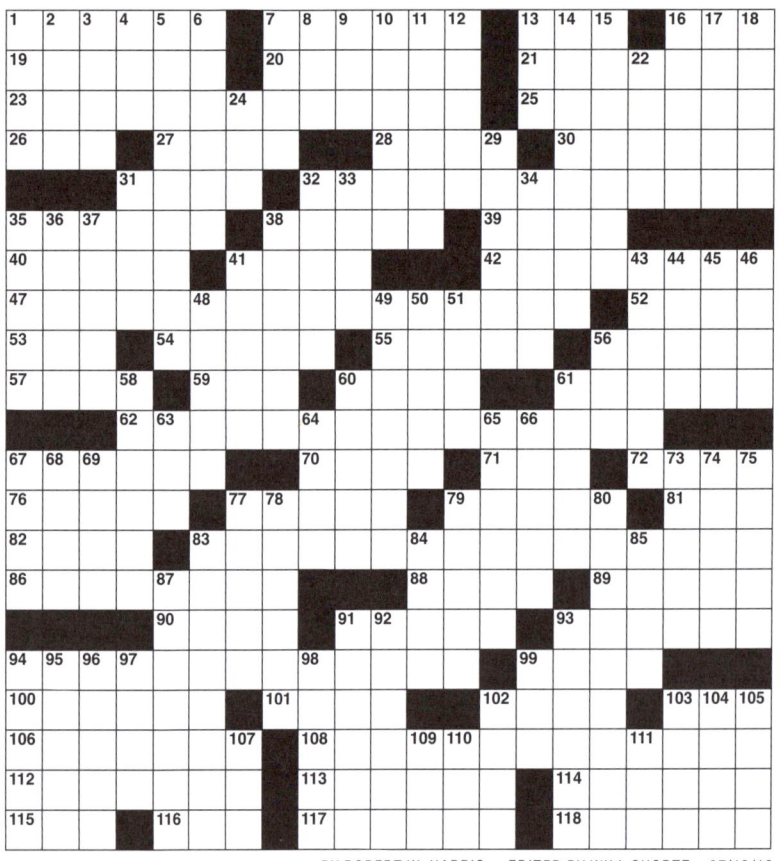

The New York Times

BY ROBERT W. HARRIS • EDITED BY WILL SHORTZ • 07/18/10

ACROSS

1. Ready for publication
7. Flag
13. Certain Internet connection: Abbr.
16. Things refs raise their arms for
19. Full chromosome set
20. Pairs' debarking point
21. Joy
23. 234, as of July 4, 2010?
25. Cash in the music business
26. 1950 noir film
27. Perfect specimens
28. Divided
30. ___ Bros.
31. Unit of force
32. Workers in a global peace organization?
35. Hard look?
38. Pass off as genuine
39. Hip
40. Unconventional
41. Remove from a talent show, maybe
42. Come under criticism
47. What gumshoes charge in the City of Bridges?
52. Kid
53. Native Coloradan
54. Some court evidence
55. Signs of spoilage
56. Group following a star?
57. Left at sea
59. Drinker's problem, for short
60. Word that comes from the Greek for "indivisible"
61. Not stay long for shots?
62. Symmetrical power conductor for appliances?
67. Hole
70. Makes holes
71. Sounds of understanding
72. Wrapped garment
76. Nimble
77. Any singer of "Hotel California"
79. "Stop!"
81. Grp. of connected PCs
82. What's borne at a funeral
83. Too much guitar work by a professor's helper?
86. Like some English muffins
88. Scullers' needs
89. Best
90. Aquatic shockers
91. "The Addams Family" co-star
93. Most easily sunburned, maybe
94. "Pay in cash and your second surgery is half-price"?
99. Small islands
100. Nuevo Laredo store
101. Get along
102. Singer Fitzgerald
103. Galoot
106. Second
108. Typical termite in a California city?
112. Inactive state
113. Using fraudulently altered checks
114. Sharpie alternatives
115. Preceder of 116-Across
116. Follower of 115-Across
117. Pack rat
118. "Opening" word

DOWN

1. "Good grief!"
2. Art ___
3. Quechua speaker
4. Low digit
5. What many older parents face
6. Locking lever
7. Rogues
8. Tulsa sch.
9. ___ Cruces
10. Elocutes
11. Seasoned stew
12. Harsh
13. "___ Fuehrer's Face" (1942 Disney short)
14. Dawdler
15. Explorer who claimed Louisiana for France
16. Thin-toned
17. Recipient
18. Bergen's foil
22. Poi ingredient
24. General dir. of Sal Paradise's return trip in "On the Road"
29. Peach ___
31. Gossip
32. Grillers' grabbers
33. On dope
34. Things that drawbridges bridge
35. Absorb
36. Headquarters of the Union of South American Nations
37. Speak
38. "Hansel and Gretel" setting
41. CNN's Sanjay
43. Northern inlets
44. Any tail in a cat-o'-nine-tails
45. Lhasa ___
46. Not spoil
48. Not well
49. Thick soups
50. Miley Cyrus and Lady Gaga, e.g.
51. Tomato type
56. Hole number
58. Some short-term investments, briefly

May-June

- 60 Seed coverings
- 61 ___ nova
- 63 Adherent: Suffix
- 64 Advantage
- 65 Site of some paintings
- 66 Informal exchanges
- 67 Li'l Abner creator
- 68 Food thickener
- 69 Loathsome
- 73 1967 Dionne Warwick hit
- 74 Some constructions on "Survivor"
- 75 Certain detail
- 77 Bobby Fischer, once
- 78 Words before "kindness" and "the Apostles"
- 79 Be of use
- 80 Like diabetes
- 83 Refinement
- 84 Tiny bit
- 85 Woes
- 87 Cross or star, often
- 91 Dexterous
- 92 Apparently do
- 93 Rice dishes
- 94 Steps that a farmer might take
- 95 Brown and Turner
- 96 "The defense ___"
- 97 Stake
- 98 Prepares to play pool, say
- 99 Tie indicator
- 102 Many an M.I.T. grad
- 103 "Che gelida manina," e.g.
- 104 Salon option
- 105 Celtic tongue
- 107 Nautical rope
- 109 Novy ___, Russian literary magazine
- 110 Low digit
- 111 International grp. since 1948

May

s	m	t	w	t	f	s
				1	2	3
4	5	6	7	8	9	10
11	12	13	14	15	16	17
18	19	20	21	22	23	24
25	26	27	28	29	30	31

June

s	m	t	w	t	f	s
1	2	3	4	5	6	7
8	9	10	11	12	13	14
15	16	17	18	19	20	21
22	23	24	25	26	27	28
29	30					

MEMORIAL DAY (USA)
SPRING BANK HOLIDAY (UK)

monday 26 146

tuesday 27 147

● NEW MOON

wednesday 28 148

thursday 29 149

friday 30 150

saturday 31 151

sunday 1 152

23. UP STARTS

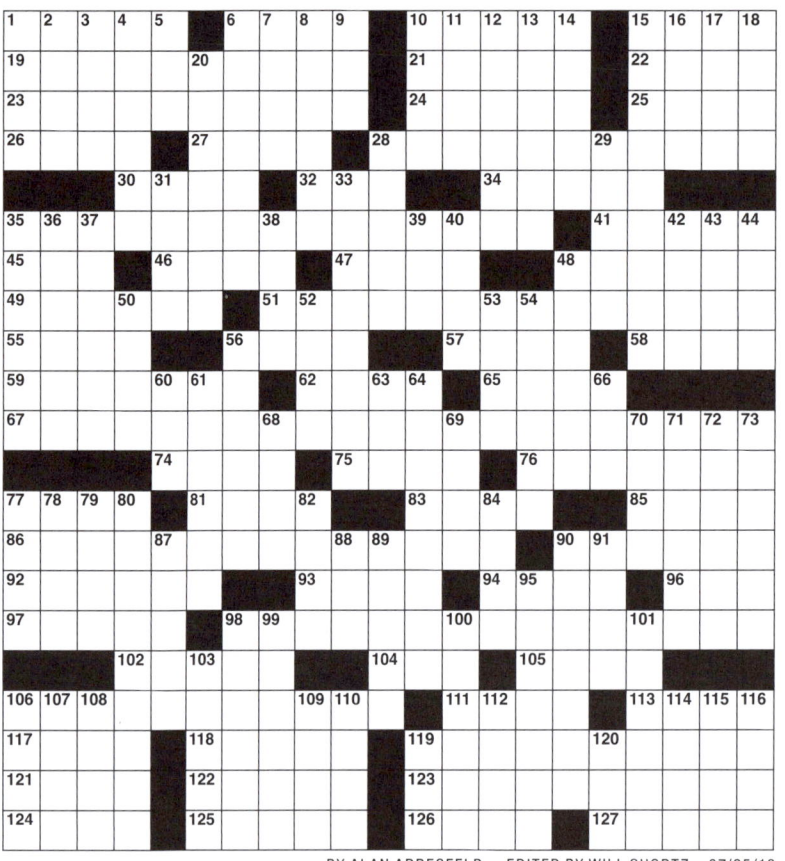

The New York Times

BY ALAN ARBESFELD • EDITED BY WILL SHORTZ • 07/25/10

ACROSS

1 "Silas Marner" foundling
6 They're schlepped on tours
10 Bruce who played Watson in Sherlock Holmes films
15 Equal
19 PBS figure from 1968 to 2001
21 Eyes
22 As well
23 Cause for Adam to refuse the apple?
24 Congested-sounding
25 Weapon in Clue
26 Feature of some Greek buildings
27 Feudal holding
28 Precamping preparation?
30 Tests for srs.
32 One-time connection
34 BMI rival
35 Christmas, for Christians?
41 Alibi, e.g.
45 Antique restorer's need, for short
46 Locale in a 1968 Beatles song
47 Beaks
48 "Really?"
49 British P.M. during the creation of Israel
51 Bountiful harvest?
55 Good source of protein
56 Saudi Arabian province
57 ___ gin fizz
58 Article in Die Zeit
59 Robert Downey Jr. title role
62 Prom rental
65 Place to pray
67 Independence Day barbecue serving?
74 Auel heroine
75 Prefix with plasm
76 Girl in a Willa Cather title
77 Shelter grp.
81 Cut
83 Serving with gâteau, maybe
85 P.T.A. member?: Abbr.
86 Unnecessary part of a jacket?
90 When streetlights go on
92 Refuse
93 The Road Runner, for one
94 Freezer brand
96 Caviar
97 Makeshift stepladder
98 Ultimatum from a spouse who wants nicer digs?
102 Single-celled organism
104 PC key
105 Some chorus members
106 Refusing to watch football on New Year's Day?
111 Tijuana fare
113 Genesis victim
117 1970s-'80s horror film franchise, with "The"
118 Lofty retreat
119 Nathan's annual hot-dog contest, e.g.?
121 It may be framed
122 ___ Chaiken, creator and writer of "The L Word"
123 Concerning
124 Eye ___
125 Grayer, perhaps
126 Scorch
127 Magnetic induction unit

DOWN

1 Pair of ruffians?
2 Rear end
3 Coin with a profile of José María Morelos
4 Conference clip-ons
5 Suffix with ranch
6 Ones prejudiced against 125-Across people
7 One subjugated by Cyrus the Great
8 Kind of housing, for short
9 1040 datum: Abbr.
10 Bar ___
11 Self-motivational mantra
12 Composer Mahler
13 Slip by
14 Eye shadow shade
15 Property that costs $350
16 Patron saint of goldsmiths
17 Where to find "Baseball Tonight"
18 Nicolas who directed "The Man Who Fell to Earth"
20 Umbrage
28 Shire in Hollywood
29 Treasure hunter's find
31 See 110-Down
33 It's WNW of Grand Canary Island
35 Interference
36 Figure at una corrida
37 Represent
38 Municipal laws: Abbr.
39 Maker of the trivia-playing computer program Watson
40 Those, in Toledo
42 Longfellow's bell town
43 "The heat ___"
44 Look down
48 Trinity component
50 Sally ___ (teacake)
52 Agitate
53 Needing tuning, maybe
54 Mr. Peanut prop
56 Hunting lodge decoration bit
60 Bird that is no more
61 "As I was saying …"
63 Casual slip-on, casually
64 Plans

June

- 66 Young newt
- 68 "Cactus Flower" Oscar winner
- 69 Alternative to chestnut
- 70 1940 Fonda role
- 71 Hesitant
- 72 Willowy: Var.
- 73 Ruth, once
- 77 Does, say
- 78 Blog comment
- 79 First name in fashion
- 80 Personal
- 82 Alternative to grounding
- 84 Media exec Robert
- 87 Person with a serious conviction
- 88 Sandal's lack
- 89 Great Lakes mnemonic
- 90 Eternal
- 91 Perfectly
- 95 There's a national park named for one
- 98 Old phone company nickname
- 99 Scented
- 100 Station identification?
- 101 Alternative to Cialis
- 103 Marsh of mysteries
- 106 "Uh-uh"
- 107 Big picture?
- 108 Lawless role
- 109 Shiraz, for one
- 110 Look from a 31-Down
- 112 Gillette product
- 114 "On&On" singer Erykah
- 115 CPR experts
- 116 Some summer births
- 119 Winter hazard in Munich
- 120 Stand-up staple

QUEEN'S BIRTHDAY (NZ)
FOUNDATION DAY (AUSTRALIA—WA)
SPRING BANK HOLIDAY (IRELAND)

monday
2 153

tuesday
3 154

wednesday
4 155

☽ FIRST QUARTER

thursday
5 156

friday
6 157

saturday
7 158

sunday
8 159

June

s	m	t	w	t	f	s
	1	2	3	4	5	6	7
8	9	10	11	12	13	14
15	16	17	18	19	20	21
22	23	24	25	26	27	28
29	30					

24. PLAY BARGAINING

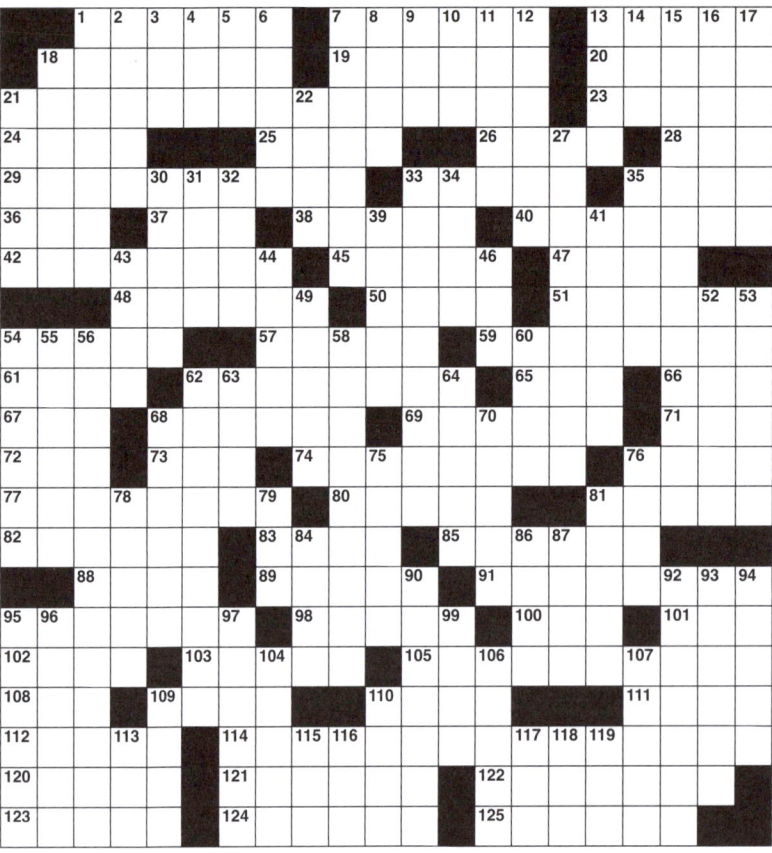

The New York Times

103 With honor
105 Floral garland for whoever?
108 Kangaroo ___
109 Character with a prominent back
110 Gillette model
111 Many P.T.A. members
112 Duel overseer in "Hamlet"
114 Indecisive wolf's question?
120 John Mason ___, English priest who wrote "Good King Wenceslas"
121 Accustoms
122 Hair-texturizing tool
123 Heretofore
124 Overage
125 Observation

DOWN
1 Battle site of 1945
2 River on the Benin border
3 -like equivalent
4 Available for purchase
5 Biomedical research agcy.
6 Secure, with "in"
7 Breastbone-related
8 Clumped
9 "Prince ___" ("Aladdin" song)
10 Basketball coach Kruger
11 Hearth
12 Take as a given
13 Sunday seats
14 W.W. II zone: Abbr.
15 Mist from a mall?
16 Leonard Bernstein called her "The Bible of opera"
17 Enlighten
18 Brazilian mister
21 "I ___ ready!"
22 Things shepherds shepherd
27 Miss who parks cars?
30 Military chaplain
31 Suffix with stink
32 Only thing between you and an open window?
33 In hell?
34 ___ close second (almost won)
35 Arterial implant
39 "Attack!"
41 Baking spuds
43 "The scavenger of misery," per Shaw
44 Served seconds, say
46 Yearbook signers: Abbr.
49 Cuts up, in a way
52 Punjabi capital
53 Oil family of TV
54 Oil unit

BY BRENDAN EMMETT QUIGLEY • EDITED BY WILL SHORTZ • 08/01/10

ACROSS
1 Grinder toppings
7 Supreme Court justice nominated by Reagan
13 Real-life actor Joe who is a character in Broadway's "Jersey Boys"
18 Bunny's covering?
19 Bent nails
20 Furniture retailer ___ Allen
21 Put a few monarchs on the scale?
23 "Orlando" novelist
24 Sister of Charlotte and Emily
25 All wrong
26 Huggies rival
28 Gaza Strip org.
29 Wrinkly dog holder?
33 Espresso topping
35 Engage in debate
36 "I said — ___!"
37 Firecracker's trajectory
38 Obama whose Secret Service code name is "Rosebud"
40 Snobbery
42 Location for a fall
45 Bank claims
47 Location for the Fall
48 Helped with the laundry
50 Political appointee
51 Cords behind a computer, often
54 Word with a German request
57 Blew by a drummer, maybe
59 Played the tourist
61 Hurting
62 Smoking character
65 Relative in the barrio
66 The golden ratio
67 Line score letters
68 Gel
69 Golfers' wear
71 N.B.A. All-Star Artest
72 Tractor-trailer
73 One with a pupil
74 Amsterdam air hub
76 Puppeteer Tony
77 Company that merged with Sony in 2001
80 Brunonian rival
81 Compromise of 1877 president
82 1996 Grammy winner for the album "The Road to Ensenada"
83 Camper's rental
85 Alternate road
88 Robert of "The Sopranos"
89 Poll answer choice
91 Famed Fokker flier
95 Toward the middle
98 "Why is this happening to me?!"
100 Its cap. is Beirut
101 Prefix with tour
102 Mensa and others: Abbr.

June

55 First player to hit an inside-the-park home run during an All-Star Game, 2007
56 Generous carhop's prop?
58 Brawl at a ball?
60 "Am ___ fat?"
62 Leno's necklace?
63 Mousse pie ingredient, maybe
64 Oily substance
68 Prynne of "The Scarlet Letter"
70 Absolute
75 Hardly a fan
76 ___ Lee bakery
78 Bird and others, once
79 Publisher of Shooting Illustrated, for short
81 When doubled, "I like!"
84 "___ in Calico" (jazz standard)
86 Prefix with copier
87 River to the Baltic
90 Game in which it's easy to make a mess
92 Change tags on
93 Mop brand that "makes your life easier"
94 Whooping
95 Dos Equis competitor
96 Clears
97 Louse
99 Austrian title
104 Where hip-hop was born, with "the"
106 F.D.R. veep John ___ Garner
107 Parkinson's battler
109 Entertainer born Tracy Marrow
110 Cries made in passing?
113 Saint-Martin, e.g.
115 Winning Super Bowl XXXVII gridder
116 Exist
117 Surgery sites, for short
118 20%, maybe
119 "I didn't need to know that," in modern lingo

QUEEN'S BIRTHDAY (AUSTRALIA—EXCEPT QLD, WA)

monday
9 160

tuesday
10 161

wednesday
11 162

thursday
12 163

○ FULL MOON

friday
13 164

FLAG DAY (USA)

saturday
14 165

FATHER'S DAY (USA, CANADA, IRELAND, UK)

sunday
15 166

June

s	m	t	w	t	f	s
1	2	3	4	5	6	7
8	9	10	11	12	13	14
15	16	17	18	19	20	21
22	23	24	25	26	27	28
29	30					

25. 3 X 8

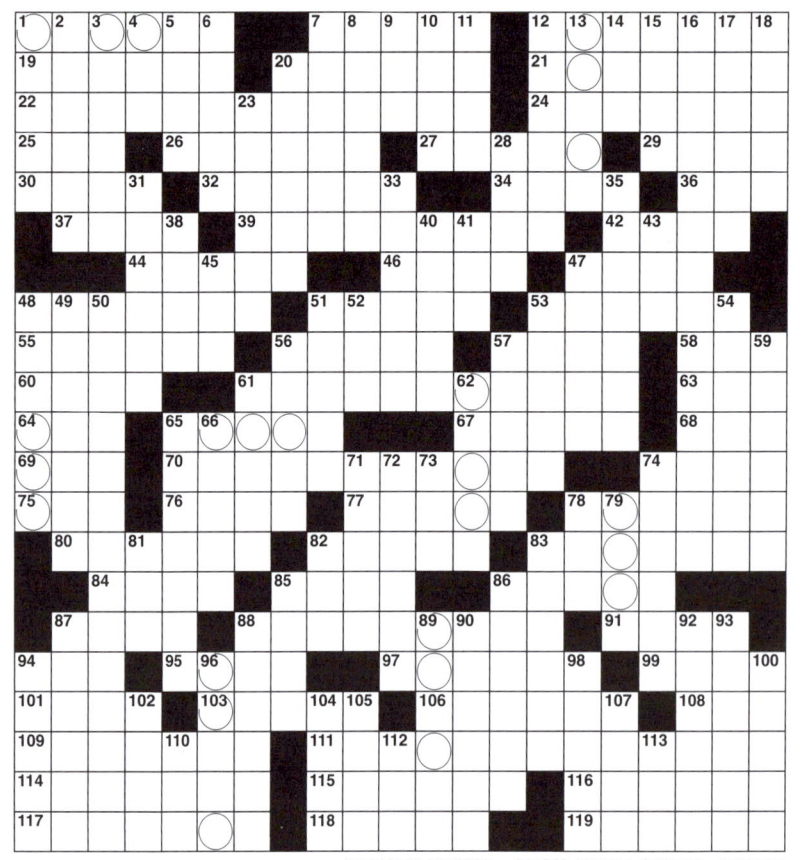

ACROSS

1. One-named teen idol of the late '50s/early '60s
7. Fashionably nostalgic
12. Came out even, in a way
19. God who killed the dragon Python four days after his birth
20. Bygone shampoo brand
21. Heads
22. See circled letters in 96-Down
24. Dow Jones publication
25. Can
26. Join the crew
27. Kind of acid found in spinach
29. Hook's right-hand man
30. Frankfurt term of address
32. Demanding overseer
34. Tennis's Nastase
36. New York subway inits.
37. In order (to)
39. … in 79-Down
42. Teen's room, stereotypically
44. Like some proverbial milk
46. Dweller on the Baltic
47. Two-baggers: Abbr.
48. People holding signs at airports
51. Dwellers on the Baltic
53. Why
55. Noted wine region
56. Underworld bosses
57. Take off
58. Stephen of "The Musketeer"
60. Does some freestyling
61. … in 13-Down
63. Big letters in fashion
64. CBS show with Laurence Fishburne
65. Very reverent
67. "Charles in Charge" co-star
68. Mathematical ordinal
69. "What was ___ think?"
70. … in 62-Down
74. Star turns
75. River to the Rhône
76. ___ place
77. New Balance competitor
78. Flatware finisher
80. Furniture mover
82. On-base percentage and others
83. At the earliest opportunity
84. Will of "The Waltons"
85. Florida city, for short
86. Word with love or honey
87. Row of stables, in Britain
88. … in 89-Down
91. Telecom hookups
94. Highway hazard
95. Spree
97. Inside flight
99. Mane, for a female lion, e.g.
101. Concerning
103. Lieu
106. Gluck works
108. Spider-Man's aunt
109. Igneous rock
111. … in 1-Across
114. Home to Mount Chimborazo
115. Brachyodont perissodactyls
116. One of the Kennedys
117. Some carry-on items
118. Apple purchases
119. Tot tender

DOWN

1. Palestinian party
2. Climbers' goals
3. 1928 musical composition originally called "Fandango"
4. Québec's Grosse-___
5. River in "Kubla Khan"
6. Tiring problem for bicyclists?
7. Soak back in
8. Drink from a bowl
9. Cycle attachment?
10. Jazz phrase
11. Aware of
12. Art installation
13. They can always be counted on
14. TiVo, for one, in brief
15. Relative of -ists
16. … in 65-Across
17. Actor Ed and family
18. Microwave button
20. Lincoln Center institution
23. Bottom-fishes
28. Melodic speech
31. Some Jamaicans, for short
33. TV marshal who frequents the Long Branch Saloon
35. Sets off
38. Job detail
40. Silly ones
41. Some sporty cars
43. P.G.A.'s Ernie
45. Heat source?
47. "The Wreck of the Mary ___"
48. Cross of "Desperate Housewives"
49. Band composition
50. … in 48-Down
51. Not in
52. Make a choice
53. Like a successful dieter's clothes
54. Candy giant, informally
56. Brilliant successes
57. Goes for, as a fly
59. Jazz great nicknamed Jumbo
61. #2 or #3
62. Rash remedies
65. Boycott, e.g.

BY PAM KLAWITTER • EDITED BY WILL SHORTZ • 08/08/10

June

- **66** ___ peace
- **71** "Coming at you!"
- **72** Jason who plays Lucius Malfoy in Harry Potter films
- **73** River island
- **74** It has a bottom but no top
- **78** Don Ho fan fare?
- **79** Laze
- **81** Singers do it
- **82** "Mamma Mia!" song
- **83** Shepherd of "The View"
- **85** Unadorned
- **86** Arrowhead Stadium team
- **87** One of the friends on "Friends"
- **88** Works a wedding, maybe
- **89** Wee
- **90** Heists
- **92** "Anything you say!"
- **93** "Make yourself ___"
- **94** Leader succeeded by his brother Raúl
- **96** Prevent
- **98** Wise ones
- **100** Orchestra leader Kay
- **102** Part of Q.E.D.
- **104** Theater opening
- **105** 60 grains
- **107** Feng ___
- **110** Swear words in a swearing-in
- **112** Pronunciation guide std.
- **113** Cause of a big bang

monday
16 167

tuesday
17 168

wednesday
18 169

☾ LAST QUARTER

thursday
19 170

friday
20 171

saturday
21 172

sunday
22 173

June

s	m	t	w	t	f	s
1	2	3	4	5	6	7
8	9	10	11	12	13	14
15	16	17	18	19	20	21
22	23	24	25	26	27	28
29	30					

26. IS THERE AN ECHO IN HERE?

ACROSS

1. Writer of the short story "The Overcoat"
6. Sitcom with three stars
10. Compos mentis
14. Some Latinas: Abbr.
19. Hersey novel setting
20. Cream, e.g.
21. Angel
22. Parts of many a still life
23. Underachiever's motto?
26. SALT topic
27. Vladimir Nabokov novel
28. It's noble
29. Sol mates?
30. Some court pleas, for short
31. U.N.-created land: Abbr.
33. Places where masseurs massage
35. Trouble's partner
37. Milk containers
38. Being debated
41. "The Mystery of ___ Vep," 1990s Off Broadway play
42. E is its lowest note
43. Majorcan affirmation?
47. She-bear: Sp.
50. 7-0 record, e.g.
51. Something for a kid to keep on hand?
52. Portuguese wines
54. Worthy of mention
56. "The lowest form of humor," per Samuel Johnson
57. Grps. that know the drill?
58. Roam and raid
61. Not yet acquired, as knowledge
65. ___-all
66. Inhabitant: Suffix
67. Registering a poodle?
71. Steve Martin's "boy king"
72. What atoms do
74. Liza Minnelli's father
75. Contents of sleeves
77. N.S.A. concern, for short
79. Ultimate
80. Hulk Hogan or Andre the Giant, slangily
83. "Vitruvian Man" artist
85. Part of batting instruction
87. "Twin Peaks" actor Jack
91. Misspeak, e.g.
92. Guy holding a Hostess snack cake?
95. Canadian curling championship, with "the"
97. Procrastinator's response
98. Decimal system
99. The beginning
101. Dom ___, "Inception" hero
102. ___ Ed
104. Letter run
105. Skyscraper support
106. 300 to 3,000 MHz range
107. ___ fixe
109. Popular fragrance
112. Slithering menace
113. Words of caution from Rodolfo?
118. "___ I might …"
119. "___ Diana's altar to protest": Shak.
120. Dinner crumbs
121. Certain Central Asian
122. Puts back in
123. Politico Gingrich
124. [Over here!]
125. Bounce

DOWN

1. Group of whales
2. Harem room
3. Annual parade subject
4. "Go ___!"
5. Fin de siècle writer Pierre ___
6. V.J.'s employer
7. The "A" of sports' A.F.L.
8. Begets
9. Red Skelton persona
10. Organizer of many a sit-in: Abbr.
11. Windblown
12. Like Bob Dylan's voice
13. Opposite of Thanatos, to Freud
14. More thin and frail
15. Modify, as software
16. Reservation at a Johannesburg restaurant?
17. Mail
18. 112-Across sound
24. Follow
25. Hors d'oeuvre follower
31. Pet food company since 1946
32. Worry
34. Constant, in product names
36. "Toe" of the Arabian Peninsula
37. Coll. in La Jolla
39. Tuscan town, home of the painter Duccio
40. Biblical correspondent
41. Very emotional
42. Designer Versace
44. Gently roast … or something that's roasted
45. Out of the office, perhaps
46. Blue pixie
48. Hipbone attachment
49. Ledger list
53. Sports org. since 1894
55. Year Columbus returned from his final voyage to the New World
56. Something that's "Miss" titled?

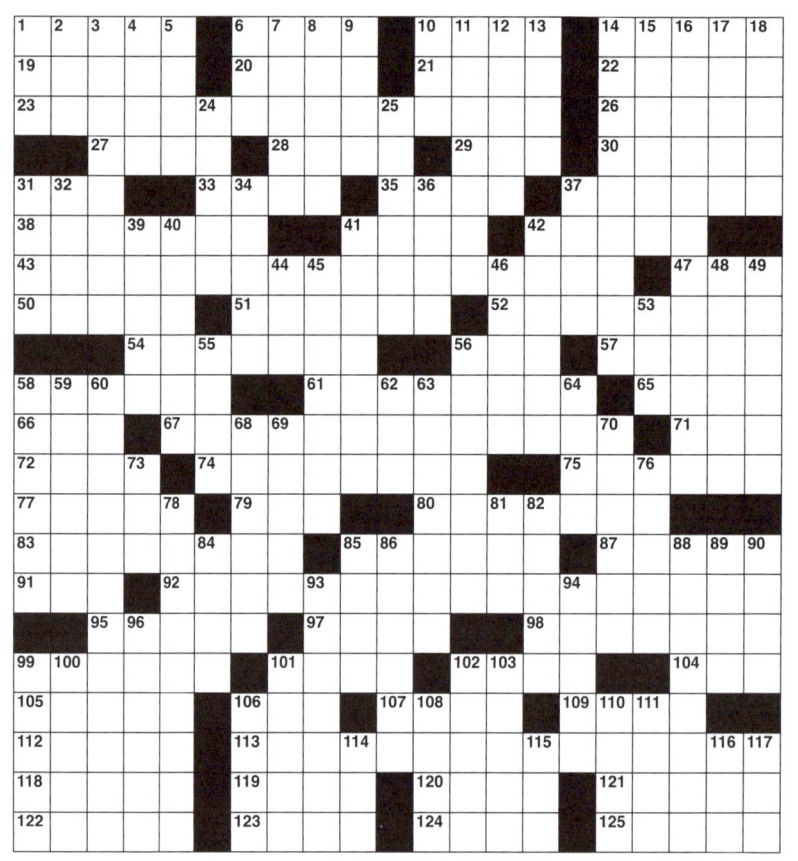

BY DANIEL C. BRYANT • EDITED BY WILL SHORTZ • 08/15/10

June

58 Where the driver is driving Miss Daisy
59 Sorry soul?
60 Landlord's ultimatum?
62 Sculptor Maya
63 Board, in a way
64 Purveyor of nonstick cookware
68 Bit of air pollution
69 Div. of biology
70 Actresses Kristen and Graff
73 Locale for a trophy display
76 Astronomer Tycho ___
78 Traditional church celebration
81 Univ., e.g.
82 Held in reserve
84 First president of South Korea
85 Supercilious sort
86 Nearly worthless
88 Almost
89 What's expensive in Paris?
90 Time on end
93 Currently
94 Must
96 Try to scare off, in a way
99 Library shelfful: Abbr.
100 End early
101 Work that's no fun
102 Jury members
103 Track meet events
106 Japanese noodle
108 Sell-off, say
110 Play money?
111 Key with five sharps: Abbr.
114 It has a blast
115 Mar. weekend shortener
116 ___ and cheese
117 Operator of the original N.Y.C. subway

monday
23 174

tuesday
24 175

wednesday
25 176

thursday
26 177

● NEW MOON

friday
27 178

RAMADAN

saturday
28 179

sunday
29 180

June

s	m	t	w	t	f	s
1	2	3	4	5	6	7
8	9	10	11	12	13	14
15	16	17	18	19	20	21
22	23	24	25	26	27	28
29	30					

27. FILM NO-R

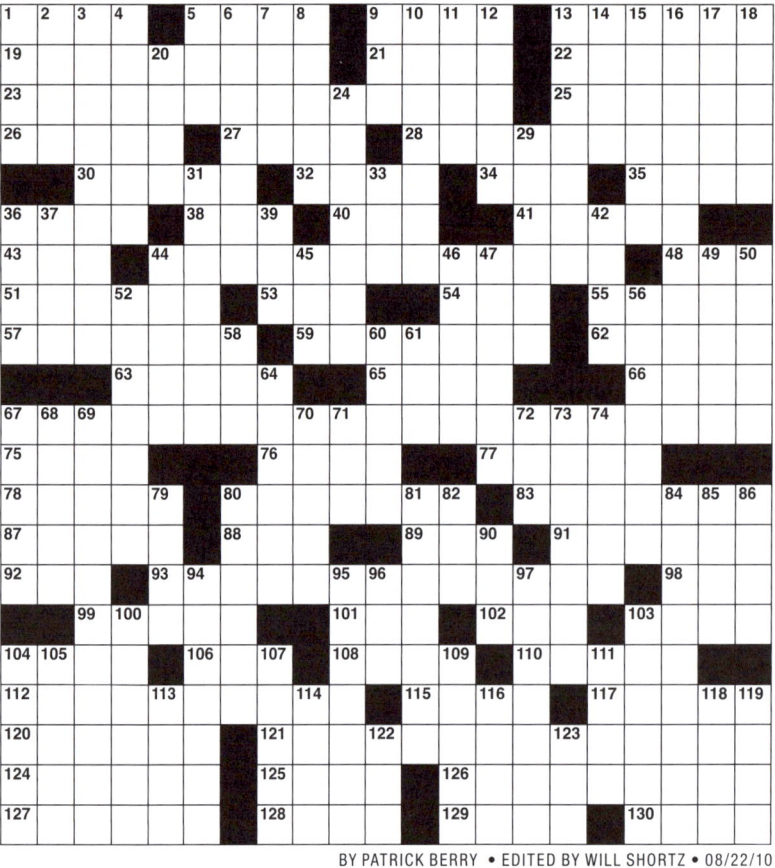

The New York Times

120 Inability to appreciate music
121 … a seedy Hollywood bar?
124 Antipathetic
125 ___ Cakesters (Nabisco offering)
126 … skinned knuckles?
127 Tenant
128 Home in the sticks?
129 Weather-stripped item
130 Sicilian province

DOWN
1 Gentle touches
2 Turkish title
3 One whose music is easy to follow?
4 What intersecting lines create
5 Maker of the Roadrunner supercomputer
6 "What nonsense!"
7 Wing-shaped
8 Novelist Bret Easton ___
9 1969 literary heroine who says "I like the words damozel, eglantine, elegant. I love when you kiss my elongated white hand"
10 Intelligent swimmer
11 Founder of an Oahu plantation
12 Tommy of ESPN
13 Papal office
14 Acknowledge
15 ___ oil (perfumery ingredient)
16 Bomb detector?
17 Name in 2000 newspapers
18 Country singer Shelby
20 Fellas
24 "Baby, It's Cold Outside" composer
29 Bygone Toyota
31 Hybrid farm animal
33 Afternoon meal, across the pond
36 Count ___ (2004 Jim Carrey role)
37 Singer/songwriter Amos
39 Ad ___
42 Exam for would-be attys.
44 Univ. overseers
45 Part of a TV dial
46 "What he said"
47 Where Excalibur was forged
49 Make watertight
50 Beasts of burden
52 Upscale restaurant requirement, maybe
56 "To Catch a Thief" setting
58 Sharpie tip
60 Author Malraux

BY PATRICK BERRY • EDITED BY WILL SHORTZ • 08/22/10

ACROSS
1 "Come to ___!"
5 Of wrath, in a Latin hymn
9 Throws in
13 "La Resurrezione" composer
19 Film about a corrida participant put to pasture?
21 Mount ___ (volcano in Mordor)
22 Too
23 … a candy-sharing confederate?
25 Lake Erie city west of Cleveland
26 As bad luck would have it
27 Vivacity
28 … a small-minded lady?
30 "Casino" actor Joe
32 TV producer MacFarlane
34 1942 Harry James hit "___ My Guy"
35 Bowler's assignment
36 ___ Day & the Knights (band in "Animal House")

38 The mythical tree Yggdrasil, for one
40 Finback whale
41 Museum piece
43 Cut off
44 … an embarrassingly one-sided tennis match?
48 David Sarnoff's company
51 Political theorist Hannah
53 "Evita" narrator
54 The Beatles' "___ Got a Feeling"
55 Some solos
57 Continuity problem
59 Geometric shape whose perimeter has infinite length
62 The Colosseum was completed during his reign
63 Paramecium's propellers
65 Part of N.F.L.: Abbr.
66 Base
67 … decorative furniture elements being blown up with dynamite?

75 Army division
76 "Lying thief," e.g.
77 ___ Dame
78 Actress Perez
80 Speaks nonsense
83 Record keeper
87 Practices, as a trade
88 Helpfulness
89 Lunch, e.g.
91 "Rainbow Six" author
92 California city name starter
93 … a demonic horse?
98 Continuity problem
99 Western star Lee Van ___
101 Center of a daisy, e.g.
102 Shuffleboard stick
103 Pixar title character
104 Recitation by Scheherazade
106 "Time ___ …"
108 Yukon, e.g.: Abbr.
110 Makes an effort
112 … drink garnishes?
115 Work like a dog
117 Rhenium or rhodium

June-July

- 61 Flagged vehicle
- 64 St. Clare's home
- 67 Consumer reports?
- 68 ___ Gay
- 69 Renders reluctant
- 70 "The Sandbox" playwright
- 71 Central point
- 72 Hip 1960s teen
- 73 "New and Improved!" might appear on one
- 74 Song syllables
- 79 Carlisle Cullen's wife in "Twilight"
- 80 Boisterous laugh
- 81 Mention
- 82 ___ volatile
- 84 Swallowing of food, e.g.
- 85 Hustle
- 86 Paper slip?
- 90 Personal quirk
- 94 English churchyard sight
- 95 Plants with stinging hairs
- 96 Indian mulberry product
- 97 Sailor's sword
- 100 Hand brakes, e.g.
- 103 Conifer leaf
- 104 Unqualified
- 105 Registering a pulse
- 107 Electronic game fad of the 1980s
- 109 Gives deep massage therapy
- 111 Web site for cinephiles
- 113 What lotus-eaters enjoy
- 114 "I'd be glad to!"
- 116 Russian figure skater Kulik
- 118 Major publisher of romance novels
- 119 Helen of Troy's mother
- 122 Wanting to be near one's fans?
- 123 Last in a series

June

s	m	t	w	t	f	s
	1	2	3	4	5	6	7
8	9	10	11	12	13	14
15	16	17	18	19	20	21
22	23	24	25	26	27	28
29	30					

July

s	m	t	w	t	f	s
		1	2	3	4	5
6	7	8	9	10	11	12
13	14	15	16	17	18	19
20	21	22	23	24	25	26
27	28	29	30	31		

monday 30 181

CANADA DAY

tuesday 1 182

wednesday 2 183

thursday 3 184

INDEPENDENCE DAY (USA)

friday 4 185

☾ FIRST QUARTER

saturday 5 186

sunday 6 187

28. GOING FOR A RUN

The New York Times

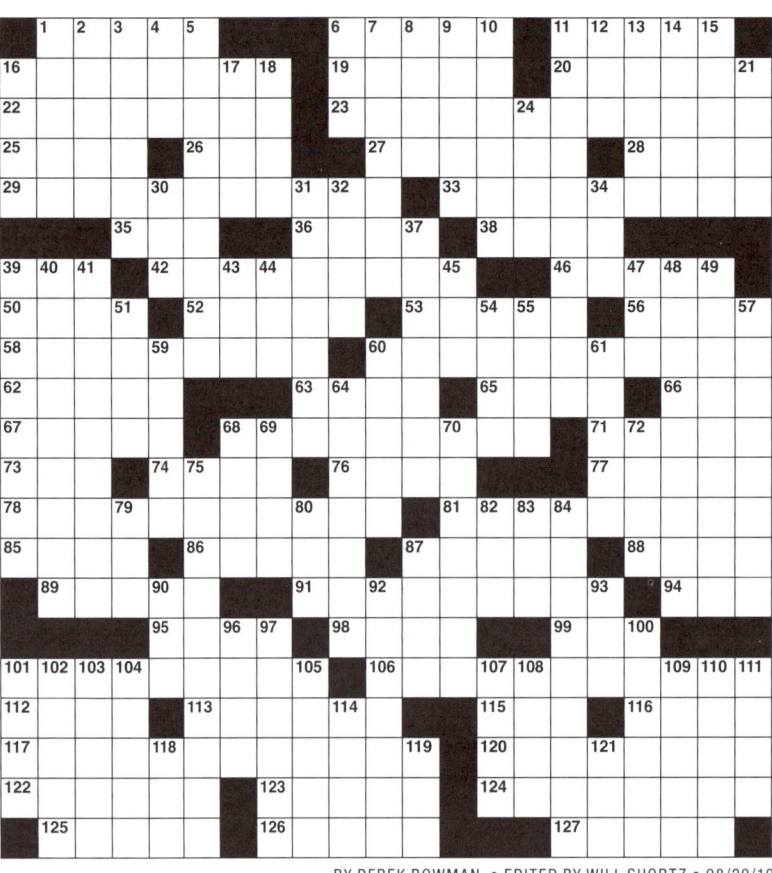

BY DEREK BOWMAN • EDITED BY WILL SHORTZ • 08/29/10

ACROSS

1. Like villains
6. Middleton who sang with Louis Armstrong
11. They might carry babies in nappies
16. Muckety-mucks
19. Cell phone feature
20. Auditorium features
22. *Kid constantly switching schools, maybe*
23. *Age-revealing method*
25. Headless Horseman's wear
26. The Wildcats, for short
27. Kind of expression
28. Real cutup
29. *Stale air removers*
33. *Supposed results of stress*
35. Danielle Steel novel about a European princess
36. Lisa with the #1 hit "Stay (I Missed You)"
38. Barks
39. "Gee," in Glasgow
42. Newer, as a car
46. "Ladies and gentlemen ...," e.g.
50. Biblical kingdom
52. Big name in dinnerware
53. "Conversations With God" author ___ Donald Walsch
56. British American Tobacco brand
58. *Embezzlement, e.g.*
60. Pet shop purchase
62. Gamble
63. Not an imit.
65. Makes one
66. Reuters competitor
67. Words a house burglar doesn't want to hear
68. *Party bowlful*
71. Highest point on the Ohio & Erie Canal
73. "___ moment"
74. Thunderbirds' org.
76. Like peacocks
77. "___ a Woman?" (Sojourner Truth speech delivered in 1851 in 71-Across)
78. *Pluto, e.g., before it was plutoed*
81. *Harlequin romance, e.g.*
85. Isthmus
86. Wine order
87. Protuberant
88. ___ precedent
89. Title dog in an Inge play
91. Delicate skill
94. Cover some ground
95. Cards once traded for Gehrigs, say
98. Part of Q.E.D.
99. ___-Boy (brand of furniture)
101. *Leadfoot's downfall*
106. *It's got some miles on it*
112. Some World Cup cheers
113. Was two under
115. Flair of pro wrestling
116. Matey's libation
117. *Annual sports event since 1997*
120. *Beginning of time?*
122. Bagel request
123. Online mag
124. Arrive continuously
125. Religious council
126. *Around the Clock is a version of this*
127. Solomons

DOWN

1. Antiseptic agent
2. Zip
3. "You bet!"
4. "Cabaret" lyricist
5. Navy, e.g.
6. Cleaner, for short
7. Went by
8. Newswoman Logan
9. "Sex and the City" character also known as John
10. Egyptian god of the universe
11. Rice source
12. Small inlet
13. "Per ardua ad ___" (Royal Air Force motto)
14. 900 years before Queen Elizabeth was crowned
15. Mister abroad
16. Tempo
17. Own, in the past
18. Double ___ (Oreo variety)
21. Some police personnel: Abbr.
24. About
30. Web address
31. Donation location
32. Cozy spot
34. Cable inits. for sales pitches
37. Oscar winner for "Life Is Beautiful"
39. Skipping
40. Carries on
41. Is not as easy as it seems
43. Atlantic City hot spot, with "the"
44. Musician Brian
45. Court cry
47. Purchase at a booth: Abbr.
48. Soldiers home from service, e.g.
49. Start of a popular children's rhyme
51. Hog
54. Elementary figure: Abbr.
55. Corrosive cleaning agents
57. Where the limbo dance originated
59. Object

July

- 60 Be a ___ heart
- 61 Chris with the top 10 hit "Wicked Game"
- 64 Woolgathering
- 68 Where the Senegal River begins
- 69 "___ all possible"
- 70 Citation's end
- 72 White wine cocktails
- 75 Like aprons, at times
- 79 Squeeze (out)
- 80 Nancy Drew's beau
- 82 Locale of an 1805 Napoleon victory
- 83 Supermarket with a red oval logo
- 84 Low-cost, lightweight autos of the 1910s-'20s
- 87 Lesage book "Gil ___"
- 90 Gymgoer's pride
- 92 Sensible
- 93 Derisive call
- 96 "Time ___" (1990s sci-fi series)
- 97 Gave under pressure
- 100 Many a path up a mountain
- 101 Foments
- 102 Wields
- 103 Teeny-tiny
- 104 "Dónde ___ los Ladrones?" (1998 platinum album by Shakira)
- 105 Square
- 107 Temperance proponents
- 108 ___ Cong
- 109 ___ de cacao
- 110 Petty and Singer
- 111 Von Furstenberg of fashion
- 114 Kuwaiti dignitary
- 118 Alternative rock genre
- 119 Parisian possessive
- 121 Actor Stephen

monday
7 188

tuesday
8 189

wednesday
9 190

thursday
10 191

friday
11 192

○ FULL MOON

saturday
12 193

sunday
13 194

July

s	m	t	w	t	f	s
		1	2	3	4	5
6	7	8	9	10	11	12
13	14	15	16	17	18	19
20	21	22	23	24	25	26
27	28	29	30	31		

29. TURNING BACK

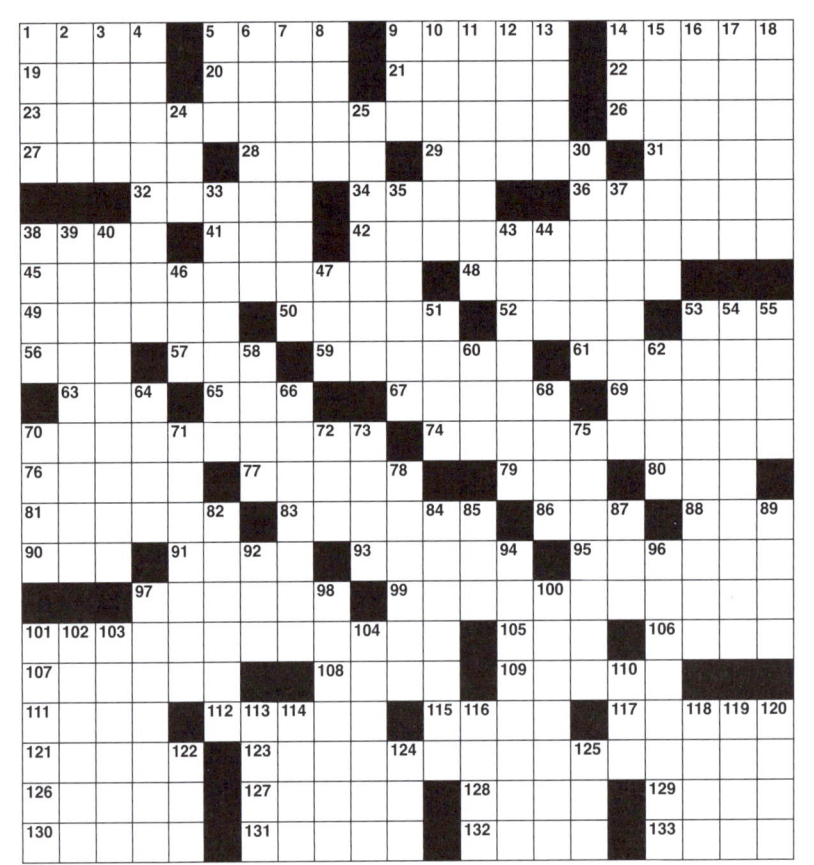

ACROSS
1. Math class, for short
5. Future doc's exam
9. Its slogan begins "15 minutes could save you …"
14. How stocks may be sold
19. Snack with a floral design
20. Ship written about by Apollonius of Rhodes
21. International relief org.
22. Went for
23. Taking the dimensions of busybodies?
26. Encircle
27. Medicare add-on
28. Fair
29. Short-billed rail
31. Starting material in coal formation
32. Some wedding guests
34. Image format
36. Her feast day is Jul. 11
38. Eminem song that samples Dido's "Thank You"
41. ___ germ
42. Done swimming?
45. Giving an award to the wrong person?
48. Capital of Albania
49. Freshen, in a way
50. Lipstick hue
52. Tofu base
53. Add (up)
56. Indian guy in National Lampoon's "Van Wilder" movies
57. Get on
59. Sense
61. Italian sculptor Nicola
63. Follower of White or Red
65. "That feels good!"
67. Wielder of the sword Tizona
69. More likely to get gifts from Santa
70. Slandering a Thanksgiving dish?
74. Othello, before Act V, Scene II?
76. "Enoch ___," Tennyson poem
77. Plum relatives
79. Palindromic preposition
80. Map abbr. before 1991
81. Many Maurice Sendak characters
83. Kazakh land feature
86. Large cask
88. Professional org. with a House of Delegates
90. It has a big mouth but can't speak
91. Friendship ender
93. Loy of "The Thin Man"
95. Custom-make
97. Awaited judgment
99. Comment in a women's mag?
101. Summary of "Raiders of the Lost Ark"?
105. Like Beethoven's "Kreutzer" Sonata
106. January 13, e.g.
107. So far
108. Site of the oldest university in South America
109. Joins
111. Letter opener
112. Fervent
115. Character in "I, Claudius"
117. Carne ___ (roasted meat dish)
121. Marion's "La Vie en Rose" character
123. Pious spouse's ultimatum?
126. Bank manager?
127. Hyundai sedan
128. Had a hunch
129. Drink in "My Big Fat Greek Wedding"
130. Wand waver, old-style
131. Like Ymir
132. Ymir, for one
133. One-eighties

DOWN
1. Give for free
2. Word with gray or rest
3. The Duke of Albany's father-in-law
4. Surname of TV's George, Frank and Estelle
5. Disfigure
6. Champagne often mentioned in hip-hop songs
7. Undecided, in a way
8. Getup
9. Suffix for shapes
10. Antiship missile used in the Falklands War
11. "It slipped my mind"
12. Cloak, in Córdoba
13. Siberian city
14. "Mein Gott!"
15. Wearer of a famous ring
16. Fruit with a thick rind
17. Crumbly cheese
18. Netflix movie
24. "___ Roi" (Alfred Jarry play)
25. Brief stay
30. F equivalent
33. Bouquet of flowers
35. Metamorphose, as a larva
37. Keeping an eye on
38. It may cause a scene
39. One who keeps one's balance?
40. Sneaker with a Jumpman logo

BY WILL NEDIGER • EDITED BY WILL SHORTZ • 09/05/10

July

- 43 Made-up
- 44 Hit 1989 biographical play
- 46 Z follower
- 47 Samoan dish
- 51 Put to sleep
- 53 Dish with greens and ground beef
- 54 A nonzero amount
- 55 Unit of pressure
- 58 Grub
- 60 "___ on parle français"
- 62 Family of games
- 64 Classic Jags
- 66 Piece keeper?
- 68 Reputation ruiner
- 70 Brand advertised as "the forbidden fragrance"
- 71 Beseech
- 72 Go to waste
- 73 Overflow
- 75 Gray, e.g.
- 78 Cuckold's purchase, perhaps
- 82 Confessional user
- 84 Charcoal alternative
- 85 One-point Scrabble tiles
- 87 "Me, ___ cheerful twinkle lights me": Robert Burns
- 89 Torah holders
- 92 Agcy. that may order recalls
- 94 "Is it not so?"
- 96 Sweetheart's telephone comment
- 97 Egyptian coin
- 98 Rescue
- 100 Bogey
- 101 "… is fear ___"
- 102 "Search me"
- 103 Certain PC storage area
- 104 Apple products
- 110 Roosevelt or Hoover
- 113 Mathematician Turing
- 114 Doofus
- 116 City in Nevada
- 118 Flu symptom
- 119 Ready for a nap
- 120 Big deals
- 122 "Get your hands off me!"
- 124 Popular middle name for a girl
- 125 Shorn female

July

s	m	t	w	t	f	s
		1	2	3	4	5
6	7	8	9	10	11	12
13	14	15	16	17	18	19
20	21	22	23	24	25	26
27	28	29	30	31		

monday
14 195

tuesday
15 196

wednesday
16 197

thursday
17 198

friday
18 199

☾ LAST QUARTER

saturday
19 200

sunday
20 201

30. IT'S GOING TO COST YOU

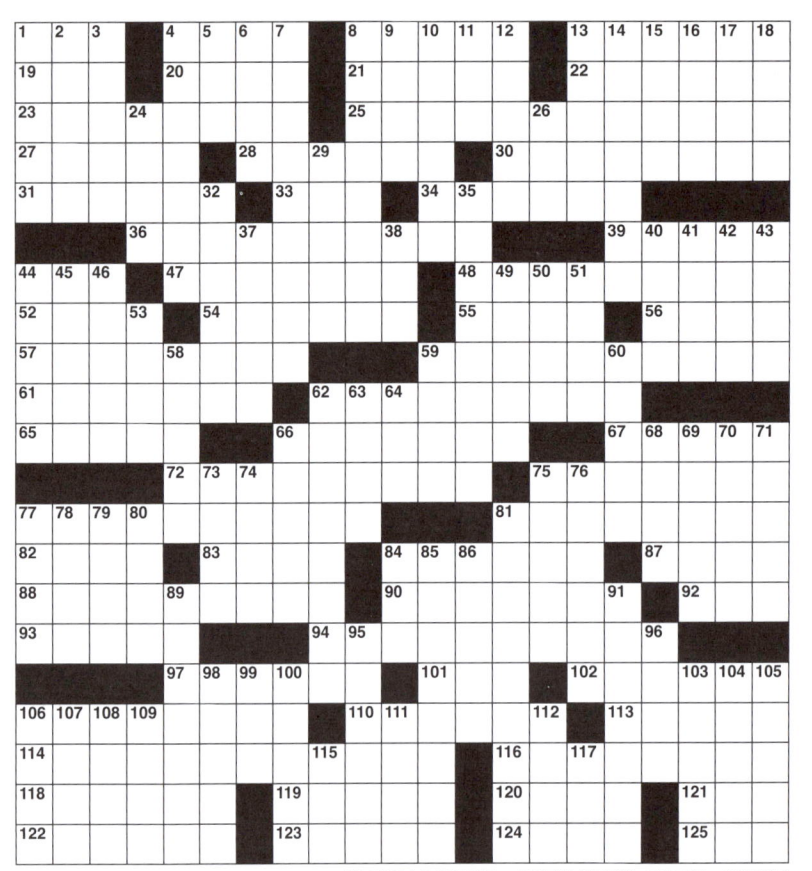

The New York Times

BY PAULA GAMACHE • EDITED BY WILL SHORTZ • 09/12/10

ACROSS
1. Obstinate type
4. Electronic music pioneer Robert
8. Boost
13. Straw hat
19. Cry after poor service?
20. River with the Reichenbach Falls
21. Some commercial signs
22. Remove ropes from
23. Bad news on Wall Street
25. What Fels-Naptha banished, in old ads
27. Where N.B.A. coach Rick Pitino played college ball
28. Relating to songbirds
30. Boost
31. French ice cream flavorer
33. "So nice!"
34. Excited call to a crew
36. Three squares
39. Classic camera maker
44. How to address a brother
47. Large group in a 23-Across
48. Heavenly body that humans will never set foot on
52. Alderaan royal
54. Jet boat brand
55. Alternatively, in Internet lingo
56. When said three times, a W.W. II cry
57. Followers
59. Like some doughnuts and windows
61. Unit of star measurement
62. Beckett's "Krapp's Last Tape," e.g.
65. Deli nosh
66. High-fiber, low-fat cereal ingredient
67. Mandela's presidential successor
72. Hazards for marine life
75. Blow it
77. Arc de Triomphe and Nelson's Column
81. Bet in craps
82. Strong
83. Part of MHz
84. Company that introduced NutraSweet
87. Botanical bristle
88. Tough rubber?
90. Relax
92. Angelo or Antonio
93. Connect with
94. Neutral space
97. Diminish
101. Mezzanotte is one
102. Crime scene evidence
106. Merely routine
110. Levels
113. Works in the music business
114. April, May and June
116. Blah-blah-blah
118. Subject of the 2008 biography "Somebody"
119. Bête ___
120. "Super!"
121. Object of many a court order
122. Some flowering shrubs
123. Overthrow, e.g.
124. Hair goops
125. Like a three-card monte player

DOWN
1. Contents of a sleeve
2. Request for face time
3. David Bowie single with the lyric "If we can sparkle he may land tonight"
4. Reed sites
5. Flavor associated with Chardonnay
6. Treat in a blue wrapper
7. Contends for valedictorian, say
8. See 9-Down
9. James known for playing an 8-Down
10. "Let's hear it!"
11. It does a bang-up job
12. Singer K. T. ___
13. Relative of Rover
14. Doing really well
15. Assert without proof
16. Butler's place
17. Those, to Tomás
18. "Seven Seas of ___" (early Queen hit)
24. Galaxy sci.
26. Squelch
29. "___, I'm sure"
32. Disgorges
35. About equal to
37. "___ Gold"
38. Kyushu volcano
40. "Do I dare to ___ peach?"
41. "Rinkitink ___" (L. Frank Baum book)
42. Smear with wax, old-style
43. Slightly
44. Hooch holder at a ballgame
45. Intel mission
46. Provençal sauce
49. Take ___ for the worse
50. Japanese noodle
51. Throat stuff
53. Frightens
58. Swiftian brute
59. Unhip sort
60. Farm newborns
62. "L'Après-midi d'un faune" poet Stéphane ___
63. Lift innovator
64. "ER" network

July

66 ___ orange
68 Crude qty.
69 Mournful songs
70 ___ Kinte of "Roots"
71 "Um … well … it's like …"
73 "___ la Douce"
74 Fabrications
75 He taught Mowgli the law of the jungle
76 Depletes
77 Slightest amount
78 Emporio ___
79 Actress Sommer
80 Sports competition
81 Dividing fairly, say
84 South of France
85 Check person
86 Brand for hay fever sufferers
89 Watts who hosted a 1990s talk show
91 Implants
95 Behind bars
96 Quick swims
98 Mathematician Paul
99 Smugness
100 It joins the Rhône at Lyon
103 Places for some newborns
104 "Perry Mason" scene
105 Tear-jerking
106 Chem. pollutants
107 In short supply
108 Pearl Buck heroine
109 George Manville ___, English adventure writer
111 "Comin' ___ the Rye"
112 Chick's tail?
115 Neither's partner
117 Permitted

monday 21 202

tuesday 22 203
Benefits enrolments
July 22 - Aug 4.
Register on Flex tool first
watch video
608 829 5500
People Support Centre — market party

wednesday 23 204

thursday 24 205

friday 25 206

● NEW MOON

saturday 26 207

sunday 27 208

July
s	m	t	w	t	f	s
		1	2	3	4	5
6	7	8	9	10	11	12
13	14	15	16	17	18	19
20	21	22	23	24	25	26
27	28	29	30	31		

31. MUSICAL PLAY

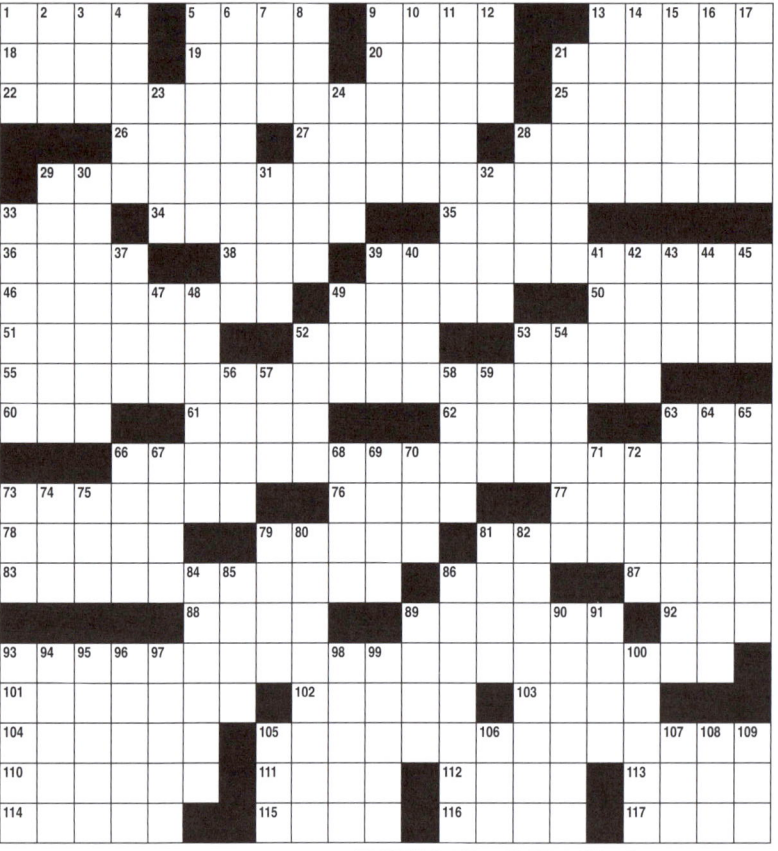

The New York Times

ACROSS

1. Diner fixture, informally
5. Not stopping the draft, say
9. Cathedral feature
13. Once-popular Olds
18. Producer of a colorful ring tone
19. It mentions the Prodigal Son
20. ___ Men ("Move It Like This" group)
21. Kind of season
22. "Carmen" composer-turned-dam builder?
25. Passé
26. It hangs around the Amazon
27. Not straight
28. Not neat
29. Embrace more than just a family of Baroque composers?
33. Org. in the "Bourne" series
34. Union representative?
35. Hawaiian fish, on some menus
36. Mine entrance
38. These, overseas
39. Romantic overindulgence in nocturnes and mazurkas?
46. Distills
49. Some gridiron yardage
50. Zoo heavyweight
51. Buzz in a rocket
52. Oblast bordering Kazakhstan
53. ___ harp
55. Singing a "Messiah" piece too quickly?
60. Sightseer?
61. Song lead-in to "di" or "da"
62. Opposing
63. It's eight hours off from 49-Down: Abbr.
66. Countrywide music celebration in Hungary?
73. If all else fails
76. Fortune
77. "This isn't looking good …"
78. Missionary Junipero ___
79. It might start a rumor
81. Ohio city named for a queen
83. Part of a children's game with the Father of the Symphony?
86. Place of corruption
87. Ja's opposite
88. Poet depicted in art alongside the Scythians
89. ___ economics
92. Otolaryngology: Abbr.
93. Grand nuptials whose only music was "Peer Gynt"?
101. Climactic
102. Cousin of a goldeneye
103. Some old runabouts
104. Physicist Schrödinger and others
105. Try to capture the Waltz King?
110. Upscale upholstery
111. Hint
112. Geezer
113. Laguna composition
114. Twisty turns
115. Command
116. Dame ___
117. Honey Nut ___

DOWN

1. It might be found in a plant
2. Longtime news inits.
3. Second baseman Matsui, to fans
4. Aromatic resin
5. Purchase of 1867
6. "Even if it'll never happen again …"
7. Alias
8. Taxpayers' hopes
9. Noisy counters
10. Smoothed over
11. Succubus
12. Pink Mr. Potato Head piece
13. Gossip topic
14. Hindu god of thunder
15. Work ___
16. It's measured at arm's length
17. Gets in the game, say
21. Peaceful protest
23. Peewee
24. Highland tongue
28. "Funny meeting you here!"
29. How current events may happen?
30. It helps you change the locks
31. Strummed instruments, for short
32. Lager sources
33. Wine order
37. Garr of "Tootsie"
39. Till fill
40. Bring up
41. Last thing
42. It can be popped
43. Upstate N.Y. school
44. Spill-fighting grp.
45. Years on end
47. Bass part
48. They're worth their weight in gold
49. See 63-Across
52. Wink ___ eye
53. 1998 film featuring Princess Bala
54. Mad person?
56. Something of yours you'll never see
57. Mel's Diner waitress
58. Greet loudly

BY KEVIN G. DER • EDITED BY WILL SHORTZ • 09/19/10

July-August

- **59** Opposite of a ques.
- **63** Many a Little Leaguer
- **64** Setting forth
- **65** Monocrat
- **66** France's ___-Pas-de-Calais
- **67** ___ Islands, group at the mouth of Galway Bay
- **68** Bide-___
- **69** Publicist's headache
- **70** Choreographer Lubovitch
- **71** ___ Beta Kappa
- **72** Port SSE of Sana
- **73** Contents of some cones
- **74** Crumpet's go-with
- **75** Not straight
- **79** "This ___" (Michael Jackson album)
- **80** It may extend about a yard
- **81** Persian's call
- **82** News anchor Cooper
- **84** Sell quickly
- **85** Like the Ford logo
- **86** Track event for gamblers
- **89** #2
- **90** "Glory, Glory" singer
- **91** It's often carried around a gym
- **93** Irish novelist Binchy
- **94** W.W. I battle site
- **95** Gets the ball rolling?
- **96** "Uncle!"
- **97** Offspring's inheritance
- **98** One thrown from a horse
- **99** "In my opinion …"
- **100** Singer of sewing machine fame
- **105** Grunts
- **106** Mann's "Der ___ in Venedig"
- **107** Cry of distaste
- **108** Go after
- **109** Big band member, for short

July

s	m	t	w	t	f	s
		1	2	3	4	5
6	7	8	9	10	11	12
13	14	15	16	17	18	19
20	21	22	23	24	25	26
27	28	29	30	31		

August

s	m	t	w	t	f	s
					1	2
3	4	5	6	7	8	9
10	11	12	13	14	15	16
17	18	19	20	21	22	23
24	25	26	27	28	29	30
31						

EID AL-FITR

monday
28 209

tuesday
29 210

wednesday
30 211

thursday
31 212

friday
1 213

saturday
2 214

sunday
3 215

32. LOCATION, LOCATION, LOCATION

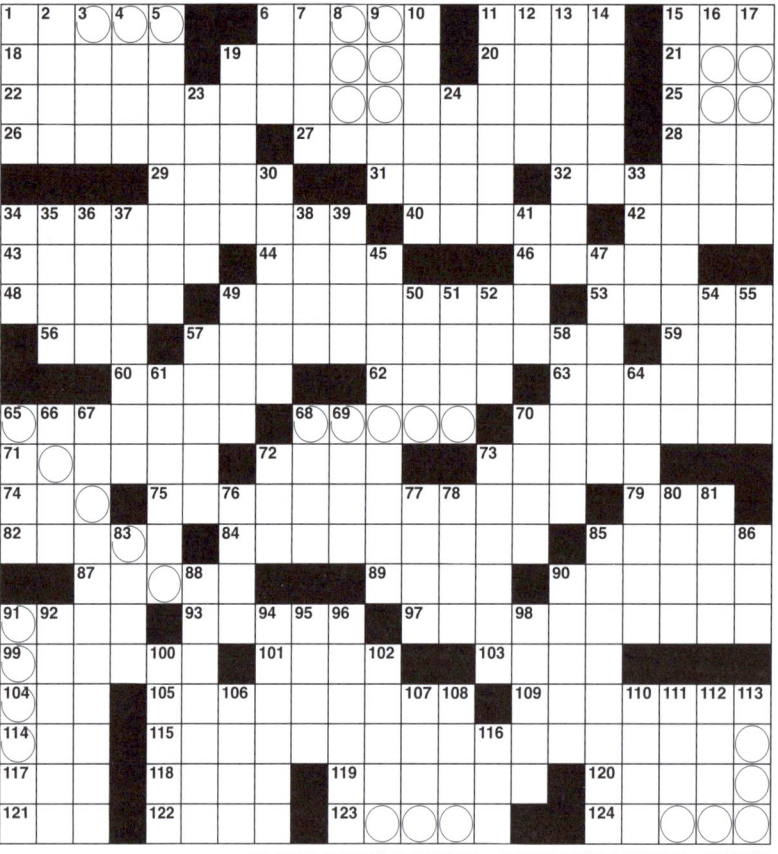

BY PAMELA AMICK KLAWITTER • EDITED BY WILL SHORTZ • 09/26/10

NOTE: Each set of circled letters is described by an answer elsewhere in the grid.

ACROSS

- 1 When repeated, a resort near the Black Forest
- 6 How things may be remembered
- 11 Beginning
- 15 Caboose, for one
- 18 In ___ (unborn)
- 19 Homeric hero
- 20 Part of Q.E.D.
- 21 ___ Miss
- 22 Specification in a salad order
- 25 A lens fits in it
- 26 Swell
- 27 Certifies, in a way
- 28 U.S.M.C. barracks boss
- 29 XXX
- 31 Homeric genre
- 32 Address part
- 34 Unit in measuring population density
- 40 As a friend, to the French
- 42 Relative of Manx
- 43 Michael who once headed Disney
- 44 Grab bag: Abbr.
- 46 Some stakes
- 48 Dreadful feeling
- 49 Worker who may create a stir?
- 53 Following
- 56 Opening
- 57 Opening for an aspiring leader
- 59 Fine and dandy, in old slang
- 60 "I don't give ___!"
- 62 Zing
- 63 Writer/critic Trilling
- 65 Hit computer game with the original working title Micropolis
- 68 First name alphabetically in the Baseball Hall of Fame
- 70 President who said "I'm an idealist without illusions"
- 71 Giggle
- 72 Suffix with lumin-
- 73 Hard, boring efforts
- 74 Directional suffix
- 75 Diagonals
- 79 "Mazel ___!"
- 82 Fix, as a shoelace
- 84 Complete
- 85 Country singer Griffith
- 87 Name on 1952 campaign buttons
- 89 Romance of 1847
- 90 Errand runners
- 91 Mid 12th-century year
- 93 Cool, very red celestial body
- 97 Carp or flounder, typically
- 99 Highly rated security
- 101 Hungarian city
- 103 Actress Ward
- 104 Fashion inits.
- 105 You might wait for it to drop
- 109 Three-wheeled vehicle
- 114 Spanish bruin
- 115 Go-between
- 117 Rapper ___-A-Che
- 118 Same: Fr.
- 119 Convict
- 120 Relative of a canary
- 121 Cinch ___ (Hefty garbage bag brand)
- 122 "Idylls of the King" lady
- 123 Falls (over)
- 124 Breast: Prefix

DOWN

- 1 Melville's "Billy ___"
- 2 Italian bell town
- 3 Dead ends?
- 4 Formerly, once
- 5 Public knowledge
- 6 Ph.D., e.g.
- 7 Barge ___
- 8 "Don't give ___ lip!"
- 9 Beverage that may be foamy
- 10 A wishbone has one
- 11 Director Vittorio
- 12 48th state: Abbr.
- 13 Begins energetically
- 14 Explosive trial, for short
- 15 Place for a date, frequently
- 16 "___ Restaurant"
- 17 Not likely
- 19 "… ___ the queen of England!"
- 23 "And to those thorns that ___ bosom lodge": Shak.
- 24 St. Patrick's land
- 30 One of the 12 tribes of Israel
- 33 Shipwreck locale
- 34 Ship locale
- 35 Last dynasty of China
- 36 Links org.
- 37 Susan who co-starred in "Five Easy Pieces"
- 38 Actor Neeson
- 39 "Cómo ___?"
- 41 Shopping locale
- 45 Indulged
- 47 Pre-broadcast activity
- 49 David Cameron, e.g.
- 50 Normandy battle town
- 51 More ___ enough
- 53 Dark time, in verse
- 54 Just got (by)
- 55 Trust, with "on"
- 57 Honey badger

August

- 58 Dinner spreads
- 61 Engine type
- 64 Employed
- 65 "Fer ___!"
- 66 French noun suffix
- 67 Cause of thoughtlessness?
- 68 Dog of old films
- 69 Didn't just pass
- 70 Noted Bauhaus artist
- 72 Dallas-to-Memphis dir.
- 73 High-hats
- 76 Large food tunas
- 77 Bausch & ___ (lens maker)
- 78 Langston Hughes poem
- 80 "The ___ Gave My Heart To" (1997 Aaliyah hit)
- 81 Tapers, briefly
- 83 Peculiar: Prefix
- 85 Bedouins' trait
- 86 It's like "-like"
- 88 "Next …"
- 90 Dimwit
- 91 City chiefs
- 92 Cinnamon tree
- 94 Swarmed
- 95 Indian tourist city
- 96 Challenger astronaut Judith
- 98 Chief dwelling?
- 100 "I'm innocent!"
- 102 Liechtenstein's western border
- 106 Certain engine
- 107 "This round's ___"
- 108 List-ending abbr.
- 110 Notion
- 111 Mil. leaders
- 112 Came to earth
- 113 "There Shall ___ Night" (Pulitzer-winning Robert E. Sherwood play)
- 116 Elevs.

August

s	m	t	w	t	f	s
					1	2
3	4	5	6	7	8	9
10	11	12	13	14	15	16
17	18	19	20	21	22	23
24	25	26	27	28	29	30
31						

SUMMER BANK HOLIDAY (IRELAND, UK—SCOTLAND, AUSTRALIA—NSW)
PICNIC DAY (AUSTRALIA—NT)
☽ FIRST QUARTER

monday
4 216

tuesday
5 217

wednesday
6 218

thursday
7 219

friday
8 220

saturday
9 221

○ FULL MOON

sunday
10 222

33. CAN I CHANGE PLACES?

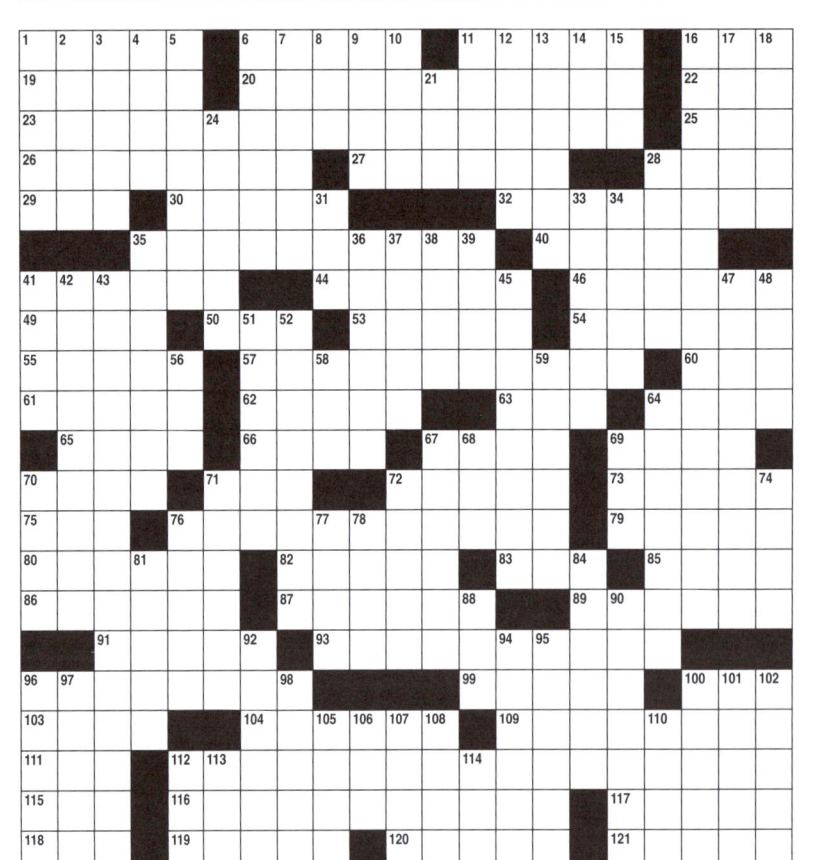

The New York Times

109 Convert, as metal into a melt?
111 Prefix with skeleton
112 Admonishment at a Surrealist museum?
115 Delivery means
116 "West Side Story" fight scene prop
117 More awesome, to a rapper
118 Slalom figure
119 Lab holder?
120 Darling
121 Like many mosaics

DOWN
1 Went (for)
2 ___ toad
3 Cold look
4 Grab bag
5 Moved on wheels, as a movie camera
6 Afraid
7 Et ___
8 Regal letters
9 Opposite of sans
10 Practical school, for short
11 Uncle ___
12 Pennies are small ones
13 Staples of action scenes
14 Poetic contraction
15 Humorless
16 Decorative piece of George Harrison tour equipment?
17 Ball's partner
18 Spring, summer, fall and winter, e.g.
21 Big suit
24 Stale
28 Eyes
31 Grade school subj.
33 Play opener
34 Wishing undone
35 Restrains
36 Boo ___, recluse in "To Kill a Mockingbird"
37 Forster's "___ With a View"
38 Crucifix letters
39 Unlikely response to "Sprechen Sie Deutsch?"
41 Actress Drescher
42 Chart showing highs and lows
43 Paintings of Marilyn Monroe, Che Guevara and the like?
45 Rests
47 Shoe insert
48 Grown-up eft
51 Anesthetic gas
52 Sharpener residue
56 Sun Devils' sch.
58 Screw up

BY DANIEL A. FINAN • EDITED BY WILL SHORTZ • 10/03/10

ACROSS
1 "This can't be happening!"
6 Apple's instant-messaging program
11 Headquartered
16 Anatomical pouch
19 Spanish fowl
20 Headquarters
22 Inquire about private matters
23 Lewis and Clark expedition, for the 1800s?
25 "Monsters, ___"
26 Student
27 Elite group, with "the"
28 Like some exams
29 Turn red, say
30 "___ you!" ("Just try it!")
32 Search the heavens
35 Spoiler of a parade for Ahmadinejad?
40 Racing boat
41 Charlie Brown's curly-haired pal
44 January birthstone
46 Attaches with string
49 Like most city blocks: Abbr.
50 Parisian possessive
53 Andrea ___ (lost ship)
54 Like some kicks
55 "___ From Hawaii," 1973 Elvis album
57 Top butcher's title?
60 Pull
61 WXY buttons
62 Sultan's group
63 Santa Barbara-to-Las Vegas dir.
64 Blemish
65 Hosiery shade
66 "Climb ___ Mountain"
67 ___ en scène (stage setting)
69 Her: Ger.
70 "Independence Day" fleet
71 Singer DiFranco
72 Brewery sights
73 South American shrubs with potent leaves
75 T-shirt sizes, in short
76 Destroyers of les forêts?
79 Glide
80 Aplenty
82 Surgeon's procedure
83 Super ___ (game console)
85 Minute fraction of a min.
86 Cave dwellers
87 Menu option
89 Upbeat
91 Chocolate substitute
93 What a family court judge enforces?
96 Where sharks are in their food chain
99 Plant ___ of doubt
100 Glimpsed à la Tweety Bird
103 Luke's princess sister
104 Yellowish-brown

August

- 59 Actually
- 64 Words said with a shrug
- 67 Tiki bar order
- 68 Medit. state
- 69 Suffix with robot
- 70 Grp. concerned with courses
- 71 Playground retort
- 72 Volunteer
- 74 Cabinet member: Abbr.
- 76 Parisian business partner, maybe
- 77 Squeeze (in)
- 78 "___ Nagila" (Hebrew folk song)
- 81 Site of the College World Series
- 84 Cornea neighbor
- 88 RR stop
- 90 Didn't shrink from the challenge
- 92 1990s war site
- 94 Member of the prosecutor's office: Abbr.
- 95 Fyodor Karamazov, for one
- 96 Advil rival
- 97 U.S.S. ___, first battleship to become a state shrine
- 98 ZaSu of film
- 100 Peewee slugger's sport
- 101 Tree-lined walk
- 102 Kooky
- 105 Permanently mark
- 106 Japanese drama
- 107 Gists
- 108 Rights org.
- 110 Year Boris Godunov was born
- 112 Broadband letters
- 113 Be behind
- 114 Witch

monday

11

tuesday

12

wednesday

13

thursday

14

friday

15

saturday

16

☾ LAST QUARTER

sunday

17

August

s	m	t	w	t	f	s
					1	2
3	4	5	6	7	8	9
10	11	12	13	14	15	16
17	18	19	20	21	22	23
24	25	26	27	28	29	30
31						

34. DRIVERS' TRANSLATIONS

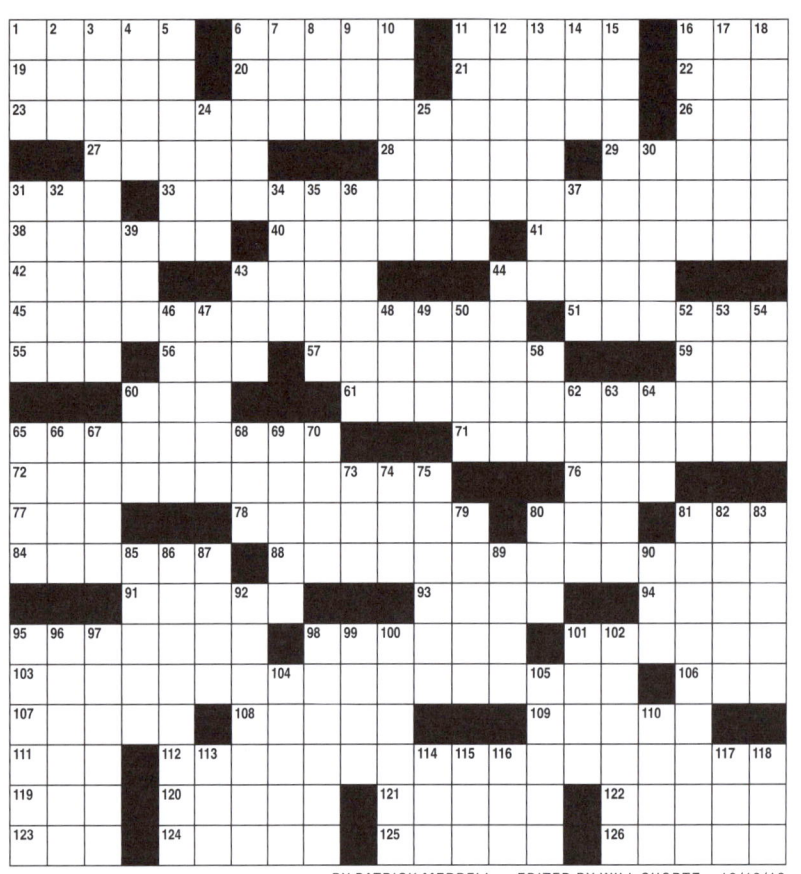

ACROSS
1. "Applesauce!"
6. The pulp in pulp fiction
11. "That ticked me off!"
16. Bob and pageboy
19. 1987 #1 Heart song that starts "I hear the ticking of the clock"
20. Sauce made with garlic and olive oil
21. Adrenaline producer
22. Dog show org.
23. YOUR TAX DOLLARS AT WORK …
26. Call of support
27. Some run to get in it
28. "Batman" fight scene sound
29. Blender brand
31. Hold 'em bullet
33. MERGING TRAFFIC …
38. Flies that don't go far from home
40. Removed fold marks
41. Places to pray
42. Know-it-___ (cocky types)
43. Cuzco native
44. Range rover
45. STOP …
51. Some '50s Fords
55. Suffix with hatch
56. Special ___
57. Reply from a polite young'un
59. It's often pointed in gymnastics
60. Ermine, e.g.
61. CONGESTION NEXT 10 MILES …
65. Wearers of jeweled turbans
71. Neurotransmitter associated with sleep
72. NO THRU TRAFFIC …
76. However, briefly
77. Genetic material
78. Open mike night format, perhaps
80. From ___ Z
81. Wizened woman
84. Winged celestial being
88. STAY IN LANE …
91. Kind of translation
93. Setting for the biggest movie of 1939
94. Sailing
95. Number system with only 0's and 1's
98. Cheesesteak capital
101. Earthlings
103. NO STOPPING OR STANDING …
106. Ultimate degree
107. Like some legal proceedings
108. Has an angle
109. Syrian president
111. Comprehend
112. SPEED LIMIT 65 M.P.H. …
119. Guffaw syllable
120. "None for me, thanks"
121. Field Marshal Rommel
122. Feeling when called to the principal's office
123. Literary monogram
124. Cockeyed
125. Requiring an umbrella
126. Brings in

DOWN
1. Unchallenging reading material
2. ___-mo
3. Roughhousing
4. Egyptian symbol of life
5. Online program
6. City in a "Can-Can" song
7. Common inhalant
8. Creator of the detective C. Auguste Dupin
9. Architectural addition
10. Oriole who played in a record 2,632 straight games
11. Small crustacean
12. Low-level position
13. Queen of double entendres
14. Cannonball's path
15. Took an alternate route
16. The Wright brothers' Ohio home
17. Michael of "Caddyshack"
18. Gobbles (down)
24. Mortgage figs.
25. Part of 24-Down
30. Awakens
31. Swiftly
32. Kind of commentator
34. Pub order
35. Don Marquis's six-legged poet
36. Lion or tiger or bear
37. Tony Hillerman detective Jim
39. ___ Intrepid
43. Connections
44. Investment unit
46. Roadies work on them
47. First name in TV talk
48. Spanish bear
49. Actress Thurman
50. Gallivants
52. School for Prince Harry
53. Anderson of "WKRP in Cincinnati"
54. Spotted
58. Harm
60. Troll dolls or Silly Bandz
62. Gambino boss after Castellano
63. Group values
64. Place with feeding times
65. Supermarket V.I.P.'s: Abbr.
66. Best-of-the-best

BY PATRICK MERRELL • EDITED BY WILL SHORTZ • 10/10/10

August

- 67 Frozen dew
- 68 Betty, Bobbie and Billie followers on "Petticoat Junction"
- 69 Bandleader Shaw
- 70 Woodlands male
- 73 "The Situation Room" airer
- 74 Japanese vegetable
- 75 Slowpoke
- 79 "The Power of Positive Thinking" author
- 80 "I get it now"
- 81 Like some matching pairs
- 82 Representative
- 83 Grind together
- 85 Anacin alternative
- 86 Famed Russian battleship
- 87 "That's just ___ feel"
- 89 "___ Little Tenderness"
- 90 Houston after whom the Texas city is named
- 92 Toilet tissue superlative
- 95 Worry for a farmer
- 96 Leader whom Virgil called "the virtuous"
- 97 Jean-Paul who wrote "Words are loaded pistols"
- 98 Particular form of government
- 99 Jabba the ___, "Star Wars" villain
- 100 Bond offerer, e.g.
- 101 It may wind up at the side of the house
- 102 All the pluses
- 104 "Criminy!"
- 105 Sideshow worker
- 110 Taj Mahal site
- 113 Bird in New South Wales
- 114 New Deal inits.
- 115 Breathalyzer determination, for short
- 116 One, for Fritz
- 117 It's often picked up at the beach
- 118 QB's stat.

August

s	m	t	w	t	f	s
					1	2
3	4	5	6	7	8	9
10	11	12	13	14	15	16
17	18	19	20	21	22	23
24	25	26	27	28	29	30
31						

monday

18

tuesday

19

wednesday

20

thursday

21

friday

22

saturday

23

sunday

24

35. FIGURE OF SPEECH

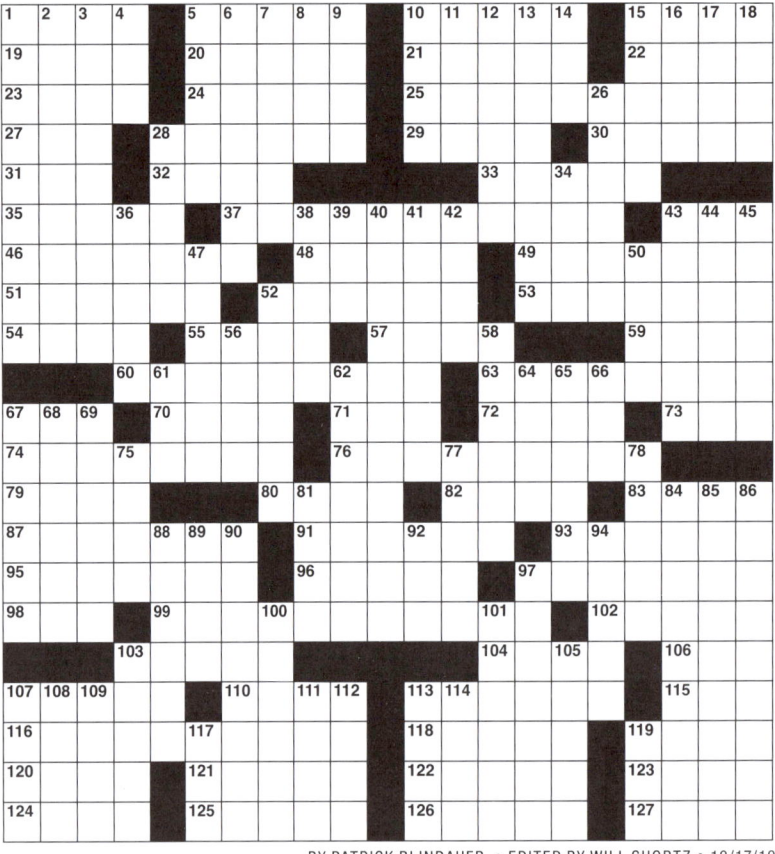

BY PATRICK BLINDAUER • EDITED BY WILL SHORTZ • 10/17/10

ACROSS
1. Alaska senator Murkowski
5. Sean who played the title role in "Rudy," 1993
10. Start to frost?
15. Pan handler
19. El océano, por ejemplo
20. Shakespeare's Lennox, Angus or Ross
21. Bitter
22. Aries or Taurus
23. Hoop grp.
24. They may be split
25. Singer with the #1 country hit "Hello Darlin'"
27. When repeated, a calming phrase
28. A whole lot
29. Debate side
30. Cartographic extra
31. Egg protector
32. Easy as falling off ___
33. Salon, for example
35. Listens, old-style
37. Suspenseful 1966 Broadway hit
43. Grp. that conducts many tests
46. Biblical liar
48. See 39-Down
49. Actress ___ Chong
51. Least welcoming
52. Wait upon
53. Gathered
54. ___ Coty, French president before de Gaulle
55. Stick in the mud
57. Subtracting
59. Cassandra, for one
60. Repeatedly raised the bar?
63. Long piece of glassware
67. N.F.C. South player
70. Noggin
71. Still product: Abbr.
72. On the safe side
73. Wave function symbol in quantum mechanics
74. Items of short-lived use
76. Racy best-selling novel of 1956
79. Take ___ (rest)
80. Hindu titles
82. Speed-skating champ Johann ___ Koss
83. Out of
87. Like an egocentric's attitude
91. Flammable fuel
93. Part of a postal address for Gannon University
95. Carry out
96. Moon of Saturn
97. Barbecue cook
98. Football linemen: Abbr.
99. Fast-talking salesman's tactic
102. Itsy-bitsy
103. Explorer ___ da Gama
104. Shout from one who's on a roll?
106. ___ loss
107. One to a customer, e.g.
110. Prime
113. Camping treats
115. B.M.O.C.'s, often
116. X Games competitor
118. Rikki-___-tavi
119. Tanned
120. Zoom
121. Florida univ. affiliated with the Catholic Church
122. ___ the hole
123. "… and ___ it again!"
124. "Twilight," e.g.
125. ___ manual
126. Gull relatives
127. Spat

DOWN
1. Common patio sight
2. Bliss, it is said
3. 1, 2, 3, 4, 5, 6 or 7, in New York City
4. Prominent tower, for short
5. Massachusetts industrial city on the Millers River
6. Trails
7. Follow too closely
8. Dictator's phrase
9. Dread loch?
10. Spotted cavy
11. H.S. class
12. Didn't buy, perhaps
13. Don Herbert's moniker on 1950s-'60s TV
14. Lessen
15. "Educating Rita" star
16. Sheds
17. Novel conclusion?
18. Track star A. J.
26. Gave a sly signal
28. Good spot for a date?
34. "Dies ___" (hymn)
36. Prepare for a dubbing
38. ___ Yucatán "you"
39. With 48-Across, mediocre
40. Insomniac's TV viewing
41. "The Chairs" playwright
42. Former Fords
43. Showing, as a deck member
44. Square sorts
45. Peace Nobelist Sakharov
47. Cost for getting money, maybe
50. Common settler
52. Bowls
56. ___-Tass news agency
58. Bread, milk or eggs

August

- 61 Tech stock
- 62 Elk
- 64 Folk singer Jenkins
- 65 Miracle Mets pitcher, 1969
- 66 Shamus
- 67 Person who's visibly happy
- 68 On deck
- 69 Rubs
- 75 Sweeping story
- 77 Schubert's "Eine kleine Trauermusik," e.g.
- 78 Use TurboTax, say
- 81 Comedian Foxx
- 84 Movie producer's time of stress
- 85 Tariffs hinder it
- 86 Oscar-winning actress for "The Great Lie," 1941
- 88 With freedom of tempo
- 89 Conditions
- 90 Some service stations
- 92 Black bird
- 94 Devotional ceremonies
- 97 Pickle type
- 100 Noggin
- 101 Ring around the collar
- 103 Lead-in to harp or phone
- 105 Dancer's controls?
- 107 W.W. II craft
- 108 Furniture giant
- 109 Largest employer in Newton, Iowa, until 2006
- 111 Not e'en once
- 112 Winged Greek god
- 113 Ballpark figure
- 114 Cheese lovers
- 117 The Sun Devils of the N.C.A.A.
- 119 Magnanimous

monday 25 237
SUMMER BANK HOLIDAY (UK—EXCEPT SCOTLAND)
● NEW MOON

tuesday 26 238

wednesday 27 239

thursday 28 240

friday 29 241

saturday 30 242

sunday 31 243

August

s	m	t	w	t	f	s
					1	2
3	4	5	6	7	8	9
10	11	12	13	14	15	16
17	18	19	20	21	22	23
24	25	26	27	28	29	30
31						

36. RISKY BUSINESS

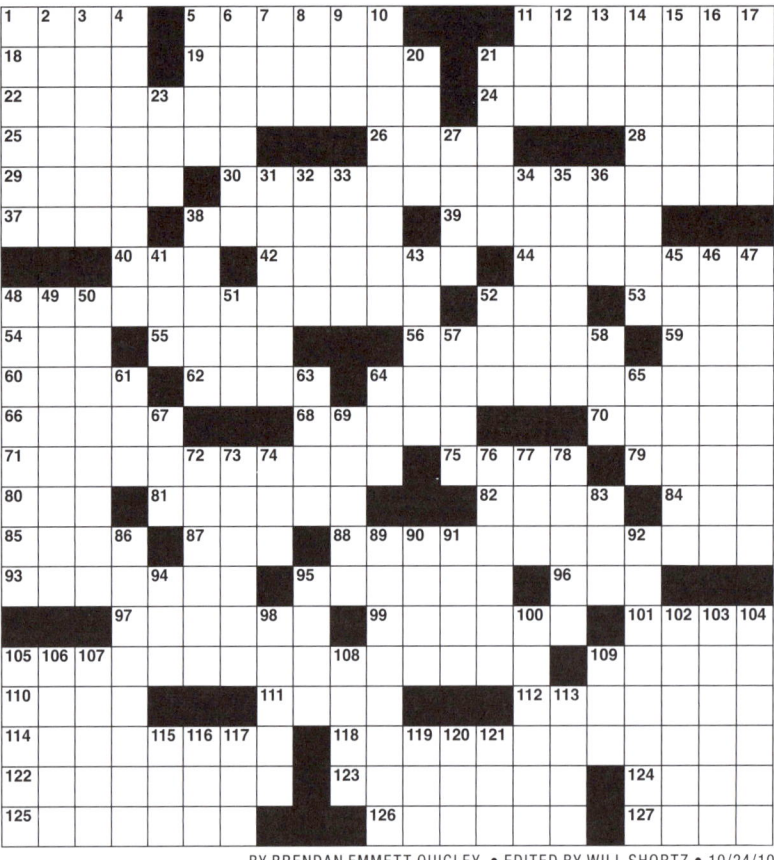

The New York Times

BY BRENDAN EMMETT QUIGLEY • EDITED BY WILL SHORTZ • 10/24/10

ACROSS

1. Charitable contributions
5. Bungalow roof
11. Part of an ice skater's shoe
18. One of the Three B's
19. Friend of Hamlet
21. Film festival name since 1990
22. London-based place to play the ponies?
24. Firm part
25. Street bordering New York's Stuyvesant Town
26. "___ Athlete Dying Young" (A. E. Housman poem)
28. 8-point X, e.g.
29. Laughing
30. J. D. Salinger character's favorite game?
37. Golfer John
38. Doughnut shape
39. Asian royalty
40. Letters on an Olympics jersey
42. Busy
44. Like Nasser's movement
48. Game played with dice set on fire?
52. "Mad Men" actor Hamm
53. "99 Luftballons" hit-maker of 1984
54. Spoilage
55. Short and detached, in mus.
56. Diva Renata
59. One-third of a game win
60. "I'm ___ you!"
62. Libido
64. One-armed bandits?
66. Arabian Peninsula native
68. Sideways on a ship
70. Participants in an annual run
71. Relative of a bingo caller?
75. Insurer's offering
79. Author McCaffrey
80. Antiquity, quaintly
81. Mitch Albom title person
82. Losing tribe in the Beaver Wars
84. Psychologist LeShan
85. Crumhorn, e.g.
87. Dearie
88. Card game played Reynolds's way?
93. Leaves high and dry
95. Poe's "rare and radiant maiden"
96. On a roll
97. "I'm not the only one?"
99. Actress Langdon
101. ___ ghanouj
105. "Please consider playing the wheel again"?
109. "Life of Brian" outfits
110. Stereotypical lab assistant's name
111. Alphabetically first inductee in the Rock and Roll Hall of Fame
112. Arriviste
114. Split personality?
118. Pot with a pile of chips?
122. Offered in payment
123. Vine-covered colonnade
124. Emphatically
125. Nods
126. Radio ___
127. Gym gear

DOWN

1. "All ___!"
2. 8-Down's home
3. TV character with dancing baby hallucinations
4. Climb, as a rope
5. What you used to be?
6. Big gun
7. The Iguazu Riv. forms part of its border
8. 1960s chess champion Mikhail
9. L overseer
10. Alluded to
11. When repeated, an admonishment
12. Mich. neighbor
13. Capital until 1868
14. Like politics, by nature
15. Hole just above a belt
16. Flashlight battery
17. Worked (up)
20. N.B.A. star nicknamed the Candy Man
21. World capital almost 1 1/2 miles above sea level
23. Bit in trail mix
27. Part of a plot
31. "The Epic of American Civilization" muralist
32. Stuff of legends
33. Effort
34. Begins to transplant
35. "Lost" shelter
36. Squishy place
38. Art collector's asset
41. Snake's warning
43. Rock band with an inventor's name
45. Football special teams player
46. Tropical menace
47. Roadster's lack
48. Frogs
49. Seven-line poem
50. One who's all there?
51. Bygone geographical inits.
52. Scribble

September

- 57 Give for free
- 58 Frequently, in brief
- 61 Well-known Tokyo-born singer
- 63 "The Open Window" story writer
- 64 Talk to the flock: Abbr.
- 65 Mau ___ (forever, in Hawaii)
- 67 School: Suffix
- 69 Former Buffalo Bills great Don
- 72 Hall & Oates, e.g.
- 73 1974 top 10 hit whose title means "You Are"
- 74 Canvases, say
- 76 Coach Dick in the N.F.L. Hall of Fame
- 77 The Altar
- 78 Recess
- 83 Prefix with warrior
- 86 Do some quick market work
- 89 Tacit
- 90 Smooth operator
- 91 Early smartphone
- 92 Basically
- 94 Neighbor of Swe.
- 95 Trial of the Century defendant
- 98 "Shanghai Express" actor
- 100 Mathematical sequence of unknown length
- 102 Annual award for mystery writers
- 103 Most meager
- 104 Texas nine
- 105 Mandates
- 106 Meanies
- 107 Common times for duels
- 108 0.5 fl. oz.
- 109 "Your safety is our priority" org.
- 113 Bit of theatrics
- 115 "Taps" hour
- 116 N.Y.C. subway line
- 117 1950s political inits.
- 119 Actress Graynor
- 120 Metric weights: Abbr.
- 121 Big stretch?

September

s	m	t	w	t	f	s
	1	2	3	4	5	6
7	8	9	10	11	12	13
14	15	16	17	18	19	20
21	22	23	24	25	26	27
28	29	30				

LABOR DAY (USA, CANADA)

monday
1 244

☽ FIRST QUARTER

tuesday
2 245

wednesday
3 246

thursday
4 247

friday
5 248

saturday
6 249

FATHER'S DAY (AUSTRALIA, NZ)

sunday
7 250

37. FANGS FOR THE MEMORIES

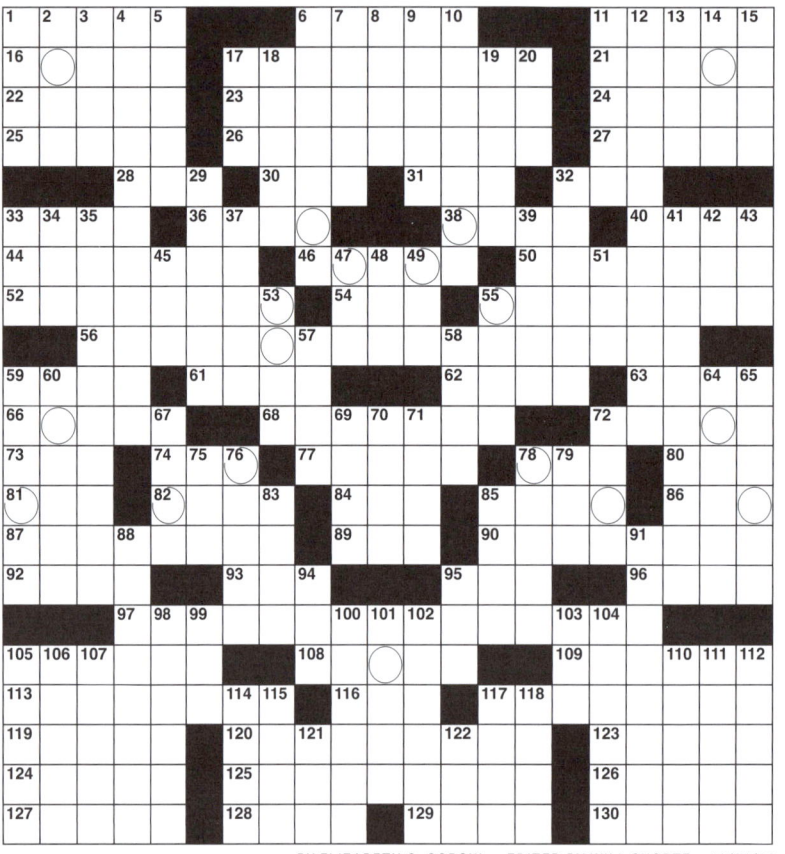

BY ELIZABETH C. GORSKI • EDITED BY WILL SHORTZ • 10/31/10

NOTE: WHEN THIS PUZZLE IS COMPLETED, CONNECT THE CIRCLED LETTERS IN ALPHABETICAL ORDER FROM A TO R TO SHOW THE OUTLINE OF AN 84-ACROSS.

ACROSS
1. Home of "Hardball"
6. "Love is blind," e.g.
11. Moolah
16. Even
17. Doltish
21. Odd Fellows' meeting place
22. Kind of acid
23. 1922 Max Schreck film
24. Words of empathy
25. Heavyweight
26. High-water mark
27. "Enough, Jorge!"
28. Super ___ (old game console)
30. It might come after you
31. ___ Balls (Hostess snack food)
32. As written
33. Tijuana table
36. Parking spot
38. Actor McGregor
40. "Beetle Bailey" dog
44. Lover of Isolde
46. Oodles
50. Cozy place?
52. Wagnerian opera setting
54. Crime scene matter
55. Saturnalia participants
56. 1995 Eddie Murphy film
59. Tech whiz
61. Athenian porch
62. Some gravesite decorations
63. Arctic herder
66. Composer Ned
68. 1931 Bela Lugosi film
72. Fix, as laces
73. Coolers, for short
74. System of beliefs
77. "The Rights of Man" writer
78. Mauna ___
80. Argentine article
81. Furry adoptee
82. Water brand
84. [See instructions]
85. Cobb of "12 Angry Men"
86. A bit of cheer?
87. Like some fondue pots
89. Halloween cry
90. Compel
92. When Italian ghouls come out?
93. Poodle's greeting
95. Bygone flightless bird
96. ___ Bator
97. 1979 George Hamilton film
105. "Fine"
108. Stage direction that means "alone"
109. Ring figures
113. 1987 Adrian Pasdar film
116. ___ Tin Tin
117. 2008 Robert Pattinson film
119. Bones also called cubiti
120. "Piece of cake!"
123. Pianist/composer Schumann
124. Tandem twosome
125. 1986 Brad Davis film
126. George who wrote "The Spanish Gypsy"
127. Walk the earth
128. "___ Ben Adhem"
129. Belonging to you and me
130. Many visitors to Legoland

DOWN
1. Coconut filler
2. Acreage fig.
3. When French ghouls come out?
4. Fruit-based fountain treat
5. Make a copy of
6. Sucks up
7. Crusoe's creator
8. Breezed through
9. Grade school door sign
10. Noted New York eatery
11. Russian pancakes
12. What Chippendale furniture was made in
13. Cheese ball?
14. "Slumdog Millionaire" locale
15. Subpar grades
17. Gershwin's "Concerto ___"
18. Canine cousin
19. "Do ___!" ("Stop procrastinating!")
20. Maestro's sign
29. Skull caps?
32. Sly sorts
33. "Jersey Shore" airer
34. All alternative
35. Medal of valor
37. Like the inside of a coffin
39. Used, as a dinner tray
41. Bernard Malamud's first novel
42. Rocky pinnacle
43. Saturn's wife
45. Souvenir from Scotland
47. Early fifth-century year
48. "Slander" author Coulter
49. Bit of Vaseline
51. Communication syst.
53. Longtime Yankee nickname
55. Roman squares
57. O.K. Corral figure
58. Exclude, with "out"
59. Bunch at a grocery store

September

60 Epoch in which mammals arose
64 One getting hit on at a party?
65 Female fowl
67 Selfish person's cry before and after "all"
69 Common rhyme scheme
70 "Later!"
71 Biblical preposition
72 N.F.L. defensive lineman B. J. ___
75 ___ soda
76 "… And I'm the queen of England!"
78 Serving on a stick
79 Sushi bar order
83 Sarah McLachlan hit
85 It may be hidden at a hideout
88 Shopping center regulars
91 Kind of warfare
94 Units of cream: Abbr.
95 Slush pile contents: Abbr.
98 Least typical
99 Cold war broadcasting inits.
100 Gift giver's words
101 Epic translated by Alexander Pope
102 Reaches altogether
103 "Vous êtes ___"
104 Sprinkled with baby powder
105 Like a locked lavatory
106 Old-style fax
107 Hawaiian veranda
110 Question shouted in exasperation
111 Spasm
112 Some of the fine print on sports pages
114 1988 #1 country album
115 Newsman Marvin
117 Layer
118 Jazz saxophonist/flutist Frank
121 Ontario's ___ Canals
122 "A ___ tardi" ("See you later," in Italy)

September

s	m	t	w	t	f	s
		1	2	3	4	5	6
7	8	9	10	11	12	13
14	15	16	17	18	19	20
21	22	23	24	25	26	27
28	29	30				

monday
8 251

○ FULL MOON

tuesday
9 252

wednesday
10 253

thursday
11 254

friday
12 255

saturday
13 256

sunday
14 257

38. LEADING ARTICLES

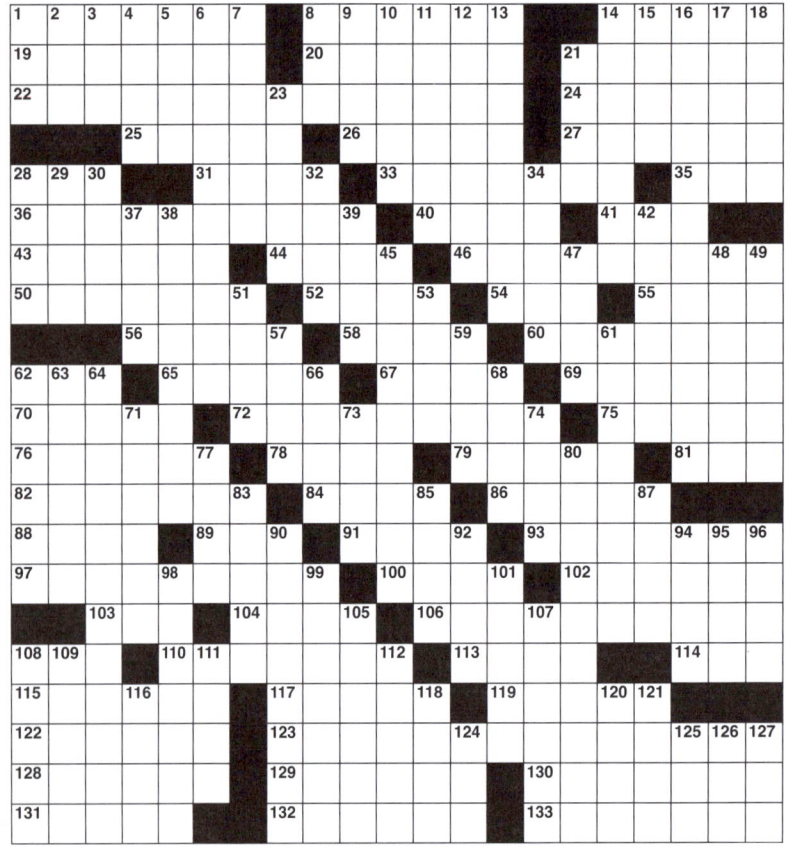

The New York Times

122 Mark who won the 1998 Masters
123 Frisking Dracula?
128 First name on "60 Minutes"
129 Rake
130 Lex Luthor alter ego, once
131 Takes nothing in
132 One of the Crusader states
133 A sixth of the way through the hour

DOWN

1 Letter start
2 Gray
3 & 4 In relation to
5 For fear that
6 Activity with flags
7 Spunk
8 Bender
9 Part of a Latin conjugation
10 Conger cousin
11 Razzed
12 Smirnoff competitor
13 Refuse to shut up
14 Jewelry designer Elsa
15 Mother of Helen and Pollux
16 Mechanic's task?
17 Neighbor of Nigeria and Togo
18 Opera singer Simon
21 Arthur C. Clarke's "Rendezvous With ___"
23 Kingdom overthrown in 2008
28 Couple
29 May event, informally
30 British P.M. between Churchill and Macmillan
32 Film you don't want to see
34 Stockholders?
37 Entrance requirement, sometimes
38 Didn't go
39 The "K" of James K. Polk
42 Partway home
45 Handyman's exclamation
47 Island do
48 Good-looker
49 Plain homes?
51 Sentence structure?
53 Gang's area
57 Any minute now
59 Furniture material
61 It may involve punitive tariffs
62 Sitcom role for Brandy Norwood
63 Ready for publication
64 What the dissatisfied female giftee might do after Christmas?
66 Certain gamete

BY WILL NEDIGER • EDITED BY WILL SHORTZ • 11/07/10

ACROSS

1 Oscar-nominated actor with the given name Aristotelis
8 Preserves holder
14 Annapolis frosh
19 "Fine, tell me"
20 Slide sight
21 Steve who played the title role of Hercules in a 1959 film
22 Trying to stay awake?
24 Fervid
25 Stockholder?
26 Deck for divining
27 No Mr. Nice Guy
28 It has 21 spots
31 Features of some jeans
33 Reads the riot act
35 Connections
36 Pinned down?
40 "Beauty and the Beast," e.g.
41 Bunch
43 Spot overseer
44 Air bag?
46 Working hard on
50 Vigorous
52 Not worth debating
54 Popular word in German product packaging
55 Requested
56 Shaggy locks
58 Get rid of
60 Lay on
62 Debussy subject
65 Northern hemisphere?
67 Took a card
69 Like grizzlies
70 Classic theater name
72 Really enjoy going to carnivals?
75 Home to fly into
76 Noncommittal reply
78 "Darn!"
79 Work, in a way
81 Un-P.C. suffix
82 Star-___
84 Early Beatles songs are in it
86 Foe of 130-Across, at birth
88 Call to a dog
89 Vinegar
91 Twice-a-month tide
93 It was developed by Apple, IBM and Motorola
97 Seemingly without end
100 Sudden fancy
102 Lake ___ City, Ariz.
103 Site of the brachial artery
104 Prepresidential title for Bill Clinton or Woodrow Wilson: Abbr.
106 Straddling one's opponent?
108 Moreover
110 They have duel purposes
113 First near-Earth asteroid to be discovered
114 Addams Family cousin
115 Skin layer
117 Scaling tool
119 Peripheral

September

- 68 Sleep unit?
- 71 "Goodness me!"
- 73 George Orwell's alma mater
- 74 Take in
- 77 Gym number
- 80 85-Down is part of it
- 83 Ocean areas
- 85 Home of the highways H1 and H2
- 87 Big name in denim
- 90 It may be elementary
- 92 Snowman's prop
- 94 Sitarist Shankar
- 95 H.S. junior's exam
- 96 Kind of film
- 98 Call makers
- 99 Freeloaded
- 101 Fool
- 105 Take to the cleaners
- 107 Nutty treat
- 108 Unpopular baby name
- 109 Site of Hercules' first labor
- 111 "Well, old chap!"
- 112 Goldman ___
- 116 Fountain order
- 118 Classic sports cars
- 120 Nobel Prize subj.
- 121 Frolic
- 124 Writer Levin
- 125 Portrayer of June in "Henry & June"
- 126 "Illmatic" rapper
- 127 Blaster

monday
15 258

☾ LAST QUARTER

tuesday
16 259

wednesday
17 260

thursday
18 261

friday
19 262

saturday
20 263

U.N. INTERNATIONAL DAY OF PEACE

sunday
21 264

September

s	m	t	w	t	f	s
	1	2	3	4	5	6
7	8	9	10	11	12	13
14	15	16	17	18	19	20
21	22	23	24	25	26	27
28	29	30				

39. DOUGHEADERS

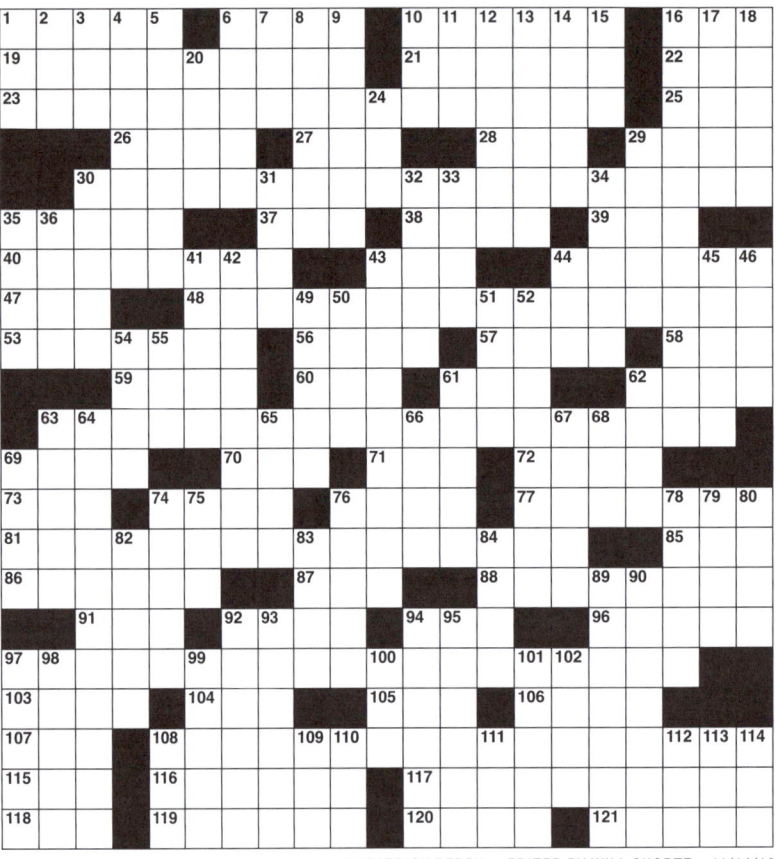

The New York Times

BY PATRICK BERRY • EDITED BY WILL SHORTZ • 11/14/10

ACROSS

1. Buggy versions, maybe
6. Big yard area
10. Expresses disbelief
16. "The Big Bang Theory" network
19. Went beyond
21. Truck driving competition
22. Muesli tidbit
23. Factors to consider while trying to sleep on a campout?
25. Upper mgmt. aspirant
26. Superior
27. You might come up for this
28. Epitome of ease
29. Arabian Peninsula sultanate
30. What the marshal declared the moonshiner's shed to be?
35. L on a T?
37. A. E. Housman's "A Shropshire ___"
38. Smelted substances
39. Preventive measure
40. Submerge
43. Upper support
44. Attend to a plot
47. "Pardonnez-___!"
48. Ohio State athlete who forgot his uniform?
53. Fighting fighting
56. Coxswain's lack
57. Relative standing
58. Publishing hirees, for short
59. Part of P.T.A.: Abbr.
60. From ___ Z
61. Name for a persona non grata
62. One who puts U in disfavor?
63. C.E.O.'s tricycle?
69. Start over on
70. Chain of life?
71. Local news hour
72. Keel's place
73. Dudgeon
74. Prologue follower
76. Request upon finishing
77. As a group
81. Wild Bill Hickok holding his aces and eights?
85. Spell
86. Respectful bow
87. Criminal charge
88. Picture that shows you what's up?
91. Platoon members, briefly
92. Competed
94. Unit of currency
96. Places to plug in peripherals
97. Garbage receptacle that you and I insult?
103. Promising good things
104. Music genre prefix
105. Ancient Rome's Appian ___
106. "What a shame!"
107. Rose of rock
108. "That high lonesome sound," as played by Atlantic crustaceans?
115. Uma's "Pulp Fiction" role
116. Many a Monopoly property
117. Singer of the 2008 #1 hit "Bleeding Love"
118. Seat facing the altar
119. Worked on in the lab
120. Cornerstone abbr.
121. Put up

DOWN

1. Rise and fall repeatedly
2. Big day preceder
3. Red Sox legend Williams
4. Call into court
5. Followed the game
6. Crooked
7. Rebel org.
8. Soprano Tebaldi
9. Went around in circles, say
10. Opposite of post-
11. Landscaper's roll
12. Zimbabwe's capital
13. Pueblo structures
14. Army-McCarthy hearings figure
15. Roman sun god
16. "Borrows" peremptorily
17. Founder of Celesteville, in children's lit
18. Roadside shop
20. Indication of teen stress, maybe
24. "Turn up the heat!"
29. Missouri's ___ Trail
30. Common dessert ingredient
31. Tess's literary seducer
32. Offers a few directions?
33. "Dies ___" (Latin hymn)
34. By surprise
35. City where TV's "Glee" is set
36. In a moment
41. Discountenance
42. Called upon
43. Fragrant cake
44. Round container
45. Singer Gorme
46. Cheeper lodging?
49. Eucalyptus eater
50. Defense grp. headquartered in Belgium
51. Pharmacopoeia selection
52. It bounces
54. Shakespearean character who says "I am not what I am"
55. Nashville-to-Memphis dir.
61. Diverse
62. Composer Bartók

September

63 Kentucky college
64 pV = nRT, to physicists
65 Geraint's wife in "Idylls of the King"
66 Aircraft, informally
67 Like a Chippendales dancer
68 Massachusetts' state tree
69 Frees (of)
74 Covered
75 Business address ender
76 Army of the Potomac commander, 1863-65
78 Pool hall pro
79 Quatre + trois
80 Former union members?
82 1989 Oscar-winning title role for Jessica Tandy
83 Took a card
84 Census form deliverer: Abbr.
89 Sequin
90 Crayon wielder
92 Moral standards
93 Focused
94 Fit for cultivation
95 Invitees who didn't R.S.V.P., say
97 Cargo vessel with no fixed route
98 ___ Hart, showgirl in "Chicago"
99 Deliver at a farm
100 Bygone rival of Delta
101 Harass nonstop
102 "Take ___ Train"
108 Be up
109 Ham helper
110 Spectrum segment
111 Auction purchase
112 What the sublime inspires
113 Verbatim quote addendum, possibly
114 J.F.K. arrival of old

monday

22 265

tuesday

23 266

● NEW MOON

wednesday

24 267

ROSH HASHANAH*

thursday

25 268

ROSH HASHANAH ENDS

friday

26 269

saturday

27 270

sunday

28 271

September

s	m	t	w	t	f	s
	1	2	3	4	5	6
7	8	9	10	11	12	13
14	15	16	17	18	19	20
21	22	23	24	25	26	27
28	29	30				

*Begins at sundown the previous day

40. HAVING ASPIRATIONS

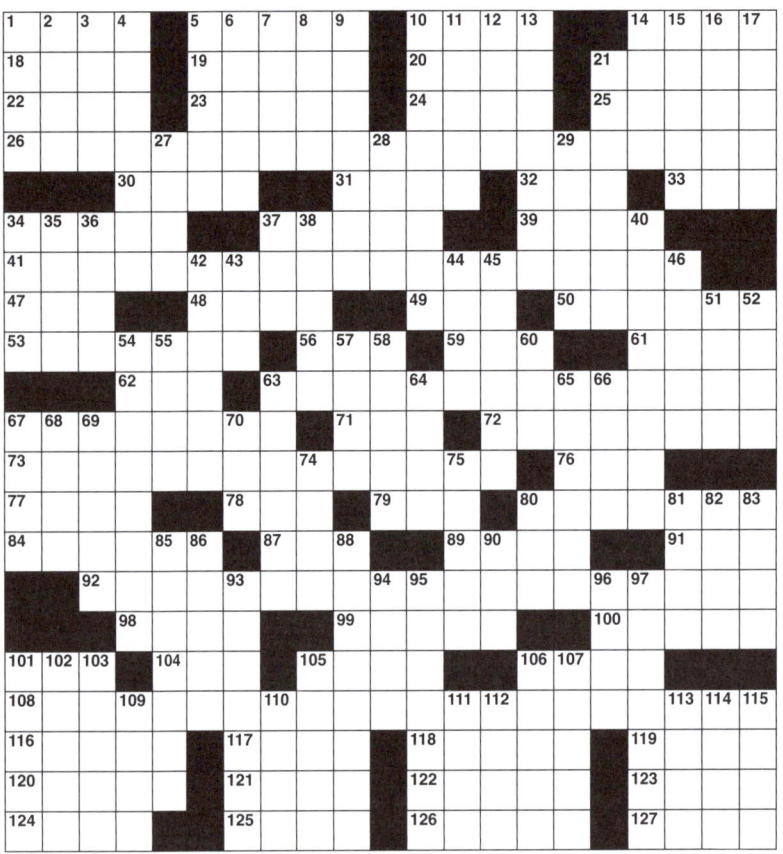

The New York Times

BY CLIVE PROBERT • EDITED BY WILL SHORTZ • 11/21/10

ACROSS

1. Judge's no-no
5. Like some responsibilities
10. German-born tennis star Tommy
14. Start of "A Visit From St. Nicholas"
18. Spree
19. "The Bad News Bears" actress
20. Film character who actually does not say "Play it again, Sam"
21. "Take it easy!"
22. Robbers' gain
23. "Winnie-the-Pooh" character
24. Signal for a programmer's jump
25. One side in the 1973 Paris Peace Accords
26. Macho guys like their pie cold?
30. Second
31. Some dates
32. "___ Day Will Come" (1963 #1 hit)
33. You might play something by this
34. Ignore
37. Potential cause of a food recall
39. Name often followed by a number
41. Bad actor's philosophy?
47. "___ doubt but they were fain o' ither": Burns
48. Org. with the motto "For the benefit of all"
49. Fair-hiring inits.
50. Kim Jong-il, for one
53. James or Jackie of Hollywood
56. Carrier with a frequent flier program called EuroBonus
59. It may be snowy or spotted
61. Emmy-winning actress ___ de Matteo
62. Johnny ___
63. Concerns of middle-aged guys in lower Louisiana?
67. Cute
71. Org. for electing candidates
72. Whales, at times
73. Lengthy military sign-up?
76. Cpl.'s inferior
77. Presidential straw poll city
78. Bauxite, e.g.
79. Place for mounted antlers, maybe
80. Club Meds, e.g.
84. Way in
87. Conductors of many exams, for short
89. R.E.M.'s "The ___ Love"
91. Chit
92. Put the dentures aside while gardening?
98. ___ Park, Queens
99. News show assemblage
100. Eye parts
101. Disco fan on "The Simpsons"
104. Reed in music
105. Shiites or Sunnis
106. View from Catania
108. Starboard food fish?
116. Contest
117. Away from the storm
118. What a beatnik beats
119. Kind of theater
120. Not so tied up
121. Sail problem
122. Maine college
123. [sigh]
124. "___ of the Storm Country"
125. Lawn starters
126. Wear away
127. Vetoes

DOWN

1. Atom modeler
2. "Dies ___"
3. Content of la mar
4. Course outlines
5. Out of one's mind, in a way, with "up"
6. Vacuous
7. Hawk
8. "Were I the Moor, I would not be ___"
9. Loud ringing
10. It's symbolized by caviar and Champagne
11. Athol Fugard's "A Lesson From ___"
12. 1930s film pooch
13. Portuguese-speaking island off the African coast
14. Like some spicy food
15. Pain result
16. Honolulu's ___ Stadium
17. More cunning
21. Very religious
27. Bearing
28. Chaucer piece
29. Actor Dennis
34. Diminutive suffix
35. List ender
36. "Get ___ hence": I Kings 17:3
37. Replies from the hard of hearing
38. Stop
40. Give due credit
42. Not smooth
43. Result of some time in a bed?
44. Cry of delight
45. Scrub over
46. Seine tributary
51. Nostradamus, for one
52. Soviet news group
54. One who takes people in

September-October

55 A Lennon
57 Xanadu river
58 Sobersided
60 Back talk
63 "Alas"
64 Part of a Molière play
65 Snag
66 Huggies competitor
67 Quick-like
68 Item in a music producer's in-box
69 Cricket units
70 MGM symbol
74 Bordeaux, e.g.
75 Benjamin
80 Old touring car
81 Fair attraction
82 Feature of much ancient Roman statuary
83 Goes after
85 Artist's workplace
86 Gain access, in a way
88 Roman square
90 Org. with a 2004-05 lockout
93 Chewy treats
94 Apiece
95 1976 rescue site
96 Go after
97 Dodge
101 Give a raw deal
102 Third planet from le soleil
103 Impulses
105 Hogan contemporary
106 Pushed, with "on"
107 "___ were the days"
109 Streets of Québec
110 Fleischmann's product
111 Surf sound
112 Word after bang, break or bump
113 Letters of faux modesty
114 Title for Helen Mirren
115 Couples no more

September

s	m	t	w	t	f	s
	1	2	3	4	5	6
7	8	9	10	11	12	13
14	15	16	17	18	19	20
21	22	23	24	25	26	27
28	29	30				

October

s	m	t	w	t	f	s
				1	2	3	4
5	6	7	8	9	10	11
12	13	14	15	16	17	18
19	20	21	22	23	24	25
26	27	28	29	30	31	

*Begins at sundown the previous day

QUEEN'S BIRTHDAY (AUSTRALIA—WA)

monday
29 272

tuesday
30 273

☽ FIRST QUARTER

wednesday
1 274

thursday
2 275

friday
3 276

YOM KIPPUR*
EID AL-ADHA

saturday
4 277

sunday
5 278

41. A SHINING MOMENT

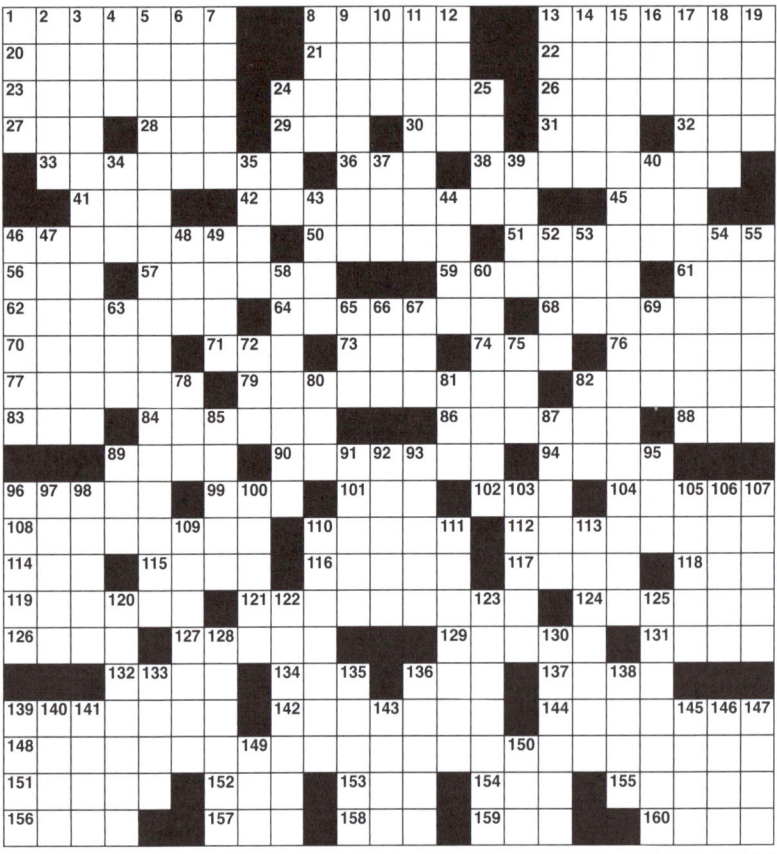

The New York Times

134 Part of a sunbow
136 Shih ___ (dog)
137 Blue stuff
139 Bitter quarrels
142 Input
144 Beatles' last studio album
148 Annual Manhattan event (represented symbolically in this puzzle)
151 Transmission repair franchise
152 Footnote abbr.
153 Zero
154 Christmas ___
155 Leader of the Silver Bullet Band
156 Lillian of silents
157 Seek damages
158 Org. that infiltrated Nazi Germany
159 Rx amount: Abbr.
160 In thing

DOWN

1 Doesn't shut up
2 Razzle-dazzle
3 With 5-Down, when 148-Across traditionally takes place
4 Pirate's realm
5 See 3-Down
6 Ceaselessly
7 Intense heat
8 La Palma, e.g.
9 Canned foods giant
10 Cosmetics giant
11 Title for Judge Judy
12 Cookie with creme
13 Wakens
14 Picker-upper
15 Where 148-Across takes place
16 "Yes, Virginia, there ___ Santa Claus"
17 Traditional centerpiece of 148-Across
18 "Diary of a Madman" author
19 December fall
24 Dinner in a can
25 "Whip It" band
34 Discus path
35 Mount in myth
37 Here, in Dijon
39 "Deus ___" (1976 sci-fi novel)
40 Low-___
43 Hardly a plain Jane
44 Capital of Iceland?
46 Winds
47 Detach, in a way
48 Movie co. behind "Wordplay" and "My Big Fat Greek Wedding"
49 Ready
52 Blind guess
53 French seasoning
54 Texas A&M athletes

BY JEREMY NEWTON • EDITED BY WILL SHORTZ • 11/28/10

ACROSS

1 Passes with flying colors
8 Home of Hells Gate State Park
13 A lot of an orchestra
20 Really, really want
21 Break off
22 "Are we not joking about that yet?"
23 Sounded sheepish?
24 Roulette bet
26 How pets may fly
27 Came to realize
28 Avant-garde composer Brian
29 Quick flight
30 Something groundbreaking?
31 N.B.A.'er Smits, a k a the Dunkin' Dutchman
32 Amaze
33 Shed thing
36 Source of some rings
38 Felt in the gut
41 Richard Gere title role of 2000
42 Peach, e.g.
45 Onetime "S.N.L." regular Tina
46 Snack food with a Harvest Cheddar flavor
50 "Butter knife" of golf
51 Deem
56 Austin-to-Waco dir.
57 Frozen, perhaps
59 Escapee from a witch in a Grimm tale
61 Swingers' grp.
62 It may be put down on a roll
64 Up for bidding
68 Strong aversion, colloquially
70 Kind of moment
71 10 Downing St. figures
73 R.V. refuge org.
74 Reflux
76 Places for needles
77 Go by
79 Exactly right
82 Mythological triad
83 Porker's place
84 Creatures known to lick their own eyeballs
86 Itty-bitty
88 "Cómo es ___?" (Spanish "Why?")
89 Nuts about
90 It guards the heart
94 Kind of romance between actors
96 One of the Gandhis
99 ___ Grand
101 Vegas opening?
102 ___ Na Na
104 What might go for a dip?
108 Worked up
110 Big name in late-night
112 "Don't try any more tricks!"
114 Brooks or Blanc
115 When repeated, an old sitcom farewell
116 Cry of self-pride
117 Beginning
118 Preceders of xis
119 Stretched figures
121 R&B funk trio with the 1990 hit "Feels Good"
124 One using twisted humor
126 Is worth doing
127 Trattoria topper
129 Letter-shaped support
131 Provides service that can't be beat?
132 Stave (off)

October

55 Asserts something
58 Magnetic disruption in space
60 1960s girl group, with "the"
63 Literary inits.
65 It's picked in Maui
66 Part of an ear
67 Torque's symbol
69 Gate projection, for short
72 Man in the hood?
75 One-named rock star
78 Stream of consciousness, for short?
80 Chu ___ (legendary Confucian sage)
81 What it must do
82 PX patrons
85 Fraudster
87 Frenchman's term of address
89 Shtick
91 Swell
92 Echo producer
93 "Right there with you"
95 Chinese "way"
96 Clean again, as a floor
97 Tiny creature
98 Like St. Nick
100 Overfills
103 Firm newbie
105 Sarcastic sort
106 Take in, as guests
107 Sends packing
109 Bingeing
110 Award named for a Hall-of-Fame pitcher
111 Blogger, e.g.
113 Just below the boiling point
120 Start for 148-Across?
122 Not benched, as in hockey
123 Not overspending
125 Set to go off, say
128 Flops in lots
130 Out
133 Extra-large top?
135 Start for -centric
136 Essays
138 Western tribe
139 Kind of party
140 Cuisine with pad see ew noodles
141 Signs of dreaming
143 Wide-lapel jackets
145 It was wrapped around the Forum
146 Rare blood type, for short
147 Jane at Thornfield
149 Funny Costello
150 Walgreens rival

October

s	m	t	w	t	f	s
			1	2	3	4
5	6	7	8	9	10	11
12	13	14	15	16	17	18
19	20	21	22	23	24	25
26	27	28	29	30	31	

QUEEN'S BIRTHDAY (AUSTRALIA—QLD)
LABOUR DAY (AUSTRALIA—ACT, SA, NSW)

monday
6 279

tuesday
7 280

○ FULL MOON

wednesday
8 281

thursday
9 282

friday
10 283

saturday
11 284

sunday
12 285

42. ON A ROLL

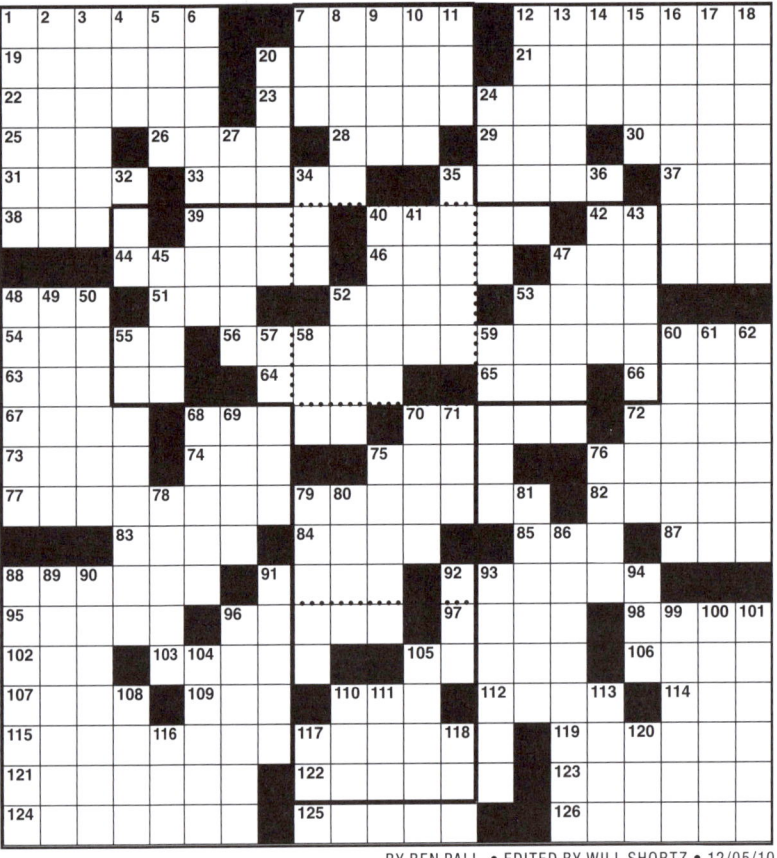

The New York Times

BY BEN PALL • EDITED BY WILL SHORTZ • 12/05/10

ACROSS

1. Hearty drinks
7. Midwest city named for an Indian tribe
12. More sentimental
19. Major diamond exporter
20. Closing to some letters
21. Trapped
22. It makes the hair stand on end
23. First step of instructions for what to do with this finished puzzle
25. N.Y.C.'s ___ of the Americas
26. Goal of a screen test
28. Many an extra on "Star Trek": Abbr.
29. Vacation conveniences, for short
30. Vitamin C source
31. Raise a big stink?
33. Kids
35. "___ Us," 1995 Joan Osborne hit
37. Path of enlightenment
38. European leader?
39. Black
40. Flavor
42. Part of PIN: Abbr.
44. Make up
46. "Where does it ___?"
47. Is
48. '60s-'70s 114-Across locale
51. Web browser provider
52. ___ fide
53. Part of every month
54. Reveals
56. Instructions, part 2
63. Prohibition's start
64. ___ Little, "The Wire" gangster
65. Old Philadelphia stadium, informally, with "the"
66. Earthen pot
67. Bygone Starfire, e.g., informally
68. ___ Rebellion of 1857-59
70. Evicts
72. Org. in 2005's Oscar-winning "Crash"
73. Hightail it
74. Alternative to plata
75. Cellar item
76. Bedouin
77. Instructions, part 3
82. Demagnetize, say
83. St. in a children's rhyme
84. Coupling
85. Previously
87. Half of many a business partnership
88. Ticks off
91. Plug's place
92. It's between green and black
95. Viceroy, e.g.
96. Snap
97. Aware of
98. Nile biters
102. "We shun it ___ it comes": Emily Dickinson
103. "Beat it!"
105. Little bit
106. Moolah
107. Except for
109. Certain tankful
110. ___ alai
112. Some funerary ware
114. See 48-Across
115. Last step of the instructions
119. Tie up
121. Cell phone plan units
122. "Pick me! Pick me!"
123. Long fights
124. Least puzzling
125. Pedestal toppers
126. Barrels along

DOWN

1. Doha native
2. Lopsided
3. Said "yea"
4. The Beatles' "___ No One"
5. Edsel
6. 1984 Olympics site
7. The Cowboys of the Big 12 Conf.
8. Portions
9. Connecticut town named for an English river
10. Coop group
11. Wall St. worker
12. Second place
13. "___ it goes"
14. Bud
15. Dr. ___
16. Charges, in a way
17. Honda model
18. Begrudges
20. Follows through with
24. Ripley's last words?
27. Insurgent group
32. Pond fish
34. Acme product in Road Runner cartoons
35. Long-running hit TV show based in Chicago
36. ___-upper
40. Farrier
41. Polly of literature, e.g.
43. Fade, maybe
45. Condé ___
47. Revises
48. Doze
49. Artemis' twin
50. Pea observer
52. Time for a party, in brief

October

53 Rapper with the 1988 platinum album "Power"
55 Plummet
57 Board
58 Latin lover's word
59 Elicit
60 Alpaca relatives
61 Home of minor-league baseball's Diablos
62 Depress
68 Undersides
69 Greek god whose name is one letter off from 118-Down
70 Soak up rays
71 Second-largest city in Kyrgyzstan
75 "No problemo"
76 "On tap" sign, sometimes
78 Affirms
79 Depressing darkness
80 Scuttlebutt
81 Device for winter sidewalks
86 Virtue
88 Take for granted
89 Superstate in Orwell's "1984"
90 Good rolls in craps
91 One-named singer/actress
92 "___-la-la!"
93 Stampede
94 [That's awful!]
96 The rite person?
99 Waste
100 Finished second
101 Gray hair producer, they say
104 Superman's closetful?
105 Vista
108 Pin holder
110 King in II Kings
111 Brouhahas
113 Trim
116 Packed away
117 Head, in slang
118 Greek goddess whose name is one letter off from 69-Down
120 Virginia's ___ Highway

October

s	m	t	w	t	f	s
			1	2	3	4
5	6	7	8	9	10	11
12	13	14	15	16	17	18
19	20	21	22	23	24	25
26	27	28	29	30	31	

COLUMBUS DAY (USA)
THANKSGIVING (CANADA)

monday
13 286

tuesday
14 287

☾ LAST QUARTER

wednesday
15 288

thursday
16 289

friday
17 290

saturday
18 291

sunday
19 292

43. THE WISH

ACROSS
1. Lady Bird Johnson's middle name
5. Butt
9. Wolf
15. Year the emperor Frederick II died
19. Phony
20. Dancer's duds
21. Last word of Kansas' motto
22. Wings on an avis
23. Tempo for a stringed instrument?
25. Nine Muses after dieting?
27. Madrileño's home
28. Cartonfuls of eggs
30. Indian musician's collection
31. Stop on many a Caribbean cruise
32. River forming the borders of parts of five states
33. Maid's supply
34. Alien attackers' goal?
39. 22 of the 26 letters of the alphabet, in D.C.
42. Part of an Egyptian headpiece
45. The Destroyer, in Hinduism
46. Part of a presidential motorcade
47. Kind of committee
49. Many unopened letters
51. Birthplace of cuneiform writing
53. Is heartbroken
55. Architect Saarinen
56. Draped item
57. Poor, as security
58. Decisive time
59. Most likely to succeed
61. Windpipe
64. Étienne's mine
66. Falling apart
68. Rush hour control?
71. Forlorn, say
74. Turner of Hollywood
75. Chicken for dinner
79. Actress de Ravin of "Roswell" and "Lost"
80. Showy coat?
82. ___ Red Seal (classical music label)
84. Score component
85. Blast
86. Royal of 27-Across
88. Mushroom-to-be
90. Ambition
91. Forcibly divides
93. Soul singer James with the 1990 #1 hit "I Don't Have the Heart"
95. "I got ___ ..."
97. Work at
98. Stout, for one
99. Choice of the right door on "Let's Make a Deal"?
102. Lorelei's locale
104. "The Time Machine" people
105. Battlefield activity
110. Hawke and Allen
112. Word before "a will" and "a way"
115. "The Sopranos" roles
116. Like tuned-in listeners?
118. Orlando team water boy, e.g.?
121. Roberts's "Pretty Woman" co-star
122. Fictitious Plaza resident
123. A reed
124. Medicinal plant
125. Billfold fillers
126. Just missed a birdie
127. Accident reminder
128. No longer carrying current

DOWN
1. Extremely pale
2. Capital city whose name means "place of the gods"
3. Rain checks?
4. Oscars org.
5. Popular German beer, informally
6. Voting day: Abbr.
7. Salt Lake City player
8. The Enlightened One
9. Manischewitz products
10. 1975 Wimbledon winner
11. Turn in many a kids' game
12. Layers
13. R.N.'s work in them
14. Gingerbread man's eye, maybe
15. Photo finish
16. Flock after a rainstorm?
17. Caleb who wrote "The Alienist"
18. Subtracting
24. Hiccups, so to speak
26. ___ different tune
29. Edmonton N.H.L.'er
32. See 50-Down
33. Lo-cal
35. Produce an egg
36. Evangeline, for one
37. Cabo da ___, westernmost spot in continental Europe
38. Robert Louis Stevenson title character
40. Trunks
41. Ivanhoe's creator
42. ___ prof.
43. Nautical pole
44. Law office worker, informally
48. Taking out
50. With 32-Down, first lady who graduated from Harvard Law
52. End-of-semester event

BY KAREN YOUNG BONIN • EDITED BY WILL SHORTZ • 12/12/10

October

54 Holy, to Horace
58 Robert who played Mr. Chips
60 Czech city
62 Mata ___
63 Poly- follower
65 Pond denizen
67 Blockade
69 Trim
70 John Irving title character
71 Winger of "Urban Cowboy"
72 Texting alternative
73 Tortoise's opponent after finishing second?
76 Coil
77 List-ending abbr.
78 Depend
81 "Bus Stop" playwright
83 Ring-tailed animal
87 German article
88 Say "cheese," say
89 Not so genteel
92 Polished
94 Stated
96 Part of songwriting
100 Synchronized (with)
101 Earth and beyond
103 Persephone's abductor
106 "___ to Be You"
107 "I Was ___ War Bride"
108 Columbus called it home
109 Was over
110 Logician's word
111 High schooler
112 God with a day of the week named after him
113 Son or daughter, typically
114 Luxury
117 Suffix with pay
119 Symbol of simplicity
120 Indian state once owned by Portugal

monday
20 ₂₉₃

tuesday
21 ₂₉₄

wednesday
22 ₂₉₅

● NEW MOON

thursday
23 ₂₉₆

UNITED NATIONS DAY

friday
24 ₂₉₇

saturday
25 ₂₉₈

October

s	m	t	w	t	f	s
			1	2	3	4
5	6	7	8	9	10	11
12	13	14	15	16	17	18
19	20	21	22	23	24	25
26	27	28	29	30	31	

sunday
26 ₂₉₉

44. HOPE FOR CLEAR SKIES

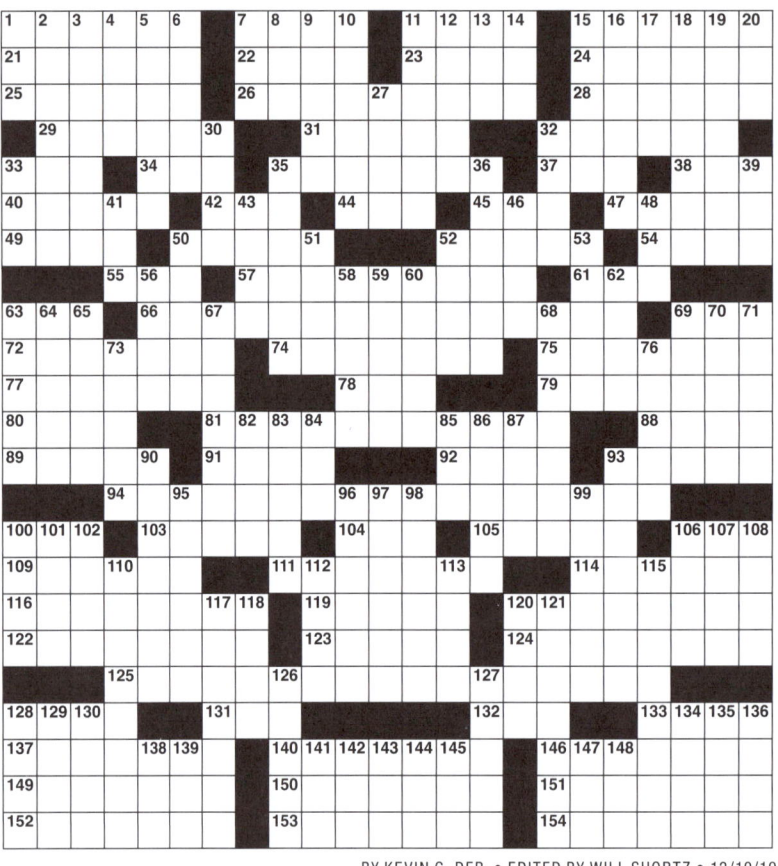

The New York Times

BY KEVIN G. DER • EDITED BY WILL SHORTZ • 12/19/10

ACROSS
1. Not live
7. Author Roald
11. Shop dresser
15. How something may be veiled
21. "Ball Four" author
22. Big name in athletic footwear
23. Rama's kingdom
24. Whence the line "I fear Greeks even when they bring gifts"
25. Feature of some pool balls
26. A long time past
28. Enthrones
29. At night
31. Football's Sanders
32. Long-shot candidate
33. ___-to
34. ___ Kippur
35. What the focus of a 125-Across will do at its climax
37. "___ said …"
38. Glossy black bird
40. One way to stop
42. Mil. address
44. Driller?: Abbr.
45. Kisser
47. Clone of an optical medium's contents
49. Wang of fashion
50. Lulus
52. Drinking and gambling
54. Basic solutions
55. Breach
57. Dummies
61. Six-time All-Star third baseman for the 1970s Dodgers
63. Remove drapes from, as a room
66. Objects of interest in a 125-Across
69. First female U.S. secretary of state
72. Not yet delivered
74. How some things are made
75. Jackie's #2
77. Think probable
78. Pliny possessive
79. Beach seen from Diamond Head
80. Once, in the past
81. 1914 Edgar Rice Burroughs novel set in an underground land
88. Like many cakes
89. "Honor is ___ scutcheon": Shak.
91. Bygone European capital
92. Subterfuge
93. Track star Owens
94. Many an avid observer of a 125-Across
100. Atlantic City locale, with "the"
103. Loser to McKinley
104. Duff Beer vendor
105. Spaceship attire
106. Slump
109. Slugger Roberto
111. Jackie's #1
114. Proust's "___ Way"
116. Book set?
119. Italian lover's coo
120. Indian royal
122. Deep-dish dishes
123. Heads outside together?
124. Novelty glasses
125. Event on Dec. 21, 2010, viewable in North and South America, depicted visually in this puzzle
128. Turkish pooh-bahs
131. Flying Cloud, e.g.
132. Student's stat.
133. Dub
137. With 146-Across, what the center of this puzzle is doing during a 125-Across
140. Folds
146. See 137-Across
149. To whom Hamlet says "Get thee to a nunnery"
150. There from the start
151. It marks the target on a curling rink
152. Munchkins
153. Pardner, say
154. Commodore's insignia

DOWN
2. Zero
3. Battle over domain
4. Haggling
5. Sailor who debuted in a 1929 comic
6. Juan's January
7. Glen Canyon ___
8. Actress Gardner
9. Dharma follower
10. Tiramisu features
11. Catalog
12. Steak ___
13. Veer back
14. Comic Philips
15. Aircraft gauges
16. Kind of couplet for Chaucer
17. "___ out?"
18. Paper for which Murray Kempton and Jim Dwyer won Pulitzers
19. Trace of blood?
20. Football meas.
27. Youthful prank in a car
30. Superhero played by Liam Neeson in a 1990 film
32. Era of ignorance
33. Kind of lane
35. How things may be laid
36. Key of Bach's "The Art of Fugue"
39. Director Anderson
41. Yankee great Joe, colloquially
43. Amorous skunk in cartoons
46. Golden State campus inits.
48. How things may be lit or remembered
50. Lincoln Center production
51. 1974 Japanese Nobelist
52. Feeling
53. Extended solo
56. Crackerjacks
58. Tundra or wetland
59. Terbium or thulium
60. Father-and-son actors
62. Actor Morales
63. Promising proposal
64. Prepare to fight
65. "Grey's Anatomy" extra
67. One of the Islamic virtues
68. Grateful response
69. Big name in athletic footwear
70. Column in a dating questionnaire
71. Optimist's focus
73. Aquarium fish

October-November

76 One getting a lift?
82 "___ yellow ribbon …"
83 Place to put bags
84 Laugh part
85 E.M.T.'s training
86 Science
87 Reagan and others
90 Tactic used against Britain by Napoleon
93 Boarding aids
95 Out-and-out
96 Protective membrane
97 Beethoven's "Appassionata," e.g.
98 One that overflows
99 Fender bender, e.g.
100 Towering
101 Jordan's Queen ___ International Airport
102 Smidgens
106 [Just like that!]
107 One of the Brontës
108 E.U. group
110 Pot-au-feu, e.g.
112 Classic rebuke
113 Observatory feature
115 Powder rooms?
117 It may be shot during a riot
118 Castaway's locale
120 The year 1045
121 Japanese "thanks"
126 Need for KenKen
127 Bistro offering
128 Rent-___
129 Hang open
130 1968 U.S. Open champ
134 Mine entrance
135 Bart Simpson's grandmother
136 Pitcher
138 Suffix with vir-
139 Never: Ger.
141 Lennon's lady
142 "Charlotte's Web" inits.
143 Dawn
144 Italian God
145 Forest game
147 Clinton or Obama, once: Abbr.
148 Laugh part

monday
LABOUR DAY (NZ)
BANK HOLIDAY (IRELAND)

27 300

tuesday
28 301

wednesday
29 302

thursday
30 303

friday
HALLOWEEN
☽ FIRST QUARTER

31 304

saturday
1 305

sunday
2 306

October

s	m	t	w	t	f	s
			1	2	3	4
5	6	7	8	9	10	11
12	13	14	15	16	17	18
19	20	21	22	23	24	25
26	27	28	29	30	31	

November

s	m	t	w	t	f	s
						1
2	3	4	5	6	7	8
9	10	11	12	13	14	15
16	17	18	19	20	21	22
23	24	25	26	27	28	29
30						

45. HEY, MISTER!

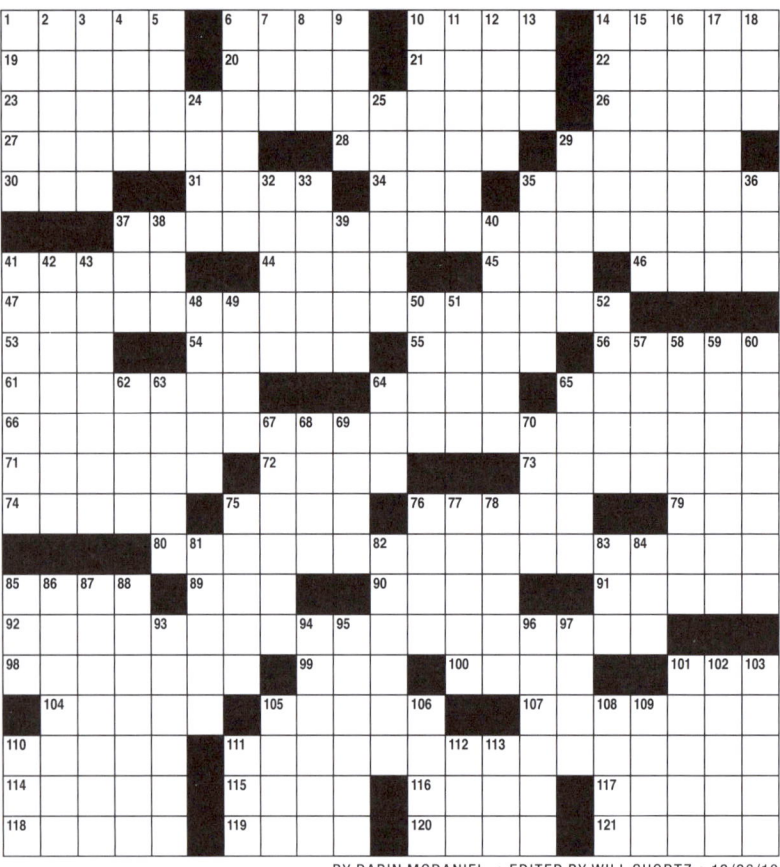

ACROSS

1. Shine
6. Intensifies, with "up"
10. High-school class
14. On the 73-Across, e.g.
19. Élan
20. Lampblack
21. Come to
22. Shifty ones?
23. Loving comment from an astronaut's wife?
26. Place from which to watch a Hawaiian sunset
27. Low tip
28. Not well
29. Throws (off)
30. Close
31. Big brass
34. Plumber's fitting
35. News offices
37. The Dark Knight rooms with Quasimodo?
41. Chili powder ingredient
44. "He wore a diamond" in "Copacabana"
45. Ryan's "Love Story" co-star
46. Origin
47. Hotel's ask-your-greeter-anything approach?
53. Popular portal
54. Swift
55. Modern pentathlon event
56. Difference in days between the lunar and solar year
61. "All clear"
64. Honoree's spot
65. Singer Carey
66. "South Park" character leading a walk around a paddock?
71. Patronized a restaurant
72. One ___ (ball game)
73. W.W. II carrier praised by Churchill for its ability to "sting twice"
74. Vaults
75. Aspersion
76. Brazilian name for six popes
79. Speak lovingly
80. What Dustin Hoffman gets to do often, thanks to royalties?
85. Advantages
89. Scoundrel
90. Steve McQueen's first major movie, with "The"
91. Sled dog
92. Actor Hugh involved in every swap shop deal?
98. W.W. I hero played by Gary Cooper
99. Pre-1868 Tokyo
100. "Don't strain"
101. Song on an album
104. ___ Gillis of 1960s TV
105. Colloquialism
107. Bar activity
110. Like some gases
111. Actor John playing Wayne Knight's role on "Seinfeld"?
114. Inhabitant of the Pribilof Islands
115. Razor brand
116. Quotable Hall-of-Famer, informally
117. Excoriate
118. "Viva ___!"
119. Pastoral sounds
120. Sign
121. Dummkopfs

DOWN

1. Modern party summons
2. Element in strobe lights
3. Confession of faith
4. Square
5. Mother of Helen
6. Retreat
7. ___ Eisley, "Star Wars" cantina town
8. Dad
9. Attempt
10. Winter Olympics powerhouse
11. Whence the phrase "Murder most foul"
12. So-so
13. Pound
14. Harshly bright
15. Prickly plants
16. Onetime home for Georgia O'Keeffe
17. Expunction
18. Sinatra's "Softly, ___ Leave You"
24. Hand, in slang
25. Charged particle
29. Third-degree, in math
32. Vermont city
33. Cartoon genre
35. Contradict
36. Old-time cartoonist Hoff
37. Hopper
38. Plus
39. Vamoose
40. Most fit
41. Funny
42. Like Rochester, N.Y.
43. Literally, "guilty mind"
48. Run ___ the mouth
49. Author Robert ___ Butler
50. Nectar flavor
51. 1960s TV boy
52. Chorus of approvals
57. Projecting front
58. The Red Baron and others
59. Clerical robe
60. Stir

BY DARIN MCDANIEL • EDITED BY WILL SHORTZ • 12/26/10

November

62 "Uncle!"
63 Something that's not optional
64 E-mail address component
65 Quark/antiquark particle
67 Slow dance with quick turns
68 S. American land
69 Actress Diane of "Numb3rs"
70 ___ Bowl
75 Shut out
76 Tiresomely disagreeable sort
77 Make ___ of
78 Planetary shadow
81 Without ___ (nonchalantly)
82 Flowering
83 "El ___ vive!" (revolutionary catchphrase)
84 Czech martyr Jan
85 Comfy bedwear
86 Ann or Andy
87 When Canada celebrates Thanksgiving
88 Azure
93 Half
94 Topper for Ol' Blue Eyes
95 Nike competitor
96 Welcomes warmly
97 Actress Cannon
101 Results of some accidents
102 Decree
103 Backpackers' gear
105 Wee bit
106 Spread for lunch, maybe
108 First name in country
109 Woodworking tools
110 Dundee dissent
111 Yak
112 Passeport info
113 Dating service datum

monday
3 307

ELECTION DAY (USA)

tuesday
4 308

wednesday
5 309

○ FULL MOON

thursday
6 310

friday
7 311

saturday
8 312

sunday
9 313

November

s	m	t	w	t	f	s
						1
2	3	4	5	6	7	8
9	10	11	12	13	14	15
16	17	18	19	20	21	22
23	24	25	26	27	28	29
30						

46. WORKS IN TRANSLATION

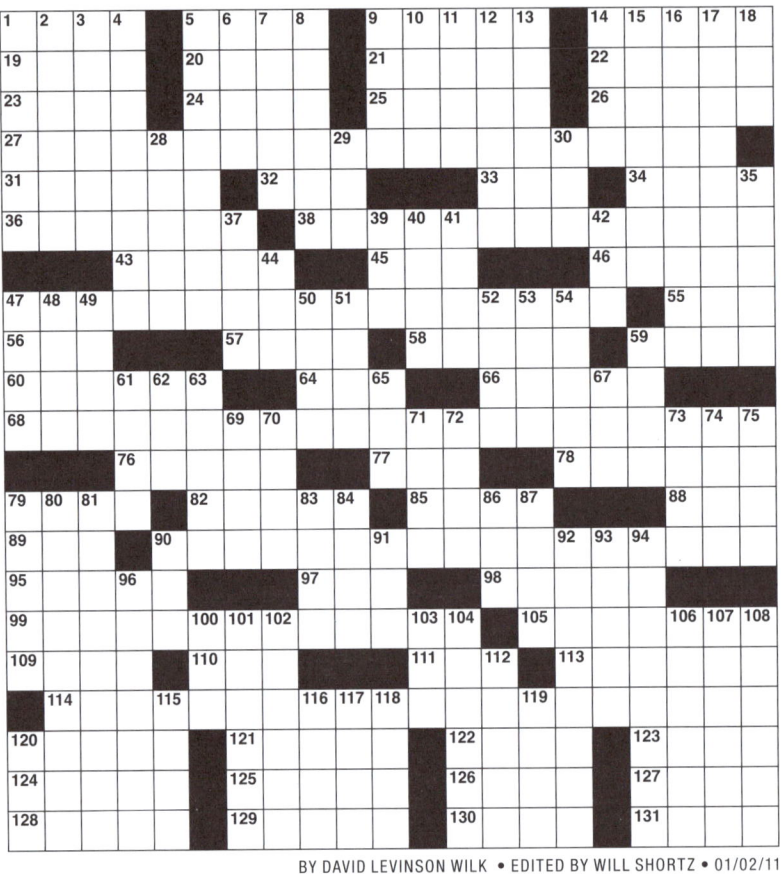

The New York Times

BY DAVID LEVINSON WILK • EDITED BY WILL SHORTZ • 01/02/11

ACROSS

1. Polite, old-fashioned assent
5. Court action
9. Baby bird?
14. Inventory
19. It's high in Peru
20. Rear
21. Where Gerald Ford went to law sch.
22. E-mail button
23. Like some points
24. Royal Norwegian Order of St. ___
25. Slur
26. Like boxers' hands
27. 1934 novel "نييعت"
31. Harold's car in "Harold and Maude"
32. Subj. of the 2005 book "Many Unhappy Returns"
33. Greeting in Lisbon
34. ___ shui
36. Creative sort
38. 1968 hit song "назад"
43. NPR host Conan and others
45. ___ for owl
46. Pitcher of milk?
47. 1985 hit song "คืนหนึ่ง"
55. Portland-to-Spokane dir.
56. "Ben-___"
57. One of the Pac-Man ghosts
58. Impassive
59. Cath. title
60. Reactions from the hoity-toity
64. Electrophorus electricus, for one
66. Light on the top?
68. 2003 film "Érase una Vez"
76. Constellation next to Ursa Major and Ursa Minor
77. Paisano
78. Film worker
79. Spanish liqueur
82. ___-Turkish War, 1911-12
85. Brilliant display
88. Sweet suffix?
89. Pep
90. 1951 film "Une Personne des États-Unis"
95. Robin Hood portrayer in "Robin Hood: Men in Tights"
97. Little pocket
98. Reveler's cry
99. 1912 novella "Morte"
105. "You're on!"
109. Irish Rose's guy
110. ___ pond
111. It contains uracil
113. 90% off?
114. 1943 novel "Whaddya Tink? A Sapling Stays a Sapling Fuhevah?"
120. Hit CBS series beginning in 2004
121. "The Story of ___" (1945 war film)
122. All's partner
123. German photographer ___ Bing
124. Bahraini buck
125. Actress Massey
126. Prefix with sphere
127. Classic brand of hair remover
128. 2003 Economics Nobelist Robert
129. Forest homes
130. Abbr. in many a mail-order address
131. Tests for coll. seniors

DOWN

1. Bike brand
2. One forming a secret union?
3. Visit during a trip
4. It's often visited during a trip
5. Failure to communicate?
6. Music on a carnival ride
7. As a friend: Fr.
8. Daily or weekly
9. Part of GPS: Abbr.
10. Novelist Hoag
11. Author Steinhauer with the 2009 best seller "The Tourist"
12. Use logic
13. "On the Road" journalist
14. Muchacha: Abbr.
15. Like some goodbyes
16. Puts under the yoke
17. Purifying
18. English dramatist Thomas
28. Immigrant from Japan
29. Ultrasecret org.
30. ___-jongg
35. Feminist Germaine
37. Pre-college yrs.
39. Cookout discard
40. Some Korean exports
41. "And who ___?"
42. "Yikes!"
44. D.C.'s Union ___
47. Très
48. Senate Armed Services Committee chairman after Goldwater
49. Hockey's Lindros
50. Retail giant whose logo has blue letters in a yellow oval
51. Dostoyevsky's denial
52. Area crossed by Marco Polo
53. Pottery need
54. Carol start
59. Year of the first Spanish settlement in Cuba
61. A.T.F. agents, e.g.
62. Some trim
63. Home of Galicia
65. Something that may be glossed over

November

- 67 "Waking ___ Devine" (1998 comedy)
- 69 Numerical prefix
- 70 Linguist Chomsky
- 71 Jacobs of fashion
- 72 "The Praise of Chimney-Sweepers" essayist
- 73 "Like ___ not …"
- 74 Mozart opera title opening
- 75 Rich rocks
- 79 Skin care brand
- 80 About 10% of Africa
- 81 "Any day now"
- 83 ___-majesté
- 84 Setting for Cervantes's "El Gallardo Español"
- 86 Turn-___
- 87 Kind of torch
- 90 Bat wood
- 91 Starting point on a French map
- 92 Eh
- 93 1990s Toyota coupe
- 94 Comic who said "A short summary of every Jewish holiday: They tried to kill us. We won. Let's eat"
- 96 Everlasting
- 100 "South Park" sibling
- 101 Gourd
- 102 Manly
- 103 ___ de coeur
- 104 The Supreme Court, e.g.
- 106 Invoice issuer
- 107 Parisian palace
- 108 Dogmata
- 112 Drop off
- 115 "Reader, I married him" heroine
- 116 Iberian eyes
- 117 Custom
- 118 They may be high or heavy
- 119 Forces on horses: Abbr.
- 120 Alphabet trio

November

s	m	t	w	t	f	s
						1
2	3	4	5	6	7	8
9	10	11	12	13	14	15
16	17	18	19	20	21	22
23	24	25	26	27	28	29
30						

monday
10 314

VETERANS' DAY (USA)
REMEMBRANCE DAY (CANADA, IRELAND, UK)

tuesday
11 315

wednesday
12 316

thursday
13 317

☾ LAST QUARTER

friday
14 318

saturday
15 319

sunday
16 320

47. THE LONG AND THE SHORT OF IT

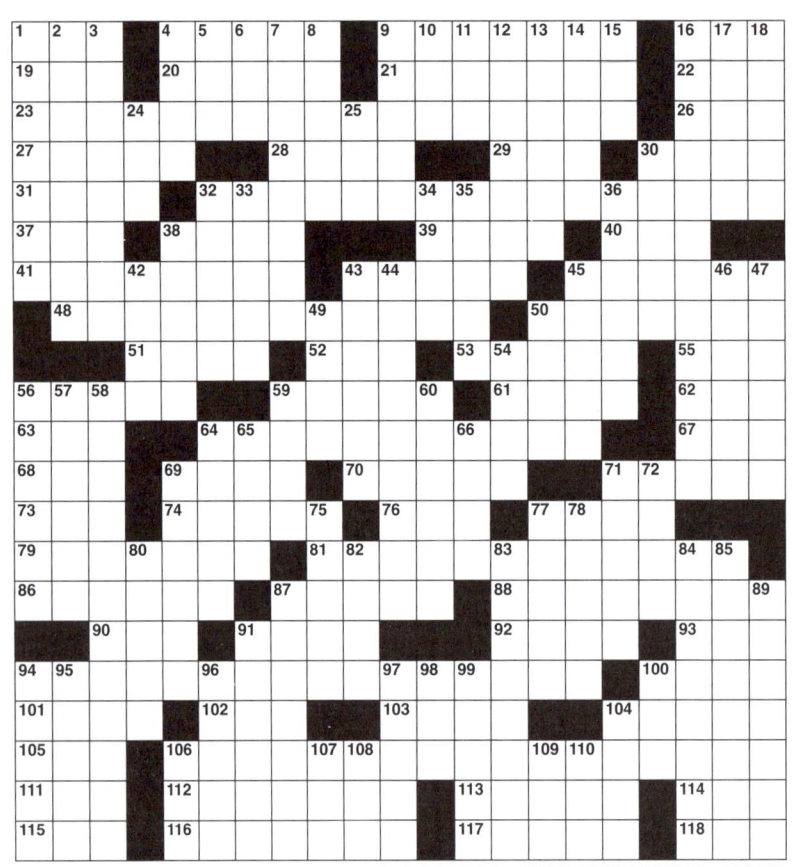

BY PATRICK BERRY • EDITED BY WILL SHORTZ • 01/09/11

ACROSS

1. Thanksgiving staple
4. "Big ___," 1995 Notorious B.I.G. hit
9. Some special deals
16. Entanglement
19. Beer buyers' needs
20. Low profile maintainer
21. Purifies
22. Exclusively
23. Manic desire to make sweaters when the weekend starts?
26. Certain corp. takeover
27. Musical virtuosity
28. Uncharitable
29. One side of a shutout
30. Put away
31. "I shouldn't have done that"
32. Contents of the Visine Gazette?
37. Empty words
38. Spot for a stream
39. Half brother of Athena
40. Naval need of old
41. Like the narrowest of wins
43. Mends
45. Hardly surprising
48. Parts of many cheerleading uniforms?
50. Where brown and white meet
51. Music category
52. Bit of chicken feed
53. Plumbing, e.g.
55. Sticky sticks
56. Disastrous
59. Chock-a-block
61. Author in the 1950s "angry young men" movement
62. "True Blood" network
63. Addison's "___ to Creation"
64. Cleanup crew's goal?
67. Badge material
68. Caterer's vessel
69. Part of a code
70. Photography problem
71. "Ghosts of the ___" (James Cameron documentary about the Titanic)
73. Whither Cain fled
74. Furnishes
76. Musician Brian
77. ___ Rosada (Argentine presidential manor)
79. Dandy things?
81. Punchophobic?
86. Layers
87. Asks for help, in a way
88. Getting help, in a way
90. London's Old ___
91. Unwelcome stocking stuffer
92. Like some highlighter colors
93. 2006 Verizon acquisition
94. Company whose motto is "Our pilots are moderately intelligent"?
100. Black
101. Repetition
102. "Giant" in "Honey, I Shrunk the Kids"
103. Layer
104. All-too-public tiff
105. Org. that supports water fluoridation
106. "That thar was an appropriate thing to say!"?
111. Many a hand sanitizer
112. Undeniable success
113. Major-league manager Joe
114. Urban rollers
115. Message in a bottle
116. Bringing forth young, as sheep
117. Springe
118. Batiking need

DOWN

1. Sinatra portrayer on "S.N.L."
2. Residents of Canyon County
3. Legal impediment
4. Three, four and five, usually
5. Outdated
6. ___ mater (cranial membrane)
7. Checks, e.g.
8. Not straight
9. Singer Lopez
10. Like some snow
11. Vacationing
12. Voldemort's portrayer in the Harry Potter films
13. Begrudges
14. Reacts to a shock
15. Div. of a former union
16. Cronkite when at the top of the ratings?
17. The radius extends from it
18. Explodes
24. Boom markets
25. "On second thought, forget it"
30. Tie-up
32. Root of diplomacy
33. Musical featuring "The Way He Makes Me Feel"
34. Like crab apples
35. John Steinbeck's middle name
36. Top-grossing concert act of 1989, '94 and '05, with "the"
38. "The Government Inspector" playwright
42. Home of Galileo Galilei Airport
43. ___ box (computer screen pop-up)
44. Big guns
45. Most hopeless moment

November

- 46 Jackal-headed god
- 47 Nonstarters?
- 49 Reagan-era surgeon general
- 50 Unexciting
- 54 Insurance quote
- 56 Water sources
- 57 Dexterous
- 58 Easily damaged major organs?
- 59 Tore
- 60 "___ Story," 1989 best seller
- 64 Ethan Frome's sickly wife
- 65 Wayhouses
- 66 Half-human counselor on "Star Trek: T.N.G."
- 69 Program problem
- 71 Drained of blood
- 72 Help (out)
- 75 ___ Hughes, 2002 Olympic skating gold medalist
- 77 Brooklyn's ___ Island
- 78 "Hair" hairstyles
- 80 Baseball Hall-of-Famer with the autobiography "Maybe I'll Pitch Forever"
- 82 1940s White House dog
- 83 Political caller's request
- 84 Covered with trees
- 85 "For another thing …"
- 87 They deliver
- 89 Savoir-faire
- 91 Industry built around shooting stars?
- 94 Talks big
- 95 Barrel racing venue
- 96 Chevy S.U.V.
- 97 Winter windshield problem
- 98 Cheap booze
- 99 Light figures?
- 100 Sphere or system starter
- 104 "Little ___' Pea" (1936 cartoon)
- 106 Your alternative
- 107 Mumbai Mr.
- 108 Beer and skittles
- 109 Big D.C. lobby
- 110 Dog's sound

monday
17 321

tuesday
18 322

wednesday
19 323

thursday
20 324

friday
21 325

● NEW MOON

saturday
22 326

sunday
23 327

November

s	m	t	w	t	f	s
						1
2	3	4	5	6	7	8
9	10	11	12	13	14	15
16	17	18	19	20	21	22
23	24	25	26	27	28	29
30						

48. A RIVER PUNS THROUGH IT

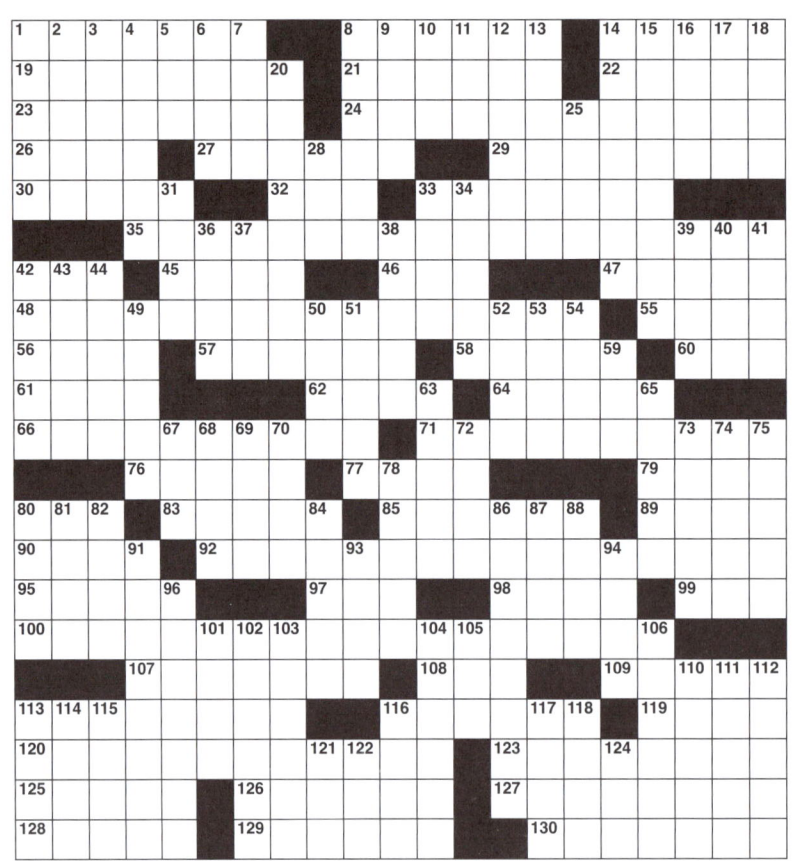

The New York Times

BY JOON PAHK • EDITED BY WILL SHORTZ • 01/16/11

ACROSS
1. Most debonair
8. Cookie with a geographical name
14. Chocolate substitute
19. More than just leaning toward
21. The Ducks of the N.C.A.A.
22. Basketmaking material
23 & 24. Why a Midwest river has so many tributaries?
26. Big name in bubbly
27. Attacks dinner
29. Popular Ford
30. Devour, with "up" or "down"
32. She's prone to brooding
33. Exemplary
35. Fop who makes idle sketches of a Chinese river?
42. They're checked at check-in
45. Move, in Realtor-ese
46. Literary title character from the planet Antiterra
47. See 69-Down
48. "If you don't meet my demands within 24 hours, I'll blow up a Russian river"?
55. Corner
56. Not give ___
57. Start of a Beatles refrain
58. Pained expression?
60. Aunt of 1960s TV
61. "I Shot Andy Warhol" actress Taylor
62. Fail to notice
64. Old-timey oath
66. Life vest worn on a Korean border river?
71. Piranhas in a German border river?
76. Speed of sound
77. ___ spell
79. One often going by limo
80. "American Beauty" director Mendes
83. Corporate shuffling, for short
85. Stand-up guy?
89. ___ dixit
90. Workers
92. Request to an Alaskan river to return to its headwaters?
95. Played one's part
97. Can of Cornwall?
98. Provoke
99. Atlanta-based cable inits.
100. Aggressive posturin' on an English river?
107. The merchant of Venice
108. Stephen of "The End of the Affair"
109. Tad
113. Bookish
116. "Buon ___"
119. Dull discomfort
120 & 123. What minor rivers of Pakistan say at their junctions?
125. Train track beam
126. Channel crosser Gertrude
127. Connected, as circuit elements
128. Fountain orders
129. Team whose home ice is the Prudential Center
130. V.M.I. athletes

DOWN
1. N.F.L. commentator Phil
2. Labor party?
3. Adrift, say
4. Priests' changing room
5. U2 collaborator on "Passengers: Original Soundtracks 1"
6. Hold 'em alternative
7. Tubes, e.g.
8. Illinois home of Black Hawk College
9. With 11-Down, prehistoric period
10. "My Name is Asher ___"
11. See 9-Down
12. Snacked
13. Reachable by pager
14. Cold war term of address
15. Hopeful
16. Narrow inlets
17. Sommelier's prefix
18. ___ Mawr
20. One who doesn't retire early
25. Shield border, in heraldry
28. "___ you!"
31. Jamie of "M*A*S*H"
33. Pop
34. Lickspittle
36. Last Julio-Claudian emperor
37. Semiliquid lump
38. California governor who was recalled in 2003
39. Workers' rights org.
40. Christine ___, "The Phantom of the Opera" heroine
41. "Wow!"
42. 2006 World Cup champion
43. Andrea ___, famous shipwreck
44. Minute
49. "Confessions of an English ___-Eater"
50. Pinpoint, say
51. Works on copy
52. Actress Skye
53. It has a big mouth
54. Father, as a mudder
59. H as in Hera
63. "I thought ___!" ("My feeling exactly!")
65. "Shrek!" author William
67. Unsettle

November

68 ___-deucey
69 With 47-Across, onetime Chinese premier
70 2009 sci-fi role for Chris Pine
72 –
73 Hemingway, once
74 Fly catcher
75 Whiff
78 Expensive bar
80 Silly singing
81 Main
82 Prefix with carpal
84 ___ apparatus (cell organelle)
86 School whose motto is Latin for "Never tickle a sleeping dragon"
87 "Typee" sequel
88 Rock, in modern lingo
91 Cry of accomplishment
93 Neighborhood west of the Bowery
94 Kicks in
96 Stonewallers' statements
101 Acronym for a small-runway aircraft
102 Sent to the free-throw line
103 Like some jokes and jobs
104 Van Gogh painting that sold for a record $53.9 million in 1987
105 Prefix with con
106 Cut a fine figure?
110 Earth shade
111 0.2% of a ream
112 Tends, as sheep
113 1960s dance, with "the"
114 Trillion: Prefix
115 Risk territory east of Ukraine
116 Rook
117 Cozy corner
118 Look badly?
121 The Silver State: Abbr.
122 Soft & ___
124 Ice cream mogul Joseph

November

s	m	t	w	t	f	s
						1
2	3	4	5	6	7	8
9	10	11	12	13	14	15
16	17	18	19	20	21	22
23	24	25	26	27	28	29
30						

monday
24 328

tuesday
25 329

wednesday
26 330

THANKSGIVING (USA)

thursday
27 331

friday
28 332

☽ FIRST QUARTER

saturday
29 333

ST. ANDREW'S DAY (UK)

sunday
30 334

49. LETTER OPENERS

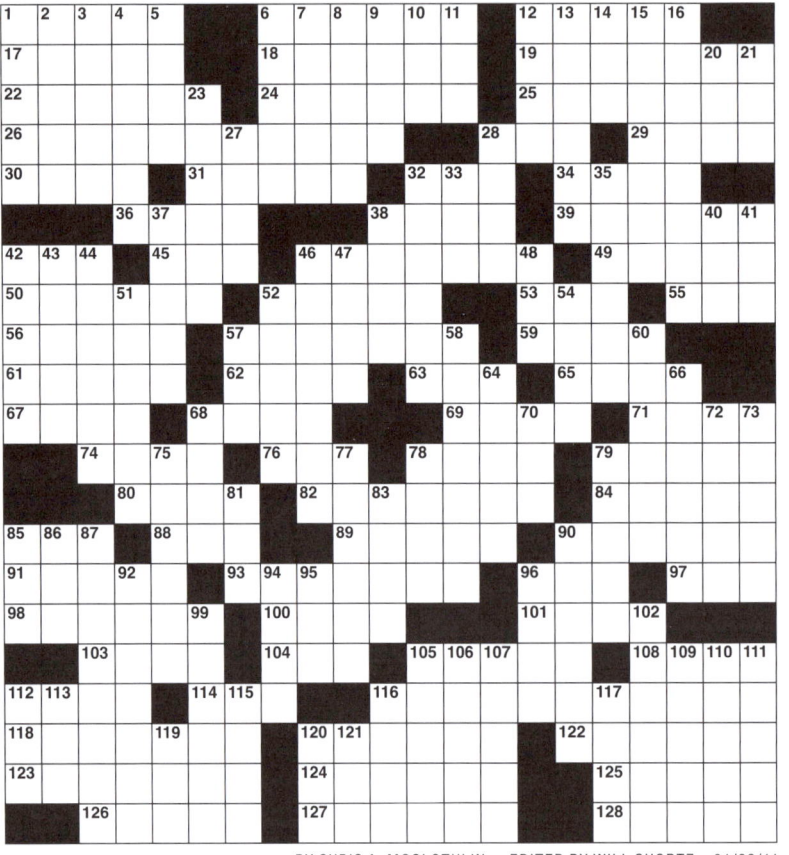

The New York Times

BY CHRIS A. McGLOTHLIN • EDITED BY WILL SHORTZ • 01/23/11

ACROSS

1. Yo, she was Adrian
6. *Insulation measure
12. *Weapon first tested in '52
17. *Gasket type
18. Bedridden, say
19. Debilitates
22. They're found in año after año
24. Oscar snubber of 1972
25. Frequently pierced place
26. *The Boss's backers
28. It may go off the road, briefly
29. *Setting for "Saving Private Ryan"
30. Taxco table
31. Winds
32. Nanki-___ of "The Mikado"
34. *Touch, e.g.
36. *Ace ___ Stories (old detective pulp magazine)
38. Swindle, slangily
39. One of the Blues Brothers
42. N N N
45. N N N
46. Stocks up
49. Slant
50. Shelled
52. *Typography symbol
53. Pilot's milieu
55. Darn
56. Workplace for a cabin boy
57. Payment type
59. Hot times on the Riviera
61. 12-Across and the like
62. Tag sale tag
63. Opposite of guerra
65. ___ Mode, female character in "The Incredibles"
67. ___ Kadiddlehopper, Red Skelton character
68. *It may be under a hood
69. The third one is a shocker
71. Barks
74. Numerical prefix
76. One carrying a toon?
78. The year 640
79. "Give it ___!"
80. Honoree's place
82. Toyota S.U.V.
84. Small
85. ___
88. *4x platinum album of 2001
89. Maurice of Nixon's cabinet
90. King protector
91. Bottle in the kitchen or bath
93. Whence the word "safari"
96. Coach Parseghian
97. Going ___
98. Numbers by a door?
100. *'Vette option
101. Actress Sofer
103. Light bulb over one's tête?
104. "Awesome!"
105. Shelter org.
108. Skewer
112. *Beam with a bend
114. Skeletal opening?
116. *Women just don't get it
118. Former Pakistani P.M. Bhutto
120. Spanish pastry
122. Last-second bidder on eBay
123. Marathoner's need
124. Mountain homes
125. *House coverer
126. Like a turkey's wattle
127. *One of Sean Combs's aliases
128. Steak ___

DOWN

1. Tribal heads?
2. "___, fair sun, and kill the envious moon": Romeo
3. Melodious speaking tones
4. Cross-dressing
5. Author who won a posthumous Pulitzer in 1958
6. Bar mitzvah party
7. Spreading fast on YouTube
8. Country singer Jackson and others
9. Jenny ___ a k a the Swedish Nightingale
10. Grand Forks sch.
11. ___ trip
12. Pointer
13. *"Plan 9 From Outer Space," e.g.
14. Saturn's spouse
15. Flatten, in a way
16. Pointers
20. Inlet
21. Like some winks
23. Trig ratio
27. Bunches
28. *Tops
32. Exercise one is prone to do
33. Places where some R.N.'s work
35. Took the part of
37. Deli array
38. Sting's instrument
40. Repeated cry in Buster Poindexter's "Hot Hot Hot"
41. ___ point
42. *Group with the 2000 #1 hit "It's Gonna Be Me"
43. *Thing that won't go off without a hitch?
44. Hit
46. Mingles (with)
47. They may have keys
48. Scranton-to-Philadelphia dir.
51. Like some amusement parks
52. Shakespeare's "food of love"

December

- 54 *"As Seen on TV" company
- 57 Vegas opening?
- 58 1909 Physics Nobelist for work in wireless telegraphy
- 60 Some drum parts
- 64 *3-D graph line
- 66 The Queen of Soul, familiarly
- 68 Colorado ski area
- 70 Dockworker's org.
- 72 *It helps one get the picture
- 73 *Midsize Jaguar
- 75 Coax
- 77 Harry Shearer's program on public radio
- 78 Kind of income
- 79 Beelike
- 81 Call letters?
- 83 *Little swab
- 85 Govt. flu-fighting org.
- 86 Mouths
- 87 ___ Trench (earth's deepest depression)
- 90 Bluegills
- 92 Obama nickname
- 94 *I.R.S. form
- 95 From ___ Z (how this puzzle goes?)
- 96 Oil company acronym
- 99 Grasping
- 102 Town in Umbria
- 105 Nose-burning
- 106 Bit
- 107 Lackluster
- 109 Old man
- 110 "Um … er …"
- 111 Lead/tin alloy
- 112 Dumbbell abbr.
- 113 Call, e.g.
- 115 *Revealing photo
- 116 Doctor Zhivago
- 117 How many oldies get rereleased
- 119 Not go straight
- 120 Limit
- 121 "If only ___ listened …"

monday
ST. ANDREW'S DAY (OBSERVED) (UK—SCOTLAND)

1 335

tuesday

2 336

wednesday

3 337

thursday

4 338

friday

5 339

saturday
○ FULL MOON

6 340

sunday

7 341

December

s	m	t	w	t	f	s
	1	2	3	4	5	6
7	8	9	10	11	12	13
14	15	16	17	18	19	20
21	22	23	24	25	26	27
28	29	30	31			

50. CIRCLE OF LIFE

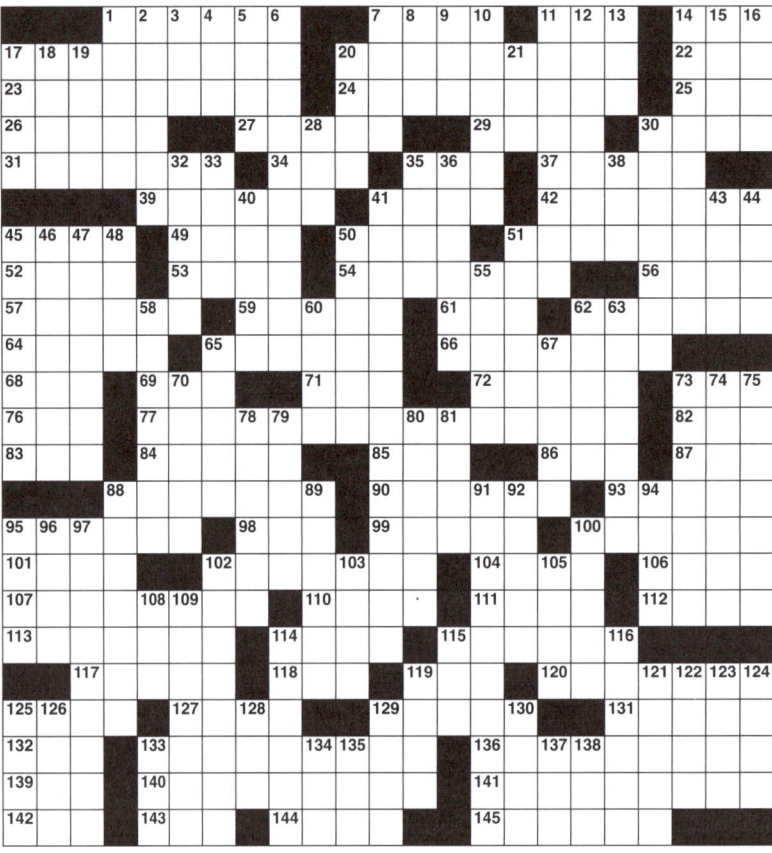

ACROSS
1. Rum, vodka and orange juice drink
7. "Little" barnyard bird with an alliterative name in a classic Willie Dixon blues song
11. "Let me think ..."
14. Costume party accessory
17. Pope after Marinus I
20. Trying
22. Turner of records
23. Felt like forever
24. Interludes
25. Cultural grp.
26. Viewable, to a camera operator
27. Author Marsh
29. EarthLink and others
30. Result of turning the corner?
31. Became annoyed
34. New England's Cape ___
35. Roman 1,150
37. Detached
39. Public person?
41. Pillow talk?
42. Cage in Hollywood
45. Fellowship foes
49. So-called "Heart of Texas"
50. Eschew
51. "See you then!"
52. Famous fiddler
53. Words to a traitor
54. Steering system parts
56. "___ bien" (Spanish for "It's good")
57. Bit of a muscle car's muscle
59. ___ Joe, "Tom Sawyer" character
61. Do-do connector
62. Looney Tunes character with a snout
64. Fashionista's concern
65. Abide
66. Surprise visitors
68. British isle
69. Suffix with torrent
71. Driller's letters
72. Poker declaration
73. Pound sound
76. Top-rated show of 2002-05
77. What the 41-Down has
82. Pooh's young pal
83. Mauna ___
84. Land of Ephesians
85. When doubled, first name in old Hollywood
86. Spanish "that"
87. ___ system (way of classifying blood)
88. Most divine
90. Rattletrap
93. Cobra product
95. Cobra products
98. Ariz. neighbor
99. Swingers in a saloon
100. Person who likes the blues?
101. Mottled
102. Soldier's meal container
104. Very
106. Palliative plant
107. Winter Olympics performance since 1976
110. Den ___, Nederland
111. Ubangi tributary
112. Phalanx's weaknesses
113. Thinned out
114. Driller's letters
115. Facing, with "from"
117. Halved
118. Be shy
119. "What?!"
120. Serves
125. King Arthur's family name
127. Make out, in York
129. Old saw
131. With craft
132. Getup
133. Italian liqueurs
136. Strip in a darkroom
139. "The Lovely Bones" composer, 2009
140. Topic at an owners/players meeting
141. Heyday
142. Source of enlightenment
143. Terminal
144. 1960 Updike novel
145. Four-time Masters winner

DOWN
1. Two-letter combinations
2. Continue, as an uncontrolled fire
3. Most common draw in Scrabble
4. Comic Caesar
5. Priory in "The Da Vinci Code"
6. Tomfoolery
7. City NNE of Tahoe
8. Bus. line
9. Patriotic women's org.
10. Wakes thrown up behind speedboats
11. Revealing 1970s wear
12. Cereal mixes
13. Ed.'s work pile
14. Portable red or white holder
15. Low-priced furniture source
16. Tent or sleeping bag, e.g.
17. Take ___ at (insult)
18. 1962 action film set in Jamaica
19. Finnish transport?
20. Mark in marble
21. Suffix with rhythm
28. Whichever
30. Samaritans
32. Galley figure
33. State in French
35. Peeved pout
36. Hotelier Hilton
38. South American tuber
40. Be part of, as a film
41. Collection of animals featured in this puzzle
43. Lawyer: Abbr.
44. Fat underwater creature
45. Like a Mountie
46. Musical echo
47. Dalmatian's home
48. Like wild oats

December

- 50 Strong
- 51 Dumbness
- 55 Foppish courtier in "Hamlet"
- 58 It may be limited or late
- 60 Revelation comes after it
- 62 Doctor's orders
- 63 Away for a while
- 65 1985 John Malkovich drama
- 67 Reggie Miller, for one
- 70 People leaving the company?
- 73 Breakfast in a bar
- 74 High-tech officer in film
- 75 Hotel figures
- 78 Mortgage holder, e.g.
- 79 Florist's supply
- 80 Comparable in reach
- 81 "Hair" co-writer James
- 88 See 91-Down
- 89 Pilot program?
- 91 With 88-Down, 2000 Ang Lee film
- 92 One of the tribes of Israel
- 94 Online publication, for short
- 95 Place where a person may be bitten
- 96 Director Vittorio De ___
- 97 Sticking with it
- 100 ___ number on (mentally abuses)
- 102 Noted Ronald
- 103 London tourist stop
- 105 Dull
- 108 Works at a museum
- 109 Blitzer, e.g.
- 114 Much-wanted toon in Toontown
- 115 Dumas's "La Dame ___ Camélias"
- 116 Combed (through)
- 119 Lock plate
- 121 Cobra products
- 122 Hindu deity
- 123 Designer Cassini
- 124 Nasdaq alternative
- 125 W. or J.F.K.
- 126 A, to Zimmermann
- 128 60 minuti
- 129 Grouse
- 130 ___ Mix
- 133 Enzyme ending
- 134 Norse war god
- 135 The Horned Frogs, for short
- 137 Mop & ___
- 138 Something about nothing?

monday

8 ₃₄₂

tuesday

9 ₃₄₃

HUMAN RIGHTS DAY

wednesday

10 ₃₄₄

thursday

11 ₃₄₅

friday

12 ₃₄₆

saturday

13 ₃₄₇

☾ LAST QUARTER

sunday

14 ₃₄₈

December

s	m	t	w	t	f	s
	1	2	3	4	5	6
7	8	9	10	11	12	13
14	15	16	17	18	19	20
21	22	23	24	25	26	27
28	29	30	31			

51. HIGH SCHOOL REUNION

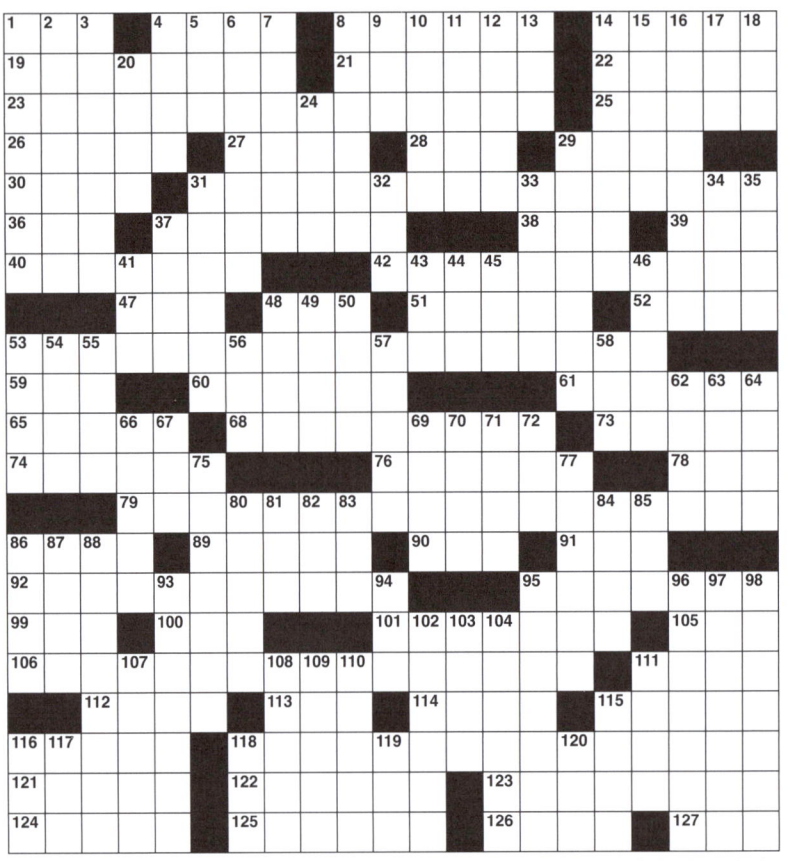

The New York Times

BY DAVID J. KAHN • EDITED BY WILL SHORTZ • 02/06/11

ACROSS
1 Many a download
4 "___ well"
8 Certain bias
14 Some storage places
19 Emu, e.g., to a chef
21 This second
22 Put down
23 *A woman went …*
25 Tricks
26 Expressionist artist James
27 Suffer vertigo
28 Fast-skating #4
29 Scratch
30 Cause of delay
31 *In his office, she noticed a …*
36 A superstar might have a big one
37 Thin overlays
38 No-goodnik
39 Michelle on a fairway
40 Not allowing
42 *She remembered having a high-school crush on a handsome, dark-haired boy with …*
47 What's that, José?
48 ___ Khan
51 BP gas brand
52 Voting side
53 *However, this man was balding, gray-haired and …*
59 North end?
60 Plains tribe
61 Had room for
65 Michelle's predecessor
68 *She thought he was much too old to have been her …*
73 Debussy piece
74 Lands' End rival
76 Bodes
78 Zero
79 *Nevertheless, she asked him if he had attended her high school, and after he said yes, she asked "…?"*
86 Carry
89 Stew
90 "One Mic" rapper
91 Actor McKellen
92 *He answered "In 1971. But …"*
95 The Dow and the Nikkei 225
99 Object
100 Turndowns
101 Go-aheads
105 1969 newlywed in the news
106 *The woman exclaimed "…!"*
111 Chorus girl
112 Spice holder
113 See 48-Down
114 Breather
115 Divorce
116 Hall-of-Famer with 10 World Series rings
118 *He looked at her closely, then asked "…?"*
121 "The Second Coming" poet
122 Thoroughly enjoys
123 One wearing cuffs
124 "Family Ties" mom
125 Check line
126 Shipped
127 Feminine suffix

DOWN
1 Not the way it was
2 Some servitude
3 1994 Sondheim musical
4 From the States: Abbr.
5 ___ Michele of "Glee"
6 Midwest capital
7 Plain
8 TV Guide's Pennsylvania headquarters
9 From ___ Z
10 Brown shade
11 Emcee's words
12 Disdain
13 113-Across, in France
14 Exhaust
15 Father of the bride, say
16 One who goes free?
17 With 34-Down, kind of pie
18 Yearbook div.
20 Superbright
24 Trick
29 Soft leather
31 From the top
32 Phoenix hrs.
33 Tail
34 See 17-Down
35 Some jeans
37 Big name in plastic
41 Still
43 Space movie villain
44 Rock genre
45 ___ Canals
46 Bother a lot
48 With 113-Across, landlocked waters
49 Blown away
50 Mellows
53 Come together
54 Russian/Kazakh river
55 Brush-off
56 Laptop key
57 Time piece?
58 At birth
62 Sushi fish
63 Take out, maybe
64 Take out
66 Say "I do" again
67 Spa reaction
69 Unstable particle
70 Rio contents
71 Canal boats
72 Mess up
75 Rome's home

December

- 77 Symbols of piety
- 80 Hanging piece
- 81 Joanne of "The Pride of St. Louis"
- 82 Org. in "The Crying Game"
- 83 Bad: Prefix
- 84 Pops
- 85 Valve opening?
- 86 Bob ___, 1986 P.G.A. Player of the Year
- 87 One of the Three Rivers
- 88 Nine-time world champion rodeo cowboy
- 93 24 bottles of beer
- 94 Mary ___ cosmetics
- 95 Coming up
- 96 Sort
- 97 Attracts by design
- 98 Palliates
- 102 Cruise lines?
- 103 Runner's place
- 104 Snap courses
- 107 ___ and all
- 108 Bandleader Jones of the 1920s-'30s
- 109 "Cool!"
- 110 Island near Quemoy
- 111 Goons
- 115 Opposite of 64-Down
- 116 "TTYL"
- 117 Reef denizen
- 118 "Are ___ pair?" ("Send in the Clowns" lyric)
- 119 Bug for payment
- 120 Table server

monday
15 349

tuesday
16 350

HANUKKAH*

wednesday
17 351

thursday
18 352

friday
19 353

saturday
20 354

sunday
21 355

December

s	m	t	w	t	f	s
	1	2	3	4	5	6
7	8	9	10	11	12	13
14	15	16	17	18	19	20
21	22	23	24	25	26	27
28	29	30	31			

*Begins at sundown the previous day

52. BARGAINING

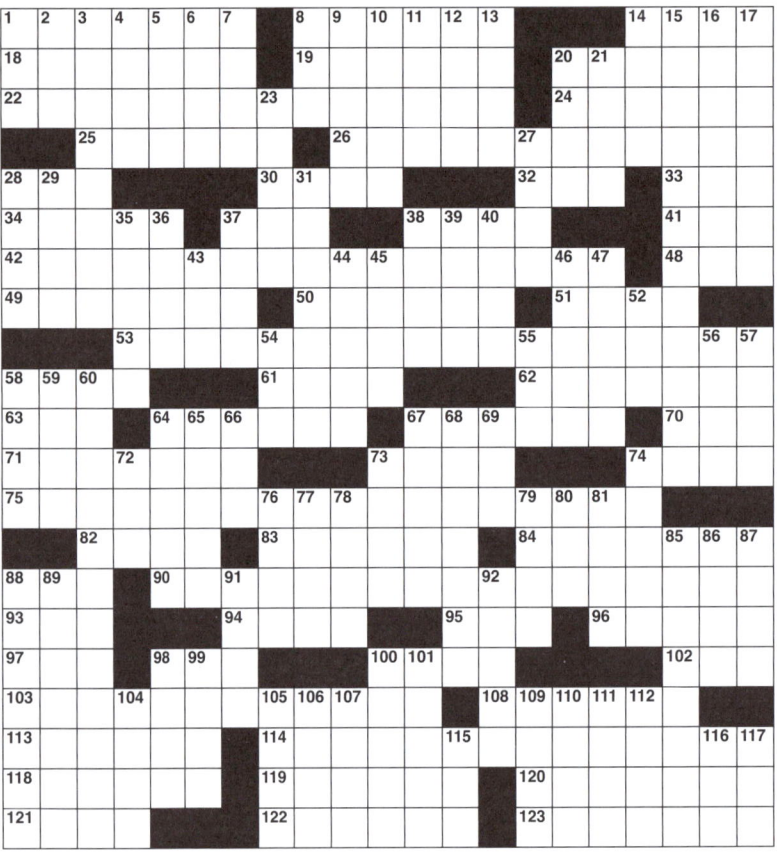

ACROSS
1. Little reminders
8. Bad record, e.g.
14. Coiled killers
18. Home of Elaine, in Arthurian legend
19. Pirate's support
20. Donne piece
22. "Should I say 'Come here often?' or 'Hey, babe!'"?
24. Recite, as a prayer
25. See 23-Down
26. Area banning pub regulars?
28. Heartache
30. "Before I forget …"
32. Losing tic-tac-toe row
33. Actor Penn of "Van Wilder"
34. Kind of jelly
37. Connecting word
38. Pirate's support?
41. Capitol Records' parent co.
42. Lines on a Dan Brown best seller?
48. "Riddle-me-___"
49. Like some yoga
50. Sworn secrecy
51. Settled (on)
53. E.T.'s ability to use the lower part of a keyboard?
58. Carpet option
61. Subject for gossip
62. Easily swayed
63. ___ Dan (Israeli archaeological site)
64. Guidebook recommendation
67. Not in the country
70. N.Y.C. avenue
71. "Welcome to the Jungle" rocker
73. Support provider
74. Crux
75. Where dimwitted people pay to drink?
82. Won
83. Some potatoes
84. Smoothie ingredients
88. Starts of some reproductions
90. Like a former 97-pound weakling?
93. It's bad to be over it
94. To be, to Augustus
95. Chemical suffix
96. When Macbeth asks "Is this a dagger which I see before me?"
97. "Holy smokes!," to a teen
98. Montréal's ___ des Soeurs
100. No. 2: Abbr.
102. Little guy
103. Dramatic production about Ivory or Dial?
108. 1974 hit whose title is sung twice after "Como una promesa"
113. Horn of Africa native
114. Certain cases of the munchies?
118. Early online forum
119. Author of the 2009 book subtitled "A Plan to Solve the Climate Crisis"
120. Protest sign
121. Quagmire
122. Midday meeting
123. Chic

DOWN
1. Mitt
2. Kyrgyzstan city
3. Attica, e.g., informally
4. Carry-on
5. Lund of "Casablanca"
6. Headwear worn over dreadlocks
7. Eye problem
8. Day ___
9. Coastal fliers
10. Home under the midnight sun
11. Silver-tongued
12. Actress Suvari
13. New ___
14. DreamWorks's first animated film
15. Where an Englishman might get a break?
16. George Orwell, e.g.
17. Agate alternative
20. Storage spot
21. Jet black
23. With 25-Across, a puzzle
27. Picture, commercially
28. Small bit of power
29. Injury-monitoring org.
31. High-end French retailer
35. Aid in lost and found
36. Co-worker of Homer on "The Simpsons"
37. Underworld activities
38. Singer Anthony
39. El Prado hangings
40. Union deserter, maybe
43. The King Henry who founded the Tudor dynasty
44. Push
45. Show of pride
46. "Our Gang" girl
47. Spanish hero of yore
52. Subj. of Form 1040's line 32
54. Tiny complaint
55. How to address a maj.?
56. Small part of a pound?
57. Modern communication
58. Opposite of leg., in music
59. Prefix with -pod
60. Annual baseball events
64. Some campfire makers

BY IAN LIVENGOOD • EDITED BY WILL SHORTZ • 02/13/11

December

65 Home of Kansai International Airport
66 Special delivery on Sun.
67 Divide up
68 Some sweet wines
69 Rembrandt van ___
72 Fraternity chapter #17
73 Bruised, say
74 Big initials in news
76 Cries of disgust
77 Betting line
78 Broccoli ___
79 Japanese port
80 Stat for Seaver or Santana
81 "Ta-___ Boom-de-ay"
85 Score on a night out
86 Lamb not found on a farm
87 Tried to make it home, say
88 Pouch bearer
89 Skedaddle
91 Tack
92 A.T.M. button
98 Suffix with contempt
99 Bébé's need
100 Match play?
101 Buffalo N.H.L.'er
104 Roasts
105 Home of the Bahla Fort and nearby oasis
106 Arizona's ___ Verde Nuclear Generating Station
107 Hence
109 Eastern blueblood
110 School near the Royal Windsor Racecourse
111 Radio choices: Abbr.
112 Strained
115 ___ Lingus
116 Kenan's old partner on Nickelodeon
117 D.C.-to-Va. Beach direction

● NEW MOON

monday
22 356

tuesday
23 357

CHRISTMAS EVE
HANUKKAH ENDS

wednesday
24 358

CHRISTMAS DAY

thursday
25 359

KWANZAA BEGINS (USA)
BOXING DAY (CANADA, NZ, UK, AUSTRALIA—EXCEPT SA)
ST. STEPHEN'S DAY (IRELAND)
PROCLAMATION DAY (AUSTRALIA—SA)

friday
26 360

saturday
27 361

☽ FIRST QUARTER

sunday
28 362

December

s	m	t	w	t	f	s
	1	2	3	4	5	6
7	8	9	10	11	12	13
14	15	16	17	18	19	20
21	22	23	24	25	26	27
28	29	30	31			

53. WUNDERBAR!

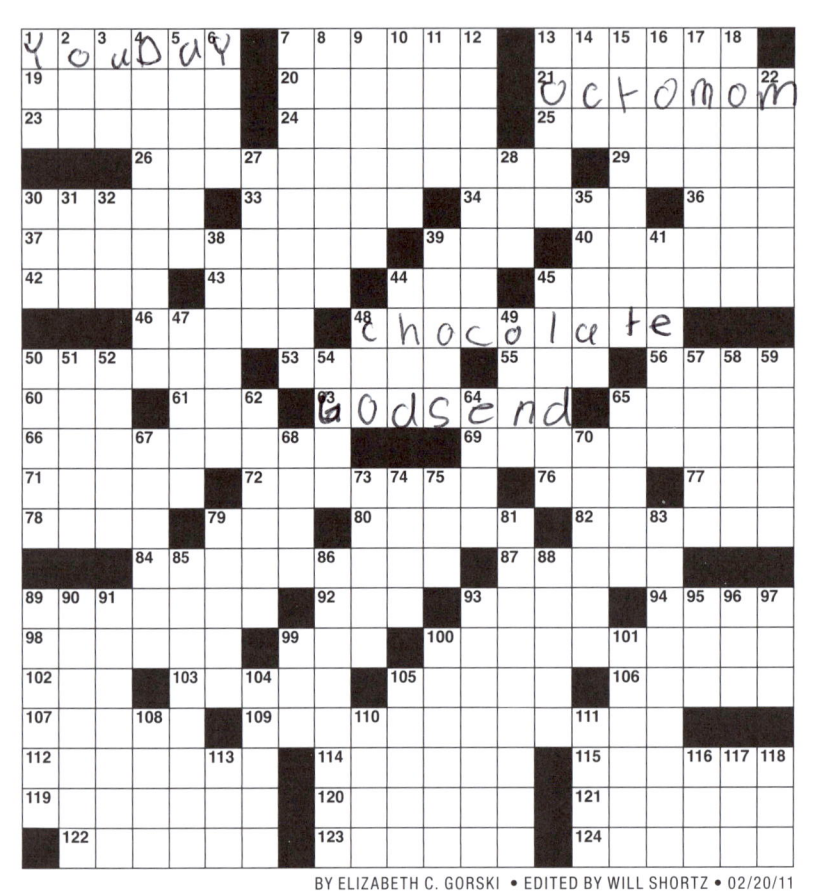

ACROSS
1. Words before a discounted price
7. TV network force
13. Pickle juices
19. Go-getter
20. Hometown of old radio's Fibber McGee and Molly
21. Noted parent in tabloids
23. Not level
24. Did sleight of hand with
25. Food often dipped in soy sauce
26. Band whose 1998 song "One Week" was #1 for one week
29. Tennis's Ivanisevic
30. Astrologer to the rich and famous
33. Softens
34. More furtive
36. PC key
37. Lab instructor?
39. Reduced amount?
40. 1950s pinup queen ___ Page
42. Spartan walkway
43. Bridge position
44. ___ generis
45. "After you"
46. Pear variety
48. Milky Way, for one
50. Didn't accept, with "on"
53. One way for drivers to turn
55. NASA recruiting site
56. In the past, once
60. "Give ___ rest!"
61. ___-ray Disc
63. Gift from above
65. Shreve who wrote "The Pilot's Wife"
66. Onetime head of the Medellín drug cartel
69. Mattel announced their breakup in 2004
71. Name in 2000 headlines
72. Set up
76. Alphabet trio
77. Tapping site
78. Big name in lens care
79. Dernier ___
80. Sandler's "Spanglish" co-star
82. With good order
84. Classic western slugfest
87. It's just below a B
89. Really use an opportunity well
92. CPR pro
93. Slinky, e.g.
94. Togo's capital
98. Writer/philosopher Hannah
99. General name on a menu?
100. Three-stringed instruments
102. Roman 1,002
103. Children's song refrain
105. "Death of a Salesman" role
106. Best Buy buy
107. Wars, in ancient Rome
109. Plan on ordering a drink, say
112. Loose
114. Actress Dolores of the silent era
115. Brand advertised with a cow
119. Member of an assaulting party
120. Leveling tool
121. Blue boys?
122. Fervid
123. Choir supports
124. Currency replaced by the euro

DOWN
1. Rushing stat: Abbr.
2. Popeye's gal
3. Juan's one
4. New Year's Eve wear
5. Egyptian god of the universe
6. "Star Wars" guru
7. Beseeches
8. Resolved
9. Suitcase convenience
10. "Aunt ___ Cope Book"
11. Multicolored
12. Really mean
13. Giving orders
14. Pioneer in quadraphonic records
15. "I love this!"
16. Big Apple neighborhood
17. Gulf state
18. Civil war locale beginning in 1991
22. Made, as money
27. Sharply reprimanded
28. Just
30. Takes too much
31. Witty saying
32. Fifth word of the Gettysburg Address
35. W.W. II craft
38. Etui item
39. Jails, in British slang
41. Finis
44. Drop
45. Quiet transportation
47. Simon of Duran Duran
48. ___-Magnon
49. Present opener?
50. Parade tootler
51. Dickens title opener
52. Vaccine pioneer
54. "The Killing Fields" actor Haing S. ___
57. "___-Tikki-Tavi"
58. Word with plate or plant
59. Like grapefruit juice

BY ELIZABETH C. GORSKI • EDITED BY WILL SHORTZ • 02/20/11

Dec 2014 - Jan 2015

62 Grp. whose seal has the words "This we'll defend"
64 Irving Bacheller novel "___ Holden"
65 Caper
67 Ralph ___ né Lifshitz
68 Steal
70 Equal in height
73 Avis alternative
74 Lizard look-alike
75 Football score abroad
79 South American animal with a snout
81 Quarantine advocates
83 Part of the next-to-last line of the Lord's Prayer
85 "My stars!"
86 Mend, in a way, as a metal joint
88 Lounge in many a hotel
89 Fearsome snakes
90 Mozart's "Un bacio di mano," e.g.
91 Garrison in Minnesota
93 More like Bette Midler stage shows
95 Green-lights
96 Common middle name for a girl
97 Biblical verb ending
99 Cravat holder
100 Recurring Matt Damon title role
101 Not out
104 "The Great Movies" author
105 Actor Waggoner and others
108 Product of fatback
110 Italian author Primo
111 Recipe abbr.
113 Brig. ___
116 Rap's Dr. ___
117 Little amphibian
118 Hush-hush grp.

December

s	m	t	w	t	f	s
	1	2	3	4	5	6
7	8	9	10	11	12	13
14	15	16	17	18	19	20
21	22	23	24	25	26	27
28	29	30	31			

January 2015

s	m	t	w	t	f	s
				1	2	3
4	5	6	7	8	9	10
11	12	13	14	15	16	17
18	19	20	21	22	23	24
25	26	27	28	29	30	31

monday
29 363

tuesday
30 364

wednesday
31 365

NEW YEAR'S DAY
KWANZAA ENDS (USA)

thursday
1 1

BANK HOLIDAY (UK—SCOTLAND)

friday
2 2

saturday
3 3

sunday
4 4

The New York Times

1. WORDS FROM THE WHITE HOUSE

2. EASE-E-DOES IT

3. COME TO ORDER

4. BOOK BINDING

5. THEM'S THE BREAKS

6. WHAT MAKES IT ITCH?

7. AFTER WORD

COACH RIB UPBOW TRIPE
ALLAY ADA SALSA HONOR
WALLPAPER FLOORLEADER
CELIA CLAW PEAR
ASSURED CHAT BLACKCAT
BEAT COLLEGEDRAFT UFO
RENT OUR EINS STIR
USDA SMUT ABUSE PETRI
PAW SWITCHBACK REVISE
TWISTED HORDE BARENTS
COREA SAG AGING
SCHLEPS CIDER BLOSSOM
ELBOWS CHEESEHEAD CRI
SIREN FAIRS KILN SHIN
APED CARL AIL COAX
MOA RUNNINGSCORE AONE
ENDTABLE ERIK AXILLAS
ACAI BAAS AKIRA
DRAWINGCARD WHITEWASH
ITINA HIREE ASS NANAS
MERYL TENDS DOH EGYPT

8. TEE TIME

UMPS CADY POWER FRAIL
POOLCUTIE ELENI LASSO
CHRISTMASTREATY ADIEU
SEMI SNAPON ACTIFED
CAPONS IDAHO
CPAS USO LOCHNESTEA
HANNABARBARITY TEHRAN
ENDOR PAYMENT SOLOIST
ENRON FINDOUT WOES
KEEPINGPASTY COCKS
SDI COLOR SLIER CSA
HAGUE SANTACLARITY
PLAY EMPEROR MAMIE
OILPANS STATUTE EDINA
OLINDA RABBITWARRANTY
HITORMISTY ORE ROSE
TEENA EDESSA
UNBINDS OSMENT ROAM
TERZA TORTOISESHELTIE
ARIEL INCUR UPTOPARTY
HOODS READY ESPN FATE

9. WHATS-ITS

BITEIT LSD CMII SAYIT
IWANNA ATASLANT ADENO
COMETOTHINKOFIT GETIT
NAME ROCKYVI BENITO
INPARK LEADOUT
ARE ICETEAS EEL ADS
MTOSSA OTB BARKCLOTH
OIL LOWBID BOLT OMNIA
ELLIE ART CROWE USTED
STILETTO FLATIRON BSA
NAPA WROUGHT OTOE
LAG OPENAREA HEMOSTAT
ONION ABNER NIL NOOSE
ENNUI SACS ROTINI NIN
WAISTHIGH GAT ATTICS
STE ALI MODULOS HTS
SCYTHES PARTER
SPACEK ITSATIE RIPS
EATIT TAKEITORLEAVEIT
ALETA OVERPAID STELMO
SEEIT MESS DTS LOSEIT

10. MONUMENTAL ACHIEVEMENT

FATSO KAPUT SCAD EDAM
ASHER OMANI ALEE AMTO
CHEERLEADINGFORMATION
TOSS ANDS RENOIR TNT
STEFANI SKICAP AURAE
IMAGEONADOLLARBILL
OFFTO DOIT ALAS
ROI TIGHT ASKNOT CTS
YOGAPOSE SLICES DAWS
DTRAIN HOTTEA SLIPON
APRES THELOUVRE OMITS
CLEATS UNEASE STRATI
MAES AMNIOS CARDGAME
ENS FLAKES AFOUL LEY
LOAD AMES BLARE
GLASSDESIGNBYIMPEI
LULUS NUCLEI AUSTRIA
USA ANOMIE CMDR CONK
THREEDIMENSIONALSHAPE
ELMS ASES CDROM RIDER
SYST KERT HEAPS ASSNS

11. FIX-A-TION

DING SMUG UNCUT ACHES
EROO CAPN CURSE SHORT
CONTRAVIOLATION SAMOA
ONTOUR SIL SPOONREST
OBDURATE ACERB IDES
MIXEDMEDIATION RITE
ACID NECTAR CITYMAP
DEC STE TUSSLES OVA
SHOWERCAPTION STEP
ASKOUT NETS UEY SEINE
CLIFT INCA SPRS ODOUR
TUNAS DEI SHOR PLANES
ORGS SOAPOPERATION
RRS CALDERA ETS FTD
SYMBOLS ATOAST SLOE
ERGS SALESQUOTATION
LANA ARTIS RUNNERUP
ARTMUSEUM CIE GETSTO
CRIBS SMITHCORONATION
TOOLS APNEA UTNE EDGE
OWNER TSGTS SEAR REAR

12. MS. CONCEPTIONS

PALTZ ANZIO YEAH STLO
IMARI GIANTPANDA CHEX
COBOLCOMPUTERLANGUAGE
ASSUCH REN DISNEY
THEMODERNBRASSIERE
MUGS NEVA SERAPE
ASO IAMS INITALICS
DRUGFORLEUKEMIA BADAT
ADRIAN AFR ARIOSE
MADEAMINT CIRCULARSAW
EMBAR NADAL
LIQUIDPAPER SCRIMMAGE
ADULTS ALA EARTHA
LEONI WINDSHIELDWIPER
ANDANTINO AMCS ANN
ONSITE ROAD ARTS
MOTHERSOFINVENTION
AVIATE NCR OBAMAS
TOLLHOUSECOOKIERECIPE
TIDE FRONTDOORS SILEX
EDEN FIBS EMOTE ENTRY

13. DOUBLE CROSSERS

F A [ST/TH] E R ■ ■ I N T H E [RE/EN] D ■ ■ S P A N O
A R E G O ■ A N D R E T T I ■ C H [EA/AT] T E R
D E F O G ■ B E A U F O R T ■ H E C T O R
E N A ■ E T E ■ K E N N Y ■ P E A H E N ■
S A N G R I A S ■ L E S ■ R E E F ■ S L R
■ ■ ■ Y A M M E R E R ■ L E S S ■ ■ T I A
■ D O N N E ■ C A V ■ [SP/PL] A T T E R ■ S G T
V O W ■ D W A Y N E ■ A B U ■ S E E T H E
I D E A M A N ■ O L D C A R S ■ T R O T ■
C O N V E [RS/NT] I O N ■ J E N N I F E R ■ ■ ■
E S S E ■ E M U ■ S I R ■ T G I ■ A R C A
■ ■ ■ D U R A T I O N ■ C O N T [RI/EN] T I O N
■ G T O S ■ S A V A N N A ■ I T S A L O T
[ST/TR] A I N E R ■ H O P ■ A N D N O T ■ E K E
U L M ■ D E T E R S ■ M A I ■ K I D D [IE/ER] ■
C L E ■ ■ P R A Y ■ C E L E R I T Y ■ ■ ■
K I L ■ P R O D ■ P H D ■ T O L U E N E S
■ P I T I E D ■ [SP/CL] E A R S ■ A L T ■ I D O
C O M I C S ■ H O L L O W E D ■ I O N I C
P L I N K S ■ S T E E P E N S ■ O R E C K
L I T T [LE/ER] ■ ■ T S E T S E S ■ ■ N E S T S

14. FLIP-FLOPS

G L A C E ■ J A W S ■ S S N S ■ O B A M A
R I V A L ■ A L A I ■ A T I T ■ A R I E S
A L I E N C R A F T S P A C E ■ K E N N Y
F O S S I L ■ S T E E P L E ■ S T A T U E
■ ■ ■ A N O D ■ ■ ■ R H E O S T A T ■ ■ ■
■ M R R O G E R S H O O D N E I G H B O R
W T A ■ ■ ■ A R T E ■ ■ ■ E E N ■ S I L O
H A N D O F F R E M A R K ■ P G S ■ M S U
O P O R T O ■ ■ T A R A W A ■ S O R B E T
S O N A T I N A ■ ■ U M A S S ■ N E O N S
■ ■ ■ P O L E F L A G S I T T I N G ■ ■ ■
A D R E M ■ I R A B U ■ ■ R Y D E R C U P
S E U R A T ■ O V U L E S ■ ■ O T E L L O
C A D ■ N A M ■ A T A S T I L L S T A N D
A L D A ■ B I C ■ ■ ■ T O N E ■ ■ ■ R A S
P S Y C H O L O G I C A L F A R E W A R ■
■ ■ ■ T O O K N O T E ■ ■ ■ R O S A ■ ■ ■
F E M U R S ■ C O S T U M E ■ A S H P I T
A T E A T ■ W E S H A L L C O M E O V E R
Q U I T O ■ I D E O ■ A V O W ■ N O T R E
S I R E N ■ Z E S T ■ N I N E ■ E S S E X

15. FULL CIRCLE

■ A G R A ■ S K O A L ■ B O O N E ■ V O L
F E L O N ■ V A N Y A ■ A R R O W ■ E T O
R O A S T T U R K E Y ■ S C A R E C R O W
O L D I S H ■ A P S ■ R E A L M ■ R I O T
T I L E ■ E S O ■ I R E D ■ ■ ■ F E L L A
H A Y S T A C K ■ R E C O R D P L A Y E R
■ ■ ■ T A R R E D ■ G O N D O L A S ■ ■ ■
O N T ■ P T A ■ I V A N ■ A N A P E S T S
F E R R I S W H E E L ■ I S T S ■ ■ A I R
T W E E N ■ L E C T E R N ■ ■ M T E T N A
■ L E S T ■ S P A T ■ E T T U ■ O L E G ■
P I S T O L ■ ■ S E A S O N S ■ C L E O N
A N A ■ ■ E T A T ■ C O T T O N C A N D Y
R E P R O V A L ■ S O D A ■ T I A ■ S S E
■ ■ ■ I M A L O S E R ■ L I O T T A ■ ■ ■
R U B B E R C E M E N T ■ M U R A L I S T
U N I O N ■ ■ ■ A P S E ■ E R A ■ B O H R
E R G S ■ I M A C S ■ R C A ■ T E E N I E
F I R E T R U C K ■ C R A N B E R R I E S
U P I ■ R O C H E ■ C O M I C ■ I T A L S
L E G ■ I N K E D ■ C R E T E ■ S A N D ■

16. TYPECASTING

A C R O S S ■ I C I E R ■ A S Y E ■ B S A
C H A R G E ■ M A N G A ■ A N A X ■ O W S
C A P I T A L P U N I S H M E N T ■ L I P
U P S ■ S L U R S ■ S P A C E K ■ C D V I
R A T E ■ ■ N O T H ■ ■ S O R E L O S E R
S L A N T E D V I E W S ■ ■ S E A T T L E
E A R T H A ■ ■ C H E E T A ■ S I T A ■ ■
■ ■ ■ R I C C I ■ ■ B R U C E ■ N O T S O
D O G ■ S H A D O W B O X I N G ■ N E E T
A R O M A ■ L I R A S ■ ■ D R Y ■ G M A T
Y E T I ■ U T T E R ■ C D R O M ■ I E R E
U G H S ■ M E A ■ ■ P A L A U ■ I N N E R
S O I T ■ S C R I P T W R I T E R ■ T D S
E N C L S ■ H O M I E ■ ■ N E R V Y ■ ■ ■
■ ■ F E L T ■ D E E R E S ■ ■ M I A S M A
D E I T I E S ■ ■ R O M A N C A N D L E S
R E C O M M E N D ■ ■ S I T H ■ ■ A I L S
A R T E ■ P E A N U T ■ N E E D S ■ M A I
W I I ■ S T R U C K O U T S W I N G I N G
E L O ■ V E E R ■ E G R E T ■ P I L E I N
R Y N ■ U R D U ■ S A N D S ■ S T O R E S

17. V-2

H U M V E E S ■ M I X E S ■ C H I V I E D
E N T I T L E ■ A R E N A ■ O U T I N L A
T E A C H E R ■ T O N A L ■ S P A N N E D
H A R E ■ V I E T N A M V E T S ■ C O M E
■ R A V E ■ F L E W ■ E O N S ■ R A C E ■
A T R E S T ■ D R O O L E D ■ S E V E N S
C H A R L E S ■ S O L E S ■ F L Y I N T O
E S T S ■ L A W ■ D A D ■ F R I ■ N T S B
■ ■ ■ A G A T E S ■ V ■ F E E D M E ■ ■ ■
M T V ■ A V A T A R ■ G A R N E R ■ V I S
C H I P S I N ■ R E P O T ■ C O S S A C K
C E L L ■ V I N C E V A U G H N ■ T R E E
A F L A T ■ C O A N C H O R S ■ R A I M I
B E A T I T ■ M S T ■ E U R ■ D U N C A N
E D G E D I N ■ M E S A S ■ T E N D O N S
■ ■ E L E V O N ■ R O D ■ S U N N I S ■ ■
L O V E D O N E S ■ V ■ W H I T E N E S S
I G O T O ■ U E L E ■ F I A T ■ R S V P S
M R I ■ V E S T A L V I R G I N S ■ E E G
A E C ■ E D E ■ S L A V E ■ O S U ■ I N T
S S E ■ R U R ■ H A T E D ■ N A P ■ N T S

18. PUBLISHING TRADE

P A S S E ■ M P A A ■ L E O N ■ B A T H E
A S C A R ■ C A N A D A D R Y ■ I C H A T
J O H N N Y G O T H I S G N U ■ K E E N E
A N I S ■ V O L S ■ A S E A ■ M I N D ■ ■
M I S E ■ O V O ■ C L O D M O U N T A I N
A A M I L N E ■ B O S S ■ E X G I ■ V S O
■ ■ ■ ■ U N R E A L ■ ■ A N Y ■ T B I L L
H A L F P E N N Y ■ F A S T ■ C O R N E A
A M O R E ■ ■ D E L A N O ■ T O P I C ■ ■
G A R E ■ T H E R A T O F W A R ■ B I E R
E N D S ■ R Y A ■ B L T ■ I R K ■ A C R E
N A O H ■ A P R E F E C T S P Y ■ B O I L
■ ■ F A B L E ■ R E S H O D ■ ■ O L E T A
A T T I L A ■ P R E S ■ S O B E R E D U P
N E H R U ■ D I S ■ ■ T A M A L E ■ ■ ■ ■
T E E ■ E L A N ■ R E M Y ■ S I L E N T C
I N F I N I T E J E T S ■ B S C ■ M A I L
■ ■ I D O L ■ S E A T ■ V I C I ■ E N N A
I D L E S ■ A F A R E W E L L T O R A M S
R E E S E ■ H O N E S T A B E ■ L I N E S
V E S T S ■ I R E D ■ O L O F ■ A L A N A

The New York Times

19. TO THINE OWN SELF BE TRUE

Completed crossword grid with answers including: SWALE, SLUR, DARTS, SAND, PISAN, TUNE, DRURY, AGEE, FILMCRITIC, ATMAN, LOVE, BIERS, OLYMPICLUGER, DEPEND, KARL, ALLSET, AMOROSO, SKOPJE, PECAN, RANT, ERAT, YAO, AGESAGO, LIZ, TABLOIDWRITER, SER, ALIBI, SIRS, SERT, MINE, SITU, TITHE, DISBANDS, LICKING, ALEVE, PEACOAT, ACHESFOR, ERINS, TROW, NEED, EROS, ACTI, ENOCH, CAM, ELECTIONLOSER, RHO, EXEMPTS, REL, OPEN, SKAL, TERIS, AISLES, EDMEESE, NORISK, IGET, SOARED, TELEMARKETER, HOURS, OLIO, YESOR, EBAYPATRON, GAEL, ONINE, TINE, LAURA, ANNA, NENES, STER, SRTAS

20. MAKING ENDS MEET

Completed crossword grid with answers including: HAHAS, ELCID, ELSE, EBBS, IMUST, JOULE, MOMA, SLAP, COMPUTERROR, ESAU, CARR, DEDUCES, ORTS, ANTI, GARRETT, ENGLISHEEPDOG, EMU, NEER, ATILT, FREAKS, LIMITEDITION, ESTOP, SAS, VOL, HAW, TOPPS, BALI, DAI, PRIMERIDIAN, TREADMILL, OPS, REC, CLE, RAN, CASENSITIVE, OLE, USE, AXL, TIE, ONESEATER, SCIENCENTER, RVS, LUST, TODAY, CEE, VIA, RED, SHUTS, PLACIDOMINGO, ORATOR, TWOAM, NITE, OUR, PERSONALITYPE, VINROSE, UGLI, LIDS, TAINTED, SEED, LINE, GUARDIANGEL, ENNE, EGGS, OPINE, REEVE, STER, INST, PILED, YESES

21. AS ELMER FUDD WOULD SAY . . .

Completed crossword grid with answers including: CARPORT, MAMBA, JOBJAR, OVERPAR, USUAL, BADMOVE, MENOTTI, SOSHALLYEWEEP, EDEN, SPICES, EONS, CRU, TOWELWHACKS, DATE, FOAL, ONS, OMAR, POST, SLOGS, SAD, THELIFEOFWILEE, DOZENS, BELIEFS, IAM, ORARE, DIALS, BBL, VAC, NADERSWADERS, TRUELOVE, ATON, HOYA, EVIL, CLAM, TOREDOWN, THINASAWHALE, ERA, OWS, DHOTI, AARON, AIM, IRANIAN, ORIENT, GARGLEANDWINCE, IBM, EVERY, SARS, STLO, SAC, NOVA, FIFE, FILTHYWITCH, ECO, TITO, CAMISE, DECO, TAKEABIGWHISK, LIEOVER, IDEATES, PUREE, OLDLINE, COSTAR, ABETS, TEASETS

22. CRITICAL PERIODS

Completed crossword grid with answers including: EDITED, COLORS, DSL, TDS, GENOME, ARARAT, ELATION, ACCEPTEDUSAGE, ROSANNE, DOA, TENS, TORN, WARNER, DYNE, THEUNEMPLOYED, SQUINT, FOIST, COOL, OUTRE, GONG, TAKEFLAK, PITTSBURGHPIRATE, JAPE, UTE, TAPES, ODORS, POSSE, PORT, DTS, ATOM, BARHOP, BILATERALACCORD, CAVITY, DIGS, AHS, SARI, AGILE, EAGLE, AVAST, LAN, PALL, EXCESSIVETARIFFS, PRESPLIT, OARS, ELITE, EELS, ASTIN, PALEST, STRANGEORDEAL, AITS, TIENDA, FARE, ELLA, APE, INSTANT, COMMONLABORER, LATENCY, KITING, FLAIRS, ESS, TEE, STORER, SESAME

23. UP STARTS

Completed crossword grid with answers including: EPPIE, AMPS, NIGEL, PEER, FREDROGERS, OCULI, ALSO, FASTOFEDEN, NASAL, ROPE, STOA, FIEF, TENTPACKING, GRES, ATA, ASCAP, SEASONTOBELIEVE, CLAIM, TLC, USSR, NIBS, THATSO, ATTLEE, DREAMOFTHECROP, TOFU, ASIR, SLOE, EINE, IRONMAN, LIMO, APSE, CORNONTHEFOURTHOFJULY, AYLA, ECTO, ANTONIA, SPCA, HEWN, LAIT, ASSN, HOODFORNOTHING, ATDUSK, ESCHEW, TOON, EGGO, ROE, STOOL, MOVEMEORLEAVEME, MONAD, ESC, ALTI, NIXINGBOWLS, TACO, ABEL, OMEN, AERIE, EATINGAME, PANE, ILENE, INREGARDTO, EXAM, OLDER, SEAR, GAUSS

24. PLAY BARGAINING

Completed crossword grid with answers including: ONIONS, SCALIA, PESCI, SKISUIT, TALONS, ETHAN, WEIGHTHREEKINGS, WOOLF, ANNE, AWRY, LUVS, PLO, SHARPEI, PEN, CREMA, SPAR, NOW, ARC, SASHA, ELITISM, TRAPDOOR, LIENS, EDEN, IRONED, CZAR, TANGLE, BITTE, FIFED, SIGHTSAW, ACHY, JOECAMEL, TIO, PHI, RHE, HARDEN, VISORS, RON, RIG, EYE, SCHIPHOL, SARG, ERICSSON, YALIE, HAYES, LOVETT, RAFT, DETOUR, ILER, AGREE, REDBARON, CENTRIC, AARGH, LEB, ECO, ORGS, NOBLY, GENERALLEI, RAT, IGOR, ATRA, DADS, OSRIC, TOBAYORNOTTOBAY, NEALE, INURES, CRIMPER, ASYET, EXCESS, ESPIAL

25. 3 X 8

FABIAN RETRO MADEPAR
APOLLO TEGRIN OBVERSE
TELEPATHSGIFT BARRONS
AXE HIREON FOLIC SMEE
HERR RAMROD ILIE IRT
SOAS WEBGIGGLE MESS
SPILT LETT DBLS
MEETERS POLES REASON
ALSACE CAPOS SOAR REA
RAPS LOSTNETWORK YSL
CSI PIOUS AAMES NTH
ITO RNSPECIALTY SOLI
AIN ONES ASICS PLATER
CASTER STATS SOONEST
GEER BOCA CHILD
MEWS CASHCACHE LANS
FOG TEAR STAIRS LACK
INRE STEAD OPERAS MAY
DIORITE CRIMEFIGHTERS
ECUADOR TAPIRS EUNICE
LAPTOPS IMACS SITTER

26. IS THERE AN ECHO IN HERE?

GOGOL MASH SANE SRTAS
ADANO TRIO DEAR PEARS
MAYITEVERBESOSO ICBMS
PNIN NEON LAS NOLOS
ISR SPAS TOIL UDDERS
ATISSUE IRMA GCLEF
MEDITERRANEANSISI OSA
SWEEP MITTEN MADEIRAS
NAMABLE PUN ROTCS
MARAUD UNLEARNT CURE
OTE LICENSINGFIFI TUT
BOND VINCENTE ALBUMS
INTEL NTH RASSLER
LEONARDO STANCE NANCE
ERR THEMANWITHTHEHOHO
BRIER SOON BASETEN
DAYONE COBB PHYS QRS
IBEAM UHF IDEE TABU
COBRA DONTTREADONMIMI
TRYAS ORON ORTS TATAR
STETS NEWT PSST EJECT

27. FILM NO-R

PAPA IRAE ADDS HANDEL
AGINGBULL DOOM OVERLY
THEGUMBALLALLY LORAIN
SADLY BRIO PETTYWOMAN
PESCI SETH HES LANE
OTIS ASH SEI RELIC
LOP ATHOUSANDACES RCA
ARENDT CHE IVE ARIAS
FIREMAN FRACTAL TITUS
CILIA NATL VILE
BEDKNOBSANDBOOMSTICKS
UNIT SLUR NOTRE
ROSIE GIBBERS DIARIST
PLIES USE EAT CLANCY
SAN MYFIENDFLICKA GAP
CLEEF EYE CUE NEMO
TALE WAS TERR TRIES
OLIVETWIST TOIL METAL
TINEAR MULHOLLANDDIVE
AVERSE OREO FISTBLOOD
LESSEE NEST SASH ENNA

28. GOING FOR A RUN

BOOED VELMA PRAMS
POOHBAHS ALARM AISLES
ARMYBRAT CARBONDATING
CAPE KSU PAINED RIOT
EXHAUSTFANS GRAYHAIRS
HRH LOEB ARFS
OCH LATEMODEL INTRO
MOAB DANSK NEALE KENT
INSIDEJOB KITTYLITTER
STAKE ORIG WEDS UPI
SICEM MIXEDNUTS AKRON
INA USAF VAIN AINTI
OUTERPLANET QUICKREAD
NECK LITER BULGY SETA
SHEBA DIPLOMACY SOD
OTTS ERAT LAZ
SPEEDTRAP USEDVEHICLE
OLES EAGLED RIC GROG
WINTERXGAMES YEARZERO
SESAME EZINE STREAMIN
SYNOD DARTS SAGES

29. TURNING BACK

CALC MCAT GEICO ATPAR
OREO ARGO OXFAM CHOSE
MEASURINGSNOOPS HEMIN
PARTB SOSO CRAKE PEAT
AUNTS JPEG STOLGA
STAN OAT OUTOFTHEPOOL
PRIZESLIPUP TIRANE
AERATE CORAL CURD TOT
TAJ AGE INTUIT PISANO
SOX AAH ELCID NICER
TURKEYTORT LIVINGMOOR
ARDEN SLOES ERE SSR
BEASTS STEPPE TUN AMA
URN RIFT MYRNA TAILOR
PENDED COSMOREMARK
INDIANARECAP INA IDES
TODATE LIMA WELDS
SIRS RABID NERO ASADA
EDITH LOVEMELOVEMYGOD
LEVEE AZERA KNEW OUZO
FAERY NORSE OGRE UEYS

30. IT'S GOING TO COST YOU

ASS MOOG ADDTO BOATER
LET AARE NEONS UNLASH
BE[ARM]ARKET TATTLETA[LEG]RAY
UMASS OSCINE INCREASE
MENTHE AHH LANDHO
REGUL[ARM]EALS LEICA
FRA SELLERS GASPLANET
LEIA SEADOO OTOH TORA
ACOLYTES DOUB[LEG]LAZED
SOL[ARM]ASS MONODRAMA
KNISH OATBRAN MBEKI
OILSLICKS BUBB[LEG]UM
W[ARM]EMORIALS PASSLINE
HALE MEGA SEARLE SETA
INKERASER UNLOOSE SAN
TIETO MIDD[LEG]ROUND
LESSEN ORA PRINTS
PROFORMA STRATA OPERA
CALEND[ARM]ONTHS ID[LEG]OSSIP
BRANDO NOIRE NEAT TAP
SENNAS ERROR GELS SLY

31. MUSICAL PLAY
32. LOCATION, LOCATION, LOCATION
33. CAN I CHANGE PLACES?
34. DRIVERS' TRANSLATIONS
35. FIGURE OF SPEECH
36. RISKY BUSINESS

37. FANGS FOR THE MEMORIES

M	S	N	B	C	■	■	■	A	D	A	G	E	■	■	■	B	R	E	A	D
E	Q	U	A	L	■	I	M	B	E	C	I	L	I	C	■	L	O	D	G	E
A	M	I	N	O	■	N	O	S	F	E	R	A	T	U	■	I	C	A	R	E
T	I	T	A	N	■	F	L	O	O	D	L	I	N	E	■	N	O	M	A	S
■	■	■	N	E	S	■	A	R	E	■	S	N	O	■	S	I	C	■	■	■
M	E	S	A	■	C	U	R	B	■	■	■	E	W	A	N	■	O	T	T	O
T	R	I	S	T	A	N	■	S	C	A	D	S	■	T	E	A	S	H	O	P
V	A	L	H	A	L	L	A	■	D	N	A	■	F	E	A	S	T	E	R	S
■	■	V	A	M	P	I	R	E	I	N	B	R	O	O	K	L	Y	N	■	■
G	E	E	K	■	S	T	O	A	■	■	■	U	R	N	S	■	L	A	P	P
R	O	R	E	M	■	■	D	R	A	C	U	L	A	■	■	R	E	T	I	E
A	C	S	■	I	S	M	■	P	A	I	N	E	■	K	E	A	■	U	N	A
P	E	T	■	N	A	Y	A	■	B	A	T	■	L	E	E	J	■	R	A	H
E	N	A	M	E	L	E	D	■	B	O	O	■	O	B	L	I	G	A	T	E
S	E	R	A	■	■	Y	I	P	■	■	■	M	O	A	■	■	U	L	A	N
■	■	■	L	O	V	E	A	T	F	I	R	S	T	B	I	T	E	■	■	■
I	T	L	L	D	O	■	■	S	O	L	U	S	■	■	C	A	R	A	T	S
N	E	A	R	D	A	R	K	■	R	I	N	■	T	W	I	L	I	G	H	T
U	L	N	A	E	■	E	A	S	Y	A	S	P	I	E	■	C	L	A	R	A
S	E	A	T	S	■	B	L	O	O	D	T	I	E	S	■	E	L	I	O	T
E	X	I	S	T	■	A	B	O	U	■	O	U	R	S	■	D	A	N	E	S

38. LEADING ARTICLES

S	A	V	A	L	A	S	■	J	A	M	J	A	R	■	■	P	L	E	B	E
I	G	I	V	E	U	P	■	A	M	O	E	B	A	■	R	E	E	V	E	S
R	E	S	I	S	T	I	N	G	A	R	E	S	T	■	A	R	D	E	N	T
■	■	■	S	T	O	R	E	■	T	A	R	O	T	■	M	E	A	N	I	E
D	I	E	■	■	R	I	P	S	■	Y	E	L	L	S	A	T	■	I	N	S
U	N	D	E	R	A	T	A	C	K	■	D	U	E	T	■	T	O	N	■	■
A	D	E	X	E	C	■	L	U	N	G	■	T	O	I	L	I	N	G	A	T
D	Y	N	A	M	I	C	■	M	O	O	T	■	N	E	U	■	B	A	D	E
■	■	■	M	A	N	E	S	■	X	O	U	T	■	S	A	T	A	T	O	P
M	E	R	■	I	G	L	O	O	■	D	R	E	W	■	U	R	S	I	N	E
O	D	E	O	N	■	L	O	V	E	A	F	A	I	R	■	A	E	R	I	E
E	I	T	H	E	R	■	N	U	T	S	■	K	N	E	A	D	■	E	S	S
S	T	U	D	D	E	D	■	M	O	N	O	■	K	A	L	E	L	■	■	■
H	E	R	E	■	P	E	P	■	N	E	A	P	■	P	O	W	E	R	P	C
A	D	N	A	U	S	E	A	M	■	W	H	I	M	■	H	A	V	A	S	U
■	■	A	R	M	■	P	R	O	F	■	U	P	O	N	A	R	I	V	A	L
A	N	D	■	P	I	S	T	O	L	S	■	E	R	O	S	■	■	I	T	T
D	E	R	M	I	S	■	I	C	E	A	X	■	O	U	T	E	R	■	■	■
O	M	E	A	R	A	■	C	H	E	C	K	I	N	G	A	C	O	U	N	T
L	E	S	L	E	Y	■	L	E	C	H	E	R	■	A	T	O	M	M	A	N
F	A	S	T	S	■	■	E	D	E	S	S	A	■	T	E	N	P	A	S	T

39. DOUBLEHEADERS

B	E	T	A	S	■	A	C	R	E	■	P	S	H	A	W	S	■	C	B	S
O	V	E	R	P	A	S	S	E	D	■	R	O	A	D	E	O	■	O	A	T
B	E	D	R	O	C	K	A	N	D	B	E	D	R	O	L	L	■	M	B	A
■	■	■	A	O	N	E	■	A	I	R	■	■	A	B	C	■	O	M	A	N
■	■	F	I	R	E	W	A	T	E	R	F	I	R	E	H	A	Z	A	R	D
L	A	R	G	E	■	■	L	A	D	■	O	R	E	S	■	B	A	N	■	■
I	N	U	N	D	A	T	E	■	■	B	R	A	■	■	G	A	R	D	E	N
M	O	I	■	■	B	U	C	K	N	A	K	E	D	B	U	C	K	E	Y	E
A	N	T	I	W	A	R	■	O	A	R	S	■	R	A	N	K	■	E	D	S
■	■	■	A	S	S	N	■	A	T	O	■	M	U	D	■	■	B	R	I	T
■	B	I	G	W	H	E	E	L	O	F	B	I	G	C	H	E	E	S	E	■
R	E	D	O	■	■	D	N	A	■	S	I	X	■	H	U	L	L	■	■	■
I	R	E	■	A	C	T	I	■	M	O	R	E	■	E	N	M	A	S	S	E
D	E	A	D	W	O	O	D	D	E	A	D	D	U	C	K	■	■	H	E	X
S	A	L	A	A	M	■	■	R	A	P	■	■	S	K	Y	S	C	A	P	E
■	■	G	I	S	■	V	I	E	D	■	A	M	P	■	■	P	O	R	T	S
T	R	A	S	H	C	A	N	W	E	T	R	A	S	H	T	A	L	K	■	■
R	O	S	Y	■	A	L	T	■	■	W	A	Y	■	O	H	N	O	■	■	■
A	X	L	■	B	L	U	E	C	R	A	B	B	L	U	E	G	R	A	S	S
M	I	A	■	A	V	E	N	U	E	■	L	E	O	N	A	L	E	W	I	S
P	E	W	■	T	E	S	T	E	D	■	E	S	T	D	■	E	R	E	C	T

40. HAVING ASPIRATIONS

B	I	A	S	■	C	I	V	I	C	■	H	A	A	S	■	■	T	W	A	S
O	R	G	Y	■	O	N	E	A	L	■	I	L	S	A	■	C	H	I	L	L
H	A	U	L	■	K	A	N	G	A	■	G	O	T	O	■	H	A	N	O	I
R	E	A	L	M	E	N	D	O	N	T	H	E	A	T	Q	U	I	C	H	E
■	■	■	A	I	D	E	■	■	G	A	L	S	■	O	U	R	■	E	A	R
L	E	T	B	E	■	■	E	C	O	L	I	■	■	M	A	C	H	■	■	■
I	T	H	I	N	K	T	H	E	R	E	F	O	R	E	I	H	A	M	■	■
N	A	E	■	■	N	A	S	A	■	■	E	O	E	■	D	Y	N	A	S	T
G	L	E	A	S	O	N	■	S	A	S	■	O	W	L	■	■	D	R	E	A
■	■	■	R	E	B	■	D	E	L	T	A	H	A	I	R	L	I	N	E	S
A	D	O	R	A	B	L	E	■	P	A	C	■	S	P	O	U	T	E	R	S
S	E	V	E	N	Y	E	A	R	H	I	T	C	H	■	P	V	T	■	■	■
A	M	E	S	■	■	O	R	E	■	D	E	N	■	R	E	S	O	R	T	S
P	O	R	T	A	L	■	M	D	S	■	■	O	N	E	I	■	■	I	O	U
■	■	S	E	T	O	N	E	S	T	E	E	T	H	O	N	H	E	D	G	E
■	■	■	R	E	G	O	■	■	P	A	N	E	L	■	■	U	V	E	A	S
S	T	U	■	L	O	U	■	S	E	C	T	■	■	E	T	N	A	■	■	■
H	E	R	R	I	N	G	O	N	T	H	E	R	I	G	H	T	S	I	D	E
A	R	G	U	E	■	A	L	E	E	■	B	O	N	G	O	■	I	M	A	X
F	R	E	E	R	■	T	E	A	R	■	B	A	T	E	S	■	O	H	M	E
T	E	S	S	■	■	S	O	D	S	■	E	R	O	D	E	■	N	O	E	S

41. A SHINING MOMENT

G	E	T	S	A	N	A	■	■	I	D	A	H	O	■	■	S	T	R	I	N	G	S
A	C	H	E	F	O	R	■	■	S	E	V	E	R	■	■	T	O	O	S	O	O	N
B	L	E	A	T	E	D	■	A	L	L	ON	R	E	D	■	I	N	C	A	R	G	O
S	A	W	■	E	N	O	■	L	A	M	■	H	O	E	■	R	I	K	■	W	O	W
■	T	E	A	R	D	R	O	P	■	ON	I	ON	■	V	I	S	C	E	R	A	L	■
■	■	D	R	T	■	■	S	O	F	T	C	O	L	O	R	■	■	F	E	Y	■	■
S	U	N	C	H	I	P	S	■	ON	E	I	R	ON	■	A	S	S	E	S	S	A	S
N	N	E	■	A	F	R	A	I	D	■	■	■	G	R	E	T	E	L	■	P	G	A
A	B	S	E	N	C	E	■	ON	A	U	C	T	I	ON	■	A	L	L	E	R	G	Y
K	O	D	A	K	■	P	M	S	■	K	O	A	■	E	B	B	■	E	T	U	I	S
E	L	A	P	S	E	■	ON	T	H	E	B	U	T	T	ON	■	G	R	A	C	E	S
S	T	Y	■	G	E	C	K	O	S	■	■	■	A	T	O	M	I	C	■	E	S	O
■	■	■	B	I	G	ON	■	R	I	B	C	A	G	E	■	ON	S	E	T	■	■	■
R	A	J	I	V	■	M	G	M	■	L	A	S	■	S	H	A	■	N	A	C	H	O
E	M	O	T	I	ON	A	L	■	C	O	N	A	N	■	I	M	ON	T	O	Y	O	U
M	E	L	■	N	A	N	U	■	Y	A	Y	M	E	■	R	I	S	E	■	N	U	S
O	B	L	ON	G	S	■	T	ON	Y	T	ON	I	T	ON	E	■	I	R	ON	I	S	T
P	A	Y	S	■	P	E	S	T	O	■	■	■	I	B	E	A	M	■	A	C	E	S
■	■	■	W	A	R	D	■	H	U	E	■	T	Z	U	■	S	M	U	T	■	■	■
S	T	R	I	F	E	S	■	E	N	T	E	R	E	D	■	L	E	T	I	T	B	E
T	H	E	T	R	E	E	L	I	G	H	T	I	N	G	C	E	R	E	M	O	N	Y
A	A	M	C	O	■	L	O	C	■	N	ON	E	■	E	V	E	■	S	E	G	E	R
G	I	S	H	■	■	S	U	E	■	O	S	S	■	T	S	P	■	■	R	A	G	E

42. ON A ROLL

Q	U	A	F	F	S	■	■	O	M	A	H	A	■	S	A	P	P	I	E	R
A	N	G	O	L	A	■	A	S	E	V	E	R	■	I	N	A	H	O	L	E
T	E	R	R	O	R	■	C	U	T	O	N	B	O	L	D	L	I	N	E	S
A	V	E	■	P	A	R	T	■	E	N	S	■	R	V	S	■	L	I	M	E
R	E	E	K	■	J	E	S	T	S	■	■	O	N	E	O	F	■	Z	E	N
I	N	D	O	■	E	B	O	N	■	S	A	P	O	R	■	I	D	E	N	T
■	■	■	I	N	V	E	N	T	■	H	U	R	T	■	E	X	I	S	T	S
N	A	M	■	A	O	L	■	■	B	O	N	A	■	I	D	E	S	■	■	■
O	P	E	N	S	■	S	H	A	D	E	T	H	E	C	I	R	C	L	E	S
D	O	N	O	T	■	■	O	M	A	R	■	■	V	E	T	■	O	L	L	A
O	L	D	S	■	S	E	P	O	Y	■	B	O	O	T	S	■	L	A	P	D
F	L	E	E	■	O	R	O	■	■	C	A	S	K	■	■	N	O	M	A	D
F	O	L	D	A	L	O	N	G	D	A	S	H	E	S	■	E	R	A	S	E
■	■	■	I	V	E	S	■	L	I	N	K	■	■	A	G	O	■	S	O	N
P	E	E	V	E	S	■	C	O	R	D	■	O	O	L	O	N	G	■	■	■
R	U	L	E	R	■	P	H	O	T	O	■	O	N	T	O	■	A	S	P	S
E	R	E	■	S	C	R	A	M	■	■	S	H	R	E	D	■	G	E	L	T
S	A	V	E	■	A	I	R	■	J	A	I	■	U	R	N	S	■	W	A	R
U	S	E	T	A	P	E	O	N	E	D	G	E	S	■	E	N	L	A	C	E
M	I	N	U	T	E	S	■	O	H	O	H	O	H	■	S	I	E	G	E	S
E	A	S	I	E	S	T	■	B	U	S	T	S	■	■	S	P	E	E	D	S

43. THE WISH

A	L	T	A		S	T	U	B		M	A	S	H	E	R		M	C	C	L
S	H	A	M		T	U	T	U		A	S	P	E	R	A		A	L	A	E
H	A	R	P	S	P	E	E	D		T	H	I	N	S	I	S	T	E	R	S
E	S	P	A	N	A			D	O	Z	E	N	S		S	I	T	A	R	S
N	A	S	S	A	U		O	H	I	O			L	I	N	E	N			
			G	L	O	B	A	L	H	A	R	M	I	N	G		S	T	S	
A	S	P		S	I	V	A			E	S	C	O	R	T		A	D	H	O	C
S	P	A	M		S	U	M	E	R		A	C	H	E	S		E	E	R	O
S	A	R	I			L	A	X		D	D	A	Y		A	B	L	E	S	T
T	R	A	C	H	E	A		A	M	O	I		D	E	C	R	E	P	I	T
		H	A	S	T	E	M	A	N	A	G	E	M	E	N	T				
D	E	S	E	R	T	E	D		L	A	N	A		B	R	O	I	L	E	R
E	M	I	L	I	E		G	I	L	T		R	C	A		N	O	T	E	
B	A	L	L		R	E	I	N	A		S	P	O	R	E		G	O	A	L
R	I	V	E	S		I	N	G	R	A	M		A	G	A	L		P	L	Y
A	L	E		H	I	N	G	E	D	V	I	C	T	O	R	Y				
		R	H	I	N	E			E	L	O	I		T	R	I	A	G	E	
E	T	H	A	N	S		T	H	E	R	E	S			H	I	T	M	E	N
R	E	A	D	Y	T	O	H	E	A	R		M	A	G	I	C	H	A	N	D
G	E	R	E			E	L	O	I	S	E		O	B	O	E		A	L	O	E
O	N	E	S		P	A	R	R	E	D			S	C	A	R		D	E	A	D

44. HOPE FOR CLEAR SKIES

O	N	T	A	P	E		D	A	H	L		A	D	Z	E		T	H	I	N	L	Y
B	O	U	T	O	N		A	V	I	A		S	I	A	M		A	E	N	E	I	D
S	T	R	I	P	E		M	A	N	Y	MOON	S	A	G	O		C	R	O	W	N	S
	A	F	T	E	R	DARK		D	E	I	O	N				DARK	H	O	R	S	E	
H	O	W		Y	O	M		T	U	R	N	R	E	D		A	S	I		D	A	W
O	N	A	DIM	E		A	P	O			S	G	T		M	U	G		C	DIM	A	G	E
V	E	R	A		O	N	E	R	S				V	I	C	E	S		L	Y	E	S
			G	A	P		P	E	A	B	R	A	I	N	S			C	E	Y		
BRIGHT	E	N		C	E	L	E	S	T	I	A	L	B	O	D	I	E	S		A	L	BRIGHT
I	N	U	T	E	R	O		T	O	O	R	D	E	R		O	N	A	S	S	I	S
D	A	R	E	S	A	Y			M	E	A				W	A	I	K	I	K	I	
E	R	S	T			A	T	T	H	E	EARTH	S	C	O	R	E			I	C	E	D
A	M	E	R	E		L	I	R	A				P	L	O	Y		J	E	S	S	E
			A	M	A	T	E	U	R	A	S	T	R	O	N	O	M	E	R			
T	A	J		B	R	Y	A	N		M	O	E			G	S	U	I	T		S	A	G
A	L	O	M	A	R			K	E	N	N	E	D	Y			S	W	A	N	N	S
L	I	T	E	R	A	T	I		T	I	A	M	O			M	A	H	A	R	A	N	I
L	A	S	A	G	N	E	S		T	O	T	E	M		X	R	A	Y	S	P	E	X
			T	O	T	A	L	L	U	N	A	R	E	C	L	I	P	S	E			
A	G	A	S			R	E	O				A	V	G				N	A	M	E	
C	A	S	T	I	N	G		G	O	E	SUN	D	E	R		A	S	H	A	D	O	W
O	P	H	E	L	I	A		I	N	B	U	I	L	T		T	E	E	L	I	N	E
P	E	E	W	E	E	S		C	O	W	P	O	K	E		O	N	E	S	T	A	R

45. HEY, MISTER!

E	X	C	E	L		A	M	P	S		S	H	O	P		A	T	S	E	A
V	E	R	V	E		S	O	O	T		W	A	K	E		G	E	A	R	S
I	N	E	E	D	M	Y	S	P	A	C	E	M	A	N		L	A	N	A	I
T	O	E	N	A	I	L			B	A	D	L	Y		C	A	S	T	S	
E	N	D		T	U	B	A		T	E	E		B	U	R	E	A	U	S	
		B	A	T	M	A	N	S	I	N	T	H	E	B	E	L	F	R	Y	
C	U	M	I	N			R	I	C	O			A	L	I		S	E	E	D
O	P	E	N	D	O	O	R	M	A	N	P	O	L	I	C	Y				
M	S	N			F	L	E	E	T		E	P	E	E		E	P	A	C	T
I	T	S	S	A	F	E			D	A	I	S		M	A	R	I	A	H	
C	A	R	T	M	A	N	B	E	F	O	R	E	T	H	E	H	O	R	S	E
A	T	E	O	U	T		O	C	A	T			U	S	S		W	A	S	P
L	E	A	P	S		S	L	U	R		P	A	U	L	O		C	O	O	
		T	A	K	E	A	R	A	I	N	M	A	N	C	H	E	C	K		
P	R	O	S		C	U	R		B	L	O	B		H	U	S	K	Y		
J	A	C	K	M	A	N	O	F	A	L	L	T	R	A	D	E	S			
S	G	T	Y	O	R	K		E	D	O		E	A	S	Y		C	U	T	
D	O	B	I	E			I	D	I	O	M			K	A	R	A	O	K	E
N	O	B	L	E		G	O	O	D	M	A	N	A	S	N	E	W	M	A	N
A	L	E	U	T		A	T	R	A		Y	O	G	I		B	L	A	S	T
E	L	R	E	Y		B	A	A	S		O	M	E	N		A	S	S	E	S

46. WORKS IN TRANSLATION

Y	E	S	M		P	L	E	A		S	T	O	R	K		S	T	O	C	K
A	L	T	O		H	I	N	D		Y	A	L	E	U		R	E	P	L	Y
M	O	O	T		O	L	A	V		S	M	E	A	R		T	A	P	E	D
A	P	P	O	I	N	T	M	E	N	T	I	N	S	A	M	A	R	R	A	
H	E	A	R	S	E		I	R	S			O	L	A		F	E	N	G	
A	R	T	I	S	T	E		B	A	C	K	I	N	T	H	E	U	S	S	R
			N	E	A	L	S		O	I	S			E	L	S	I	E		
O	N	E	N	I	G	H	T	I	N	B	A	N	G	K	O	K		E	N	E
H	U	R			I	N	K	Y			S	T	O	I	C		M	S	G	R
S	N	I	F	F	S		E	E	L			B	L	O	N	D				
O	N	C	E	U	P	O	N	A	T	I	M	E	I	N	M	E	X	I	C	O
			D	R	A	C	O		P	A	L			E	D	I	T	O	R	
A	N	I	S		I	T	A	L	O		R	I	O	T			O	S	E	
V	I	M		A	N	A	M	E	R	I	C	A	N	I	N	P	A	R	I	S
E	L	W	E	S			S	A	C			S	K	O	A	L				
D	E	A	T	H	I	N	V	E	N	I	C	E			I	T	S	A	B	E	T
A	B	I	E		K	O	I			R	N	A		S	E	N	I	L	E	
A	T	R	E	E	G	R	O	W	S	I	N	B	R	O	O	K	L	Y	N	
C	S	I	N	Y		G	I	J	O	E		E	A	C	H		I	L	S	E
D	I	N	A	R		I	L	O	N	A		A	T	M	O		N	E	E	T
E	N	G	L	E		N	E	S	T	S			D	E	P	T		G	R	E	S

47. THE LONG AND THE SHORT OF IT

P	I	E		P	O	P	P	A		T	W	O	F	E	R	S		W	E	B
I	D	S		A	L	I	A	S		R	E	F	I	N	E	S		A	L	L
S	A	T	U	R	D	A	Y	K	N	I	T	F	E	V	E	R		L	B	O
C	H	O	P	S			M	E	A	N			N	I	L		S	T	O	W
O	O	P	S		E	Y	E	W	H	I	T	E	N	E	S	S	N	E	W	S
P	A	P		G	L	E	N			A	R	E	S		T	A	R			
O	N	E	P	O	I	N	T		D	A	R	N	S		N	O	R	M	A	L
	S	L	I	G	H	T	S	K	I	R	T	S		T	A	N	L	I	N	E
			S	O	U	L		O	A	T		T	R	A	D	E		G	U	M
F	A	T	A	L			S	O	L	I	D		A	M	I	S		H	B	O
O	D	E			Z	I	P	P	O	L	I	T	T	E	R			T	I	N
U	R	N		G	E	N	E			G	L	A	R	E		A	B	Y	S	S
N	O	D		L	E	N	D	S		E	N	O		C	A	S	A			
T	I	E	P	I	N	S		A	F	R	A	I	D	O	F	H	I	T	S	
S	T	R	A	T	A		P	R	A	Y	S		O	N	R	E	L	I	E	F
			V	I	C		C	O	A	L		N	E	O	N			M	C	I
B	R	I	G	H	T	I	S	H	A	I	R	W	A	Y	S		E	B	O	N
R	O	T	E		A	N	T			C	O	A	T			S	C	E	N	E
A	D	A		T	H	E	M	S	F	I	T	T	I	N	G	W	O	R	D	S
G	E	L		H	O	M	E	R	U	N		T	O	R	R	E		E	L	S
S	O	S		Y	E	A	N	I	N	G		S	N	A	R	E		D	Y	E

48. A RIVER PUNS THROUGH IT

S	U	A	V	E	S	T		M	I	L	A	N	O		C	A	R	O	B
I	N	T	E	N	T	O	N		O	R	E	G	O	N		O	S	I	E	R
M	I	S	S	O	U	R	I		L	O	V	E	S	C	O	M	P	A	N	Y
M	O	E	T		D	I	G	S	I	N			H	A	R	R	I	S	O	N
S	N	A	R	F		H	E	N			S	T	E	L	L	A	R			
			Y	A	N	G	T	Z	E	D	O	O	D	L	E	D	A	N	D	Y
I	D	S		R	E	L	O			A	D	A			E	N	L	A	I	
T	O	M	O	R	R	O	W	N	E	V	A	D	I	E	S		T	R	A	P
A	R	A	P		O	B	L	A	D	I			Y	O	W	I	E		B	E	E
L	I	L	I				M	I	S	S		N	E	R	T	S				
Y	A	L	U	J	A	C	K	E	T		O	D	E	R	E	A	T	E	R	S
			M	A	C	H	I			S	I	T	A			E	X	E	C	
S	A	M		R	E	O	R	G		N	O	S	H	O	W		I	P	S	E
C	R	E	W		Y	U	K	O	N	G	O	H	O	M	E	A	G	A	I	N
A	C	T	E	D			L	O	O				G	O	A	D		T	N	T
T	H	A	M	E	S	F	I	G	H	T	I	N	W	O	R	D	S			
			A	N	T	O	N	I	O		R	E	A			S	K	O	S	H
S	T	U	D	I	O	U	S			G	I	O	R	N	O			A	C	H	E
W	E	R	E	A	L	L	I	N	D	U	S			T	O	G	E	T	H	E	R
I	R	A	I	L			E	D	E	R	L	E		S	O	L	D	E	R	E	D
M	A	L	T	S			D	E	V	I	L	S		K	E	Y	D	E	T	S	

49. LETTER OPENERS

T	A	L	I	A		R	V	A	L	U	E		H	B	O	M	B
O	R	I	N	G		A	I	L	I	N	G		I	M	P	A	I	R	S
T	I	L	D	E	S		B	R	A	N	D	O		N	O	S	T	R	I	L
E	S	T	R	E	E	T	B	A	N	D			A	T	V		D	D	A	Y
M	E	S	A		C	O	I	L	S			P	O	O		I	P	O	D
		G	M	A	N			B	U	R	N			E	L	W	O	O	D
N	U	S		E	N	S		A	M	A	S	S	E	S		A	N	G	L	E
S	H	O	T	A	T		M	D	A	S	H		S	K	Y		S	E	W
Y	A	C	H	T		L	U	M	P	S	U	M		E	T	E	S
B	R	A	N	D		A	S	I	S		P	A	Z		E	D	N	A
C	L	E	M		V	S	I	X			R	A	I	L		A	R	F	S
	D	E	C	A		C	E	L		D	C	X	L		A	R	E	S	T
		D	A	I	S			S	E	Q	U	O	I	A		P	E	T	T	Y
C	O	M		J	L	O		S	T	A	N	S		B	I	S	H	O	P
D	R	A	N	O		S	W	A	H	I	L	I		A	R	A		A	P	E
C	A	R	O	L	S		T	T	O	P			R	E	N	A
	I	D	E	E		W	O	W		A	S	P	C	A		S	P	I	T
L	B	A	R		E	X	O		Y	C	H	R	O	M	O	S	O	M	E
B	E	N	A	Z	I	R			C	H	U	R	R	O		S	N	I	P	E	R
S	T	A	M	I	N	A		A	E	R	I	E	S			C	S	P	A	N
				S	A	G	G	Y		P	D	I	D	D	Y		D	I	A	N	E

50. CIRCLE OF LIFE

	B	R	A	S	S	9		R	E	D	10		H	M	M		W	I	G
A	D	R	I	A	N	I	I	I		V	E	X	A	T	I	O	U	S		I	K	E
D	R	A	G	G	E	D	O	N		E	N	T	R	A	C	T	E	S		N	E	A
I	N	F	8	E		N	G	A	I	O			I	S	P	S		11	E	A	R
G	O	T	S	O	R	E		A	N	N		M	C	L		A	L	O	O	F
		N	O	T	A	R	Y		C	O	O	S			N	I	C	O	L	A	S
O	R	C	S		W	A	C	O		S	H	U	N		I	T	S	A	D	A	T	E
N	E	R	O		E	T	T	U		T	I	E	R	O	D	S		E	S	T	A
7	P	O	W	E	R		I	N	J	U	N		A	S	I		P	O	R	K	Y	12
B	R	A	N	D		E	N	D	U	R	E		D	R	O	P	I	N	S
A	I	T		I	A	L		D	D	S			I	C	A	L	L		G	R	R
C	S	I		T	W	E	L	V	E	Y	E	A	R	C	Y	C	L	E		R	O	O
K	E	A			I	O	N	I	A		Z	S	A		E	S	A		A	B	O
			H	O	L	I	E	S	T		O	L	D	C	A	R		V	E	N	O	M
6	S	K	I	N	S		N	E	V		D	O	O	R	S		D	E	M	O	C	1
P	I	E	D			M	E	S	S	T	I	N		O	H	S	O		A	L	O	E
I	C	E	D	A	N	C	E		H	A	A	G		U	E	L	E		G	A	P	S
T	A	P	E	R	E	D		R	O	T	C		A	C	R	O	S	S
		I	N	T	W	O		O	W	E		H	U	H		W	A	I	T	S	O	N
P	E	N	5		S	N	O	G			M	A	X	I	M		F	2	I	L	Y
R	I	G		A	M	A	R	E	T	T	O	S		N	E	G	A	T	I	V	E	S
E	N	O		S	A	L	A	R	Y	C	A	P		G	O	L	D	E	N	A	G	E
Z	E	N		E	N	D		4	R	U	N			3	W	O	O	D	S

Answer Key: 1 - Rat, 2 - Ox, 3 - Tiger, 4 - Rabbit, 5 - Dragon, 6 - Snake, 7 - Horse, 8 - Ram, 9 - Monkey, 10 - Rooster, 11 - Dog, 12 - Pig

51. HIGH SCHOOL REUNION

A	P	P		A	L	L	S		R	A	C	I	S	M		D	I	S	K	S
L	E	A	N	M	E	A	T		A	T	O	N	C	E		E	N	T	E	R
T	O	S	E	E	A	N	E	W	D	O	C	T	O	R		P	L	O	Y	S
E	N	S	O	R		S	P	I	N		O	R	R		C	L	A	W
R	A	I	N		D	I	P	L	O	M	A	O	N	T	H	E	W	A	L	L
E	G	O		V	E	N	E	E	R	S			R	A	T		W	I	E
D	E	N	Y	I	N	G			T	H	E	S	A	M	E	N	A	M	E
			E	S	O		A	G	A		A	M	O	C	O		A	Y	E	S
J	U	S	T	A	V	E	R	A	G	E	L	O	O	K	I	N	G
E	R	N			O	S	A	G	E	S			S	E	A	T	E	D
L	A	U	R	A		C	L	A	S	S	M	A	T	E		E	T	U	D	E
L	L	B	E	A	N		A	U	G	U	R	S			N	I	L
		W	H	E	N	D	I	D	Y	O	U	G	R	A	D	U	A	T	E
T	O	T	E		W	O	R	R	Y		N	A	S		I	A	N
W	H	Y	D	O	Y	O	U	A	S	K			I	N	D	I	C	E	S
A	I	M		N	O	S		A	S	S	E	N	T	S		O	N	O
Y	O	U	W	E	R	E	I	N	M	Y	C	L	A	S	S		A	L	T	O
			R	A	C	K		S	E	A		R	E	S	T		S	P	L	I	T
B	E	R	R	A		W	H	A	T	D	I	D	Y	O	U	T	E	A	C	H
Y	E	A	T	S		E	A	T	S	U	P		A	R	R	E	S	T	E	E
E	L	Y	S	E		A	M	O	U	N	T		S	E	N	T		E	S	S

52. BARGAINING

P	O	S	T	I	T	S		S	T	I	G	M	A			A	S	P	S
A	S	T	O	L	A	T		P	E	G	L	E	G		S	O	N	N	E	T
W	H	A	T	S	M	Y	B	A	R	L	I	N	E		I	N	T	O	N	E
			T	E	A	S	E	R		N	O	B	A	R	F	L	Y	Z	O	N	E
W	O	E			A	L	S	O				O	O	X			K	A	L
A	S	P	I	C			V	I	A		M	A	S	T			E	M	I
T	H	E	D	A	V	I	N	C	I	B	A	R	C	O	D	E		R	E	E
T	A	N	T	R	I	C			O	M	E	R	T	A			A	L	I	T
				A	L	I	E	N	S	P	A	C	E	B	A	R	C	R	A	F	T
S	H	A	G				I	T	E	M				P	L	I	A	B	L	E
T	E	L		H	O	S	T	E	L		A	B	R	O	A	D		L	E	X
A	X	L	R	O	S	E			A	L	L	Y				M	E	A	T
C	A	S	H	B	A	R	F	O	R	C	L	U	N	K	E	R	S
			T	O	O	K		I	D	A	H	O	S		O	R	A	N	G	E	S
O	V	A			S	A	V	E	D	B	Y	T	H	E	B	A	R	B	E	L	L
P	A	R		E	S	S	E			E	N	E		A	C	T	I	I	I
O	M	G		I	L	E		A	S	S	T				L	A	D
S	O	A	P	B	A	R	O	P	E	R	A		E	R	E	S	T	U
S	O	M	A	L	I		M	A	R	S	B	A	R	A	T	T	A	C	K	S
U	S	E	N	E	T		A	L	G	O	R	E		N	O	N	U	K	E	S
M	E	S	S			N	O	O	N	E	R		I	N	S	T	Y	L	E

53. WUNDERBAR!

Y	O	U	P	A	Y		A	D	R	E	P	S		B	R	I	N	E	S
D	Y	N	A	M	O		P	E	O	R	I	A		O	C	T	O	M	O	M
S	L	O	P	E	D		P	A	L	M	E	D		S	A	S	H	I	M	I
		E	N	A	K	E	D	L	A	D	I	E	S		G	O	R	A	N
O	M	A	R	R		E	A	S	E	S		S	L	Y	E	R		A	L	T
D	O	G	H	A	N	D	L	E	R		Q	T	Y			B	E	T	T	I	E
S	T	O	A		T	L	E	T	T		C	H	O	C	O	L	A	T	E
P	A	S	S	E	D		O	N	R	E	D		M	I	T		E	R	S	T
I	T	A		B	L	U		G	O	D	S	E	N	D		A	N	I	T	A
P	A	B	L	O	E	S	C	O		B	I	E	A	N	D	K	E	N
E	L	I	A	N		A	R	R	A	N	G	E		R	S	T		K	E	G
R	E	N	U		C	R	I		L	E	O	N	I		T	I	D	I	L	Y
		R	O	O	M	B	R	A	W	L		S	P	A	C	E
M	A	K	E	H	A	Y		E	M	T		C	O	I	L		L	O	M	E
A	R	E	N	D	T		T	S	O		B	A	L	A	L	A	I	K	A	S
M	I	I		E	I	E	I	O		L	O	M	A	N		T	V	S	E	T
B	E	L	L	A		B	E	L	L	Y	U	P	T	O	T	H	E
A	T	L	A	R	G	E		D	E	L	R	I	O		B	O	R	D	E	N
S	T	O	R	M	E	R		E	V	E	N	E	R		S	M	U	R	F	S
A	R	D	E	N	T		R	I	S	E	R	S		P	E	S	E	T	A

NOTES

WORLD TIME ZONE MAP

This map is based on Coordinated Universal Time (UTC), the worldwide system of civil timekeeping. UTC is essentially equivalent to Greenwich Mean Time. Zone boundaries are approximate and subject to change. Time differences relative to UTC shown here are based on the use of standard time; where Daylight Saving Time (Summer Time) is employed, add one hour to local standard time.

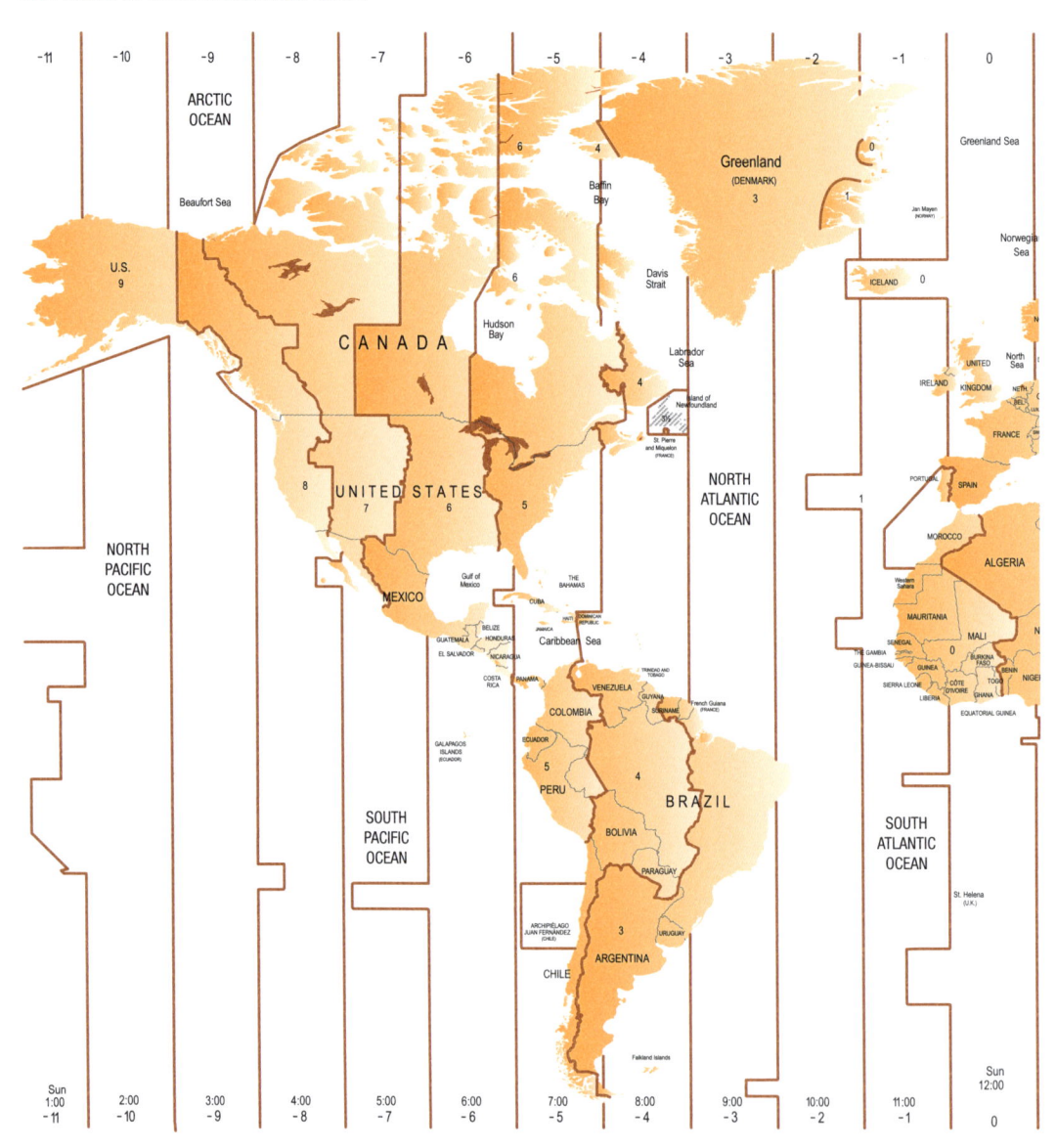

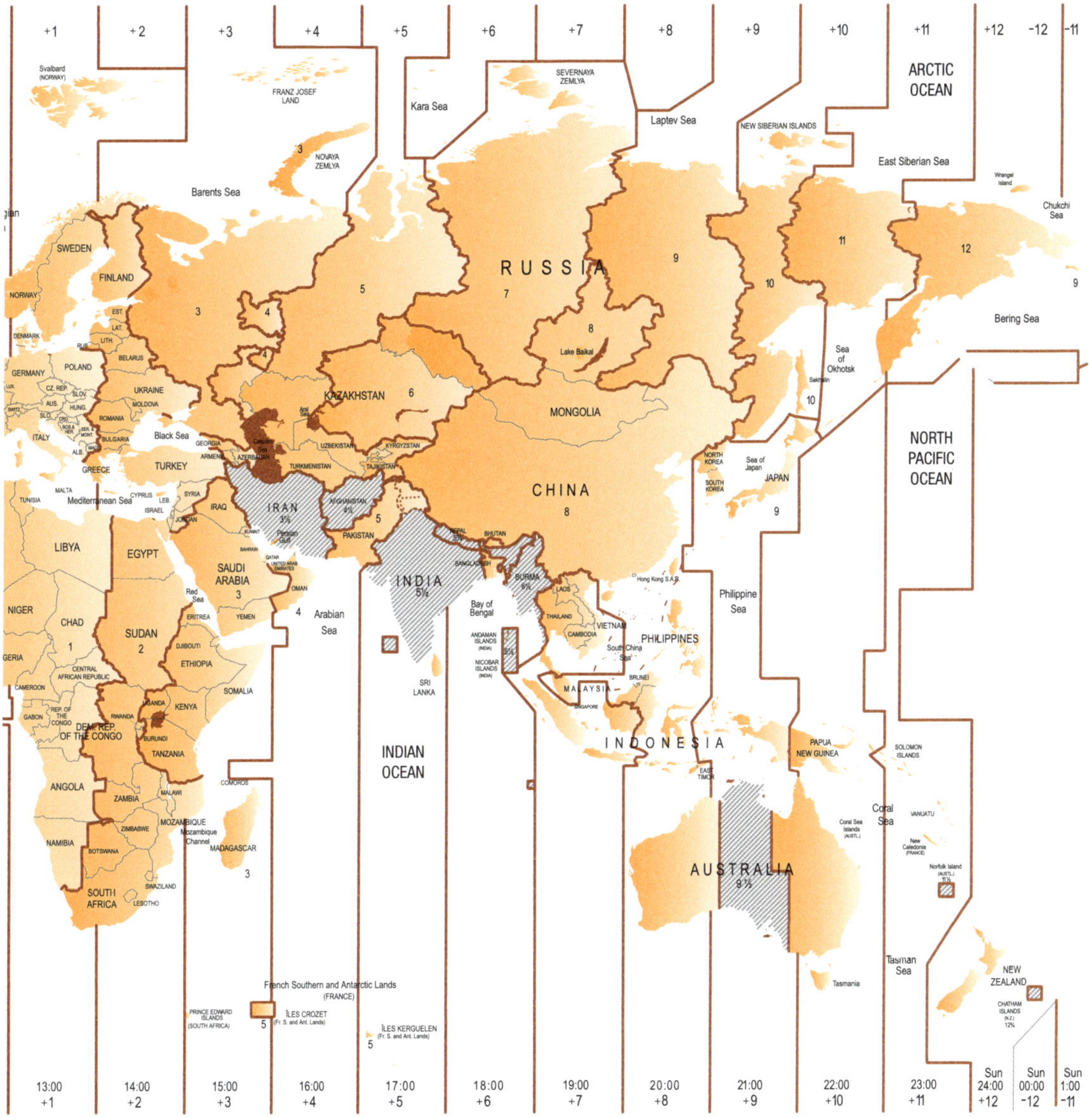

+1
+2
+3
+4
+5
+6
+7
+8
+9
+10
+11
+12
-12
-11
ARCTIC OCEAN
Svalbard (NORWAY)
FRANZ JOSEF LAND
Kara Sea
SEVERNAYA ZEMLYA
Laptev Sea
NEW SIBERIAN ISLANDS
East Siberian Sea
NOVAYA ZEMLYA
Barents Sea
Wrangel Island
Chukchi Sea
SWEDEN
FINLAND
NORWAY
RUSSIA
Bering Sea
Sea of Okhotsk
Sakhalin
Lake Baikal
KAZAKHSTAN
MONGOLIA
Aral Sea
GERMANY
POLAND
UKRAINE
BELARUS
ROMANIA
BULGARIA
ITALY
GREECE
TURKEY
Black Sea
GEORGIA
ARMENIA
AZERBAIJAN
Caspian Sea
UZBEKISTAN
KYRGYZSTAN
TURKMENISTAN
TAJIKISTAN
NORTH KOREA
SOUTH KOREA
Sea of Japan
JAPAN
NORTH PACIFIC OCEAN
CHINA
MALTA
TUNISIA
Mediterranean Sea
CYPRUS
SYRIA
LEB.
ISRAEL
JORDAN
IRAQ
IRAN 3½
AFGHANISTAN 4½
PAKISTAN
KUWAIT
Persian Gulf
NEPAL
BHUTAN
BANGLADESH
LIBYA
EGYPT
SAUDI ARABIA
QATAR
UNITED ARAB EMIRATES
OMAN
INDIA 5½
BURMA 6½
Hong Kong S.A.R.
Philippine Sea
LAOS
THAILAND
VIETNAM
CAMBODIA
PHILIPPINES
South China Sea
Red Sea
ERITREA
YEMEN
Arabian Sea
Bay of Bengal
ANDAMAN ISLANDS (INDIA)
NICOBAR ISLANDS (INDIA)
NIGER
CHAD
SUDAN
DJIBOUTI
ETHIOPIA
SOMALIA
CENTRAL AFRICAN REPUBLIC
CAMEROON
GABON
REP. OF THE CONGO
DEM. REP. OF THE CONGO
UGANDA
KENYA
RWANDA
BURUNDI
TANZANIA
SRI LANKA
BRUNEI
MALAYSIA
SINGAPORE
INDONESIA
PAPUA NEW GUINEA
SOLOMON ISLANDS
EAST TIMOR
INDIAN OCEAN
ANGOLA
ZAMBIA
MALAWI
COMOROS
MOZAMBIQUE
Mozambique Channel
ZIMBABWE
NAMIBIA
BOTSWANA
MADAGASCAR
SWAZILAND
SOUTH AFRICA
LESOTHO
Coral Sea
Coral Sea Islands (AUSTL.)
VANUATU
New Caledonia (FRANCE)
AUSTRALIA 9½
Norfolk Island (AUSTL.) 11½
Tasman Sea
Tasmania
NEW ZEALAND
CHATHAM ISLANDS (N.Z.) 12¾
French Southern and Antarctic Lands (FRANCE)
PRINCE EDWARD ISLANDS (SOUTH AFRICA)
ÎLES CROZET (Fr. S. and Ant. Lands)
ÎLES KERGUELEN (Fr. S. and Ant. Lands)
13:00 +1
14:00 +2
15:00 +3
16:00 +4
17:00 +5
18:00 +6
19:00 +7
20:00 +8
21:00 +9
22:00 +10
23:00 +11
Sun 24:00 +12
Sun 00:00 -12
Sun 1:00 -11

2015

January

s	m	t	w	t	f	s
				1	2	3
4	5	6	7	8	9	10
11	12	13	14	15	16	17
18	19	20	21	22	23	24
25	26	27	28	29	30	31

February

s	m	t	w	t	f	s
1	2	3	4	5	6	7
8	9	10	11	12	13	14
15	16	17	18	19	20	21
22	23	24	25	26	27	28

March

s	m	t	w	t	f	s
1	2	3	4	5	6	7
8	9	10	11	12	13	14
15	16	17	18	19	20	21
22	23	24	25	26	27	28
29	30	31				

April

s	m	t	w	t	f	s
			1	2	3	4
5	6	7	8	9	10	11
12	13	14	15	16	17	18
19	20	21	22	23	24	25
26	27	28	29	30		

May

s	m	t	w	t	f	s
					1	2
3	4	5	6	7	8	9
10	11	12	13	14	15	16
17	18	19	20	21	22	23
24	25	26	27	28	29	30
31						

June

s	m	t	w	t	f	s
	1	2	3	4	5	6
7	8	9	10	11	12	13
14	15	16	17	18	19	20
21	22	23	24	25	26	27
28	29	30				

_____ 2015

July

s	m	t	w	t	f	s
			1	2	3	4
5	6	7	8	9	10	11
12	13	14	15	16	17	18
19	20	21	22	23	24	25
26	27	28	29	30	31	

August

s	m	t	w	t	f	s
						1
2	3	4	5	6	7	8
9	10	11	12	13	14	15
16	17	18	19	20	21	22
23	24	25	26	27	28	29
30	31					

September

s	m	t	w	t	f	s
		1	2	3	4	5
6	7	8	9	10	11	12
13	14	15	16	17	18	19
20	21	22	23	24	25	26
27	28	29	30			

October

s	m	t	w	t	f	s
				1	2	3
4	5	6	7	8	9	10
11	12	13	14	15	16	17
18	19	20	21	22	23	24
25	26	27	28	29	30	31

November

s	m	t	w	t	f	s
1	2	3	4	5	6	7
8	9	10	11	12	13	14
15	16	17	18	19	20	21
22	23	24	25	26	27	28
29	30					

December

s	m	t	w	t	f	s
		1	2	3	4	5
6	7	8	9	10	11	12
13	14	15	16	17	18	19
20	21	22	23	24	25	26
27	28	29	30	31		

2016

January

s	m	t	w	t	f	s
					1	2
3	4	5	6	7	8	9
10	11	12	13	14	15	16
17	18	19	20	21	22	23
24	25	26	27	28	29	30
31						

February

s	m	t	w	t	f	s
	1	⟦2⟧	3	4	5	6
7	8	9	10	11	12	13
14	15	16	17	18	19	20
21	22	23	24	25	26	27
28	29					

March

s	m	t	w	t	f	s
		1	2	3	4	5
6	7	8	9	10	11	12
13	14	15	16	17	18	19
20	21	22	23	24	25	26
27	28	29	30	31		

April

s	m	t	w	t	f	s
					1	2
3	4	5	6	7	8	9
10	11	12	13	14	15	16
17	18	19	20	21	22	23
24	25	26	27	28	29	30

May

s	m	t	w	t	f	s
1	2	3	4	5	6	7
8	9	10	11	12	13	14
15	16	17	18	19	20	21
22	23	24	25	26	27	28
29	30	31				

June

s	m	t	w	t	f	s
			1	2	3	4
5	6	7	8	9	10	11
12	13	14	15	16	17	18
19	20	21	22	23	24	25
26	27	28	29	30		